ATURE'S MOST TERRIFYING PREDATORS

ISLANDS FORSAKEN BY CIVILIZATION

A FASCINATION BEYOND REASON

Praise for *The Devil's Teeth*

"Susan Casey's lively portrait of life among Northern California's white sharks and the dogged researchers who study them indulges in just the right mix of anxiety, gore and reassuring shark science. One can find reason to fear the waves and then muster the courage to enter them, usually within the same chapter. . . . The sharks are the stars of Casey's story, but the Farallones steal the show."
—*The New York Times Book Review*

"Extraordinary." —*Men's Journal*

"[A] page-turner . . . 'Los Farallones' remain icons of the elemental and the wild. Most visitors can only glimpse them from afar, from a whale watch or dive boat. So true insight has to come from someone privileged to live on the rocks with the tiny crew of professional biologists that dwell in weathered old Coast Guard housing. This book makes the most of that sort of insider access. . . . A fine read. The book gives you a way of reaching these mysterious isles without getting wet. Or seasick." —*San Francisco Chronicle*

"Casey's chronicle of how this unique environment survived nuclear contamination and endless harebrained development schemes (including the proposed relocation of Alcatraz) is one of many stranger-than-fiction elements. As the shark trivia and anecdotes about the islands' Wild West past give way to a hair-raising account of an ill-fated shark-tagging mission, Casey becomes an increasingly active participant in the story while offering skillfully wrought descriptions of nature's inscrutable fury. B + ." —*Entertainment Weekly*

"A chilling dispatch from the great white shark-filled waters off San Francisco." —*Life*

"Chilling . . . A lively and detailed account . . . vivid." —*USA Today*

"An evocative and entertaining account of the cutting edge of marine biology." —*New Scientist*

"Casey has a flair for dramatic descriptions, able to capture the characters she encounters or the landscape around her with equal aplomb . . . [Paints] a gripping portrait of scientists on the outer fringes of society and nature." —*Seattle Post-Intelligencer*

"Casey creates compelling portraits of the legendary predators, as well as of the scientists." —*People*

"You can't help but be entertained by a writer who is affectionate about a shark's 'maniac smile' and thinks a petrel smells 'musky and heavy and sort of smoky, like the bird had been part of an all-night poker game.' Being seduced into caring about the survival of a '20-foot-long, eight-foot-wide, six-foot-deep' nightmare beast is a much harder job, and Casey accomplishes even that without hardly trying. Her book is an exhilarating reminder that there are elements of both wonder and revulsion in all things sublime." —*Newsday*

"Guaranteed to scare people right out of the water." —*Associated Press*

"A rare sort of adventure story, which she tells with verve and great sympathy for the islands, the sharks and the biologists. But another poignant theme resonates through the book as well . . . Great whites provide Casey a meaning to life beyond the human, Thoreau's 'tonic of wildness.'" —*The Oregonian*

"Casey delivers amazing details . . . *The Devil's Teeth* will surely satisfy your appetite for all things fanged and finned." —*National Geographic Adventure*

"Riveting and colorful you-are-there adventure." —*Santa Cruz Sentinel*

"I read Susan Casey's book in a feeding frenzy, satisfying my curiosity while fueling my fascination with sharks. A thoroughly researched and well-written piece of literature that raises hairs as well as tickling funny bones, *The Devil's Teeth* artfully reveals what lurks in the shadows of the mysterious great white and the people obsessed with them. The true triumph of the book, though, is in Casey's transcendence of mere journalism—she's clearly embraced by the world of which she writes."
—Linda Greenlaw, author of *The Hungry Ocean*
and *All Fishermen Are Liars*

"A marvelous book—part adventure, part meditation, part natural history—that takes the reader on a wild ride into a strange and seductive world. Casey is the perfect diving companion; her account of life among San Francisco's shark population is engaging, smart, and irresistible."
—Susan Orlean, author of *My Kind of Place* and *The Orchid Thief*

"In delivering us to the Farallon Islands, and then into the souls of the magnificent great white sharks that populate its waters, Susan Casey has really delivered us into the DNA of our own beings. *The Devil's Teeth* is more than a shark story; it is an account of our instincts, our appetites, even our futures, all beautifully told by a writer compelled to know." —Robert Kurson, author of *Shadow Divers*

" 'There's another world, and it's in this one,'" declares Susan Casey, reveling in the surreality of her days and nights spent among the world's coolest, cold-eyed customers, great white sharks. Who knew these beasts lived so close to San Francisco, within the pizza delivery zone of that fair city? Casey is a poet, a bare-knuckled spirit, unabashed and funny, and hers is an entrancing ride to a beautiful, forbidding place, a new world, close by. Hang on."
—Doug Stanton, author of *In Harm's Way*

"Susan Casey could write about guppies, and I'd want to read her book. I devoured this book like a shark." —Mary Roach, author of *Stiff*

THE
DEVIL'S TEETH

THE
DEVIL'S TEETH

A True Story of
Obsession and Survival Among
America's Great White Sharks

SUSAN CASEY

ST. MARTIN'S GRIFFIN
NEW YORK

Published in the United States by St. Martin's Griffin,
an imprint of St. Martin's Publishing Group

THE DEVIL'S TEETH. Copyright © 2005 by Susan Casey. All rights reserved.
Printed in the United States of America. For information, address
St. Martin's Publishing Group, 120 Broadway, New York, NY 10271.

www.stmartins.com

Title page photograph and photograph on page 139 © Christ
Fallows/apexpredators.com, photograph on page 13 © Susan Casey

Map © 2005 by David Cain

Designed by Kelly S. Too

The Library of Congress has cataloged the Henry Holt edition as follows:

Casey, Susan, 1962–
  The devil's teeth : a true story of obsession and survival among
America's great white sharks / Susan Casey.—1st ed.
  p. cm.
  ISBN-13: 978-0-8050-8011-7
  ISBN-10: 0-8050-8011-2
  1. White shark—California—Farallon Islands—Anecdotes.
I. Casey, Susan, 1962– II. Title.
QL638.95.L3C37 2005
597.3'3'09794—dc22

                                              2004060782

ISBN 978-0-805-08011-7 (trade paperback)

Our books may be purchased in bulk for promotional, educational, or business
use. Please contact your local bookseller or the Macmillan Corporate and
Premium Sales Department at 800-221-7945, extension 5442, or by email
at MacmillanSpecialMarkets@macmillan.com.

Originally published in the United States by Henry Holt and Company

First St. Martin's Griffin Edition: May 2006

D   20

To my family:
Ron, Angela, Bob, and Bill,
who taught me to love the wild things.

Humanity is exalted not because we are so far above all living creatures, but because knowing them well elevates the very concept of life.

—EDWARD O. WILSON

Every angel is terrifying.

—RAINER MARIA RILKE

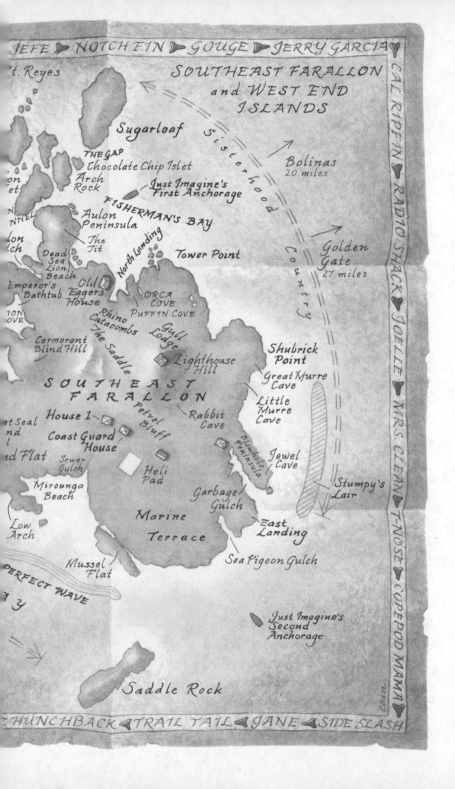

INTRODUCTION

An ocean without its unnamed monsters would be like a
completely dreamless sleep.

—JOHN STEINBECK, *THE LOG FROM THE SEA OF CORTEZ*

The killing took place at dawn and as usual it was a decapitation,
accomplished by a single vicious swipe. Blood geysered into the
air, creating a vivid slick that stood out on the water like the work
of a violent abstract painter. Five hundred yards away, outside of a
lighthouse on the island's highest peak, a man watched through a
telescope. First he noticed the frenzy of gulls, bird gestalt that signaled trouble. And then he saw the blood. Grabbing his radio, he
turned and began to run.

His transmission jolted awake the four other people on the island. "We've got an attack off Sugarloaf, big one it looks like. Lotta
blood." The house at the bottom of the hill echoed with the sounds
of scientist Peter Pyle hurrying, running down the stairs, pulling
on his knee-high rubber boots, slamming the old door behind him
as he sprinted to the boat launch.

Peter and his colleague Scot Anderson, the voice on the radio,
jumped into their seventeen-foot Boston Whaler. The boat rested
on a bed of rubber tires beside a cliff; it was attached to a crane
which lifted it up and into the air. The crane swung the whaler

over the lip and lowered it thirty feet, into the massive early winter swells of the Pacific.

Peter unhooked the winch, an inch-thick cable of steel, as the whaler rose and fell into troughs big enough to swallow it. He started the engine and powered two hundred yards toward the birds, where the object of all the attention floated in a cloud of blood: a quarter-ton elephant seal that was missing its head. The odor was dense and oily, rancid Crisco mixed with seawater.

"Oh yeah," Peter said. "That's the smell of a shark attack."

In a world where very little is known for certain, they knew that below them a great white shark was orbiting, waiting for the seal to bleed some more, and that this shark would soon be returning for breakfast. It might be Betty or Mama or the Cadillac, one of the huge females that patrolled the east side of the island. These big girls, all of them over seventeen feet long, were known as the Sisterhood. Or it might be a "smaller" male (thirteen or fourteen feet), like Spotty or T-Nose or the sneaky Cal Ripfin. These sharks were called the Rat Pack. It might be any number of great whites. At this time of the year there were scores of them cruising this 120-acre patch of sea, swimming close to the shoreline of Southeast Farallon Island as hapless seals washed out of finger gulleys at high tide and into the danger zone.

In any given year more than a thousand people will be maimed by toilet bowl cleaning products or killed by cattle. Fewer than a dozen will be attacked by a great white shark. In this neighborhood, however, those odds do not count. At the Farallon Islands, during the months of September through November, your chance of meeting a great white face-to-face is better than even money, should you be crazy enough or unlucky enough to end up in the water.

The two men stood at the stern holding long poles capped with video cameras. There were several beats of the kind of absolute silence that you hardly ever get in life, eerie moments when time seemed to stop and even the birds became quiet. Then, fifty yards away, the ocean swirled into a boil.

The dorsal fin of myth and nightmare rose from below and came tunneling toward them like a German U-boat, creating a sizable wake. The shark made a tight pass around the boat, pulling up just short of the stern. Its body, which was almost black as it broke the surface, glowed with cobalt and turquoise highlights underwater. "He's coming up!" Peter yelled. The whaler rocked. A massive triangle of a head lifted out of the water and, in a surprisingly delicate way, bit the back corner of the boat. Scot leaned closer and filmed. The shark's black eyes rolled; they could plainly see the scars all over its head and its two-inch-long teeth, backed by rows of *spare* two-inch-long teeth. Then, as quickly as it had come, the shark slipped beneath the surface, dove under the boat, and reemerged next to the seal. As the great white snatched the carcass, shaking it, bright orange blood burst from the sides of its mouth.

"It's Bitehead!" Scot said. He broke into a full-face smile beneath his wraparound sunglasses.

"Ah, Bitehead," Peter said. There was a moment of pleased recognition, as if greeting a fond acquaintance they had just happened to run into on the street. "We've known this shark for ten years."

EVERY SEPTEMBER, ONE OF THE WORLD'S LARGEST AND DENSEST congregations of great white sharks assembles in the waters surrounding the Farallon Islands, a 211-acre archipelago of ten islets in the Pacific, twenty-seven miles due west of the Golden Gate Bridge. No one fully understands what this gathering represents, why great whites, the ocean's most solitary hunters, choose to reside for a period of time in such close quarters. What's known for sure is that the sharks remain at this location for approximately three months. And this: having studied them for over a decade and a half in the Farallon White Shark Project, Scot Anderson and Peter Pyle have discovered that year after year, the same sharks return to exactly the same spot.

This annual reunion is at least partly about hunting. Despite strange inventories of items found in the bellies of sharks—a cuckoo clock, a fur cape, license plates and lobster traps, a buffalo head, an entire reindeer, and even, in one unlikely scenario, a man dressed in a full suit of armor—what great whites really love to eat are seals. And the Farallones are dripping with seals—northern elephant seals, harbor seals, fur seals, seals, seals, seals—all barking and bellowing, draped on the rocks like a blubbery carpet.

It wasn't always this way. The islands' seals, which once numbered in the tens of thousands, were hunted almost to extinction 150 years ago. Only after Southeast Farallon Island, the largest in the group, became a wildlife refuge in 1969 did the populations begin to recover. And as the seals returned, no one was happier to see them than the sharks. In 1970 Farallon biologists witnessed their first shark attack, on a Steller's sea lion, a brawny animal that itself looks like a predator. During the next fifteen years, more than one hundred attacks on seals and sea lions were observed at close range. But the sharks were only warming up. By the year 2000, Peter and Scot were logging almost eighty attacks in a single season. Still, even accounting for the allure of a seal smorgasbord, why did these *particular* sharks keep returning? And why were they clustered together so tightly? No one had ever documented such behavior among great whites before.

Not that anyone's had the opportunity. The Farallon Islands are the only place on Earth where it's possible to study great white sharks behaving naturally in the wild. Unsubjected, that is, to the presence and fumblings of humans. In South Africa's "Shark Alley," near the town of Gaansbai, the channel is stained red with chum, and often there are a dozen boats banging up against each other while as many as sixty divers sardined into steel cages clog the thousand-yard-wide passage. In Australia, great white sharks contend with underwater electrical charges, beaches ringed by netting, trophy fishing, and more chumming. The Farallon great whites, on the other hand, are largely unharassed. They might cross paths with the occasional boatload of day-trippers from San Francisco, but they're subjected to none of the behavior-altering coercion that nature's top predators regularly endure so that people can sit in the Winnebago or tundra buggy or safari truck and get a look at them.

This is important because despite their visibility at the Farallones, and despite the impressive truth that sharks are so old they predate *trees*, great whites have remained among the most mysterious of creatures. Even now, after the human genome has been reduced to an alphabet set and spaceships are trolling around on Mars, scientists are still missing some basic information about the species.

How long do they live? Unknown. (But probably at least thirty years, considering that white sharks don't mature until they're over ten years old, all the sharks at the Farallones are adults, and some individuals have been showing up for more than a decade. There are scientists who speculate that they live as long as sixty years, but that remains unproven.)

Where do they mate, or when, or how often, or even *how?* There are clues to the sex lives of great white sharks, but no facts. Scot and Peter have discovered that, while the males return annually, the females return only every other year, often with fresh, deep bites around their heads. Are these wounds related to mating? Do the females spend their off years giving birth in warmer waters? For that matter, how many great whites are there in the oceans? All of this is a complete mystery. Even the seasonal population at the Farallones is a wild guess: anywhere from thirty to one hundred.

Then, of course, there's the question of size: Exactly how big can these sharks get? And once again there are no straight answers. Because their skeletons are made of cartilage rather than bone, they've left virtually no fossil record aside from teeth. The largest great white shark to have been caught and precisely measured was nineteen and a half feet long, but there have been credible, if unverifiable, reports of much larger animals. Nothing would be too surprising. Sharks are the heavyweight champions of evolution; they've been fine-tuning their act for ages, hundreds of millions of years before party-crashing humans were even a glimmer in the primordial eye. They're resistant to infections, circulatory disease, and, to a large extent, cancer. They heal rapidly from severe injuries such as lacerated corneas or deep gouges. Everything about the animal is stacked toward survival. From the moment baby whites are born, four-foot-long replicas of their mother, they are already in pursuit of their first meal; from hundreds of yards away they can detect minute millivolt electrical impulses given off by their prey's heartbeat.

Like the great white itself, the Farallon Islands are a nearly perfect freak of nature. Their ecology is a house of cards—an intricate confluence of ocean and seals and birds and sharks, all circling back on each other, everything existing in sublime balance. But in nature, complexity also means fragility. Though the islands are part of the 1,255-square-mile Gulf of the Farallones National Marine Sanctuary, that sanctuary happens to straddle the West Coast's busiest shipping lanes. In 1971, 840,000 gallons of oil oozed into the Gulf of the Farallones, killing more than twenty thousand seabirds. Thirteen years later, in 1984, a tanker exploded and deposited 1.4 million gallons of crude. And right now, hundreds of ships are scattered on the nearby seafloor, poised to begin blurping up oil like toxic lava lamps as the salt water slowly eats away their hulls. Factor in the presence of a sunken ten-thousand-ton aircraft carrier once used for nuclear target practice and forty-eight thousand barrels of radioactive waste, and the picture gets even more precarious.

The islands themselves are fragile, hollow in places, and made of eighty-nine-million-year-old granite, much of which has gone rotten and crumbles to the touch. The word *farallon* is Spanish for "rocky islet in the ocean" (the plural is *farallones*, pronounced "fair-alons"), and some, like Middle Farallon, known locally as "the Pimple," are really more like protruding rocks than actual islands. All ten are part of the ragged edge of the continental shelf as it juts out of the Pacific before plunging two miles—the depth of the Grand Canyon—into darkness. Technically, the Farallones are just an exotic suburb of San Francisco, as they lie within the city limits. But few of the Bay Area's seven million residents are aware of their existence. And even supposing someone knew that the Farallones were out there, he surely wouldn't have any idea of the violent, desperate history of the place: the accidents, the murders, the forgotten town, the homegrown war. Each year there are fewer and fewer people alive who remember the stories. On satellite photos of the Bay Area, the Farallones are usually cropped out of the frame.

This obscurity is understandable. The boat ride from the mainland is a riot of turbulence and nausea that can last more than six hours—and that's on a day when a captain is willing to attempt the voyage. Even coast guard crews balk at the crossing, admitting that they try to take a helicopter when possible. No one lives year-round at the Farallones. Peter, Scot, and a revolving handful of colleagues bunk in the only habitable building, a 120-year-old, no-nonsense house on Southeast Farallon that looks like it could stand up to anything. And it has: The place gets regular lashings of the meanest weather the Pacific can dish out. Thirty-knot winds, blanketing fog, and fifteen-foot seas are standard.

Even if a visitor is hearty enough or curious enough to make the trip to the Farallones, upon arrival he cannot set foot aground—it is a tightly supervised National Wildlife Refuge, within a National Marine Sanctuary, and the only people allowed there by federal law are the biologists who monitor the wildlife. In any case, there's nowhere to land a boat. The islands are perimetered by sheer cliffs and treacherous hidden rocks that create abrupt surf breaks. A quarter million seabirds spend the year painting these rocks, and the stench of ammonia will knock a person back on his heels. Noisemaking is prohibited, planes may not fly directly overhead, and all boats are required to remain at least three hundred feet offshore. And you sure as hell don't want to go in for a dip. When all the impediments are taken into account, there is really only one reason to visit the Farallon Islands: because it is the spookiest, wildest place on Earth.

I BECAME HAUNTED BY THE FARALLONES IN 1998, WHEN I HAPPENED TO see a BBC documentary about Scot and Peter's work. Television tends to make even magnificent things seem puny, but this program managed to convey how enormous the sharks were, how toylike the men's research boat was by comparison, the extraterrestrial nature of the place. When the show came on I was lying on my living room floor, bleary with mononucleosis, and I wondered if I might be hallucinating.

On-screen, the islands jutted from the Pacific like the fangs of a sea monster badly in need of dental work. The water was a fathomless black; fog crept through savage rock archways. But the islands' most surreal feature lay beneath the surface. When the blond man identified as "Scot Anderson, biologist" leaned over the edge of their eleven-foot boat and lowered an underwater video camera, it was only seconds before a great white shark appeared in the frame. And then another, and then another. There was no chum in the water, no bait. The sharks were just there, swimming around, stacked like planes over O'Hare. Is this some kind of hoax? I wondered. A camera montage? *This cannot be real.* How on earth could great white sharks the size of cube vans be hanging out in a pack within the San Francisco delivery radius for a pizza? And who were the two crazies sitting in the middle of it all in a *rowboat*?

Great white sharks elicit a kind of universal awe—and not just because of their ability to snack on us. Grizzly bears can devour people with equal proficiency, and while they certainly command a healthy respect, it's nothing like our primal response to seeing that black flag shearing the water. Ask the Discovery Channel; its annual Shark Week is a ratings bonanza that has drawn as much as a 100 percent increase in viewers, and the network invariably schedules it during the sweeps.

Even to the most dedicated control freak, white sharks represent the terrible, powerful unknown. They live in a different element than we do, they're not cute, they're not at all cuddly, and on some level they seem like the closest thing we've got to living dinosaurs. Their *otherness* is what both compels us and scares the pants off us.

That, and their several sets of teeth. It's a complicated relationship. The biologist Edward O. Wilson summed it up beautifully when he wrote, "In a deeply tribal way, we love our monsters."

Most prefer to love the monster from a distance, or perhaps only in photographs, rather than marching right up to pet its fur or examine its claws (or stroke its fin, as Scot did on the BBC program when a shark passed alongside him). Survival usually trumps curiosity and that's good because those are the people we can count on to stick around and continue the race, passing their sage judgment down to their children. Then there are the others. Like me.

As far back as I can remember, I've had the feeling that the most exciting things in life were locked away somewhere, like Fabergé eggs or hundred-year-old Scotch. And that the only way to get to them was by relentless searching. You weren't going to stumble across a lost civilization on your way to catch the commuter bus, for instance, or find a goblin shark lying in the seafood section of Safeway. Seeing the moon on TV, visiting the wildest creatures in cages, nose-pressing museum cases to admire a souvenir of history—all this added up to an unacceptable trade-off. And yet pretty much everyone I knew had already made it.

And in truth I had too. But at the age of thirty-four, ten years into a successful career in the magazine world, there was still more restlessness and curiosity in me than I knew how to handle, and I wouldn't say that I ever felt content. Bodies of water caused the most distraction. They drew me in deep, like a hypnotist's coin, and I could never look at one without wondering what was under its skin. The green-black Canadian lakes where I spent my summers, the gin-clear Caribbean, the fathomless Pacific, the shallow, antiseptic glint of a swimming pool: I wanted them all the same.

My fascination with water led to an athletic career as a swimmer that has lasted for twenty-five years. For up to six hours a day I stared at the bottom of every possible kind of pool, did millions of laps and countless flipturns, and I still couldn't get enough water. The only thing more satisfying than being in the pool was swimming in a lake or a river or the ocean, where I might possibly see fish. Even the lowliest trash fish, a crappie or a perch or a rock bass, worked a kind of spell on me, an irrational mix of captivation and terror. While other people were looking up into space, wondering about black holes and distant galaxies, I was staring down into some expanse of water, hoping for a glimpse of fin.

Oceans cover 71 percent of the earth, and it's estimated that no one has ever laid eyes on 95 percent of the life-forms that live there; only a piddling fraction of this aquatic real estate has been explored. Breakthroughs in deep exploration have made it possible to venture farther into the abyss, and in recent years jaw-dropping images of formerly unknown creatures have come back from below—beings that stretch the imagination such as the fangtooth fish and the vampire squid and the gulper eel. Scientists have only just discovered hot vents on the ocean floors—boiling, mineral-saturated water that spews up from the Earth's crust into the sea through chimneylike formations. (These chimneys might be the very source of life, that's all.) Through the use of new technologies like side-scan sonar, astonishing treasures have been found: Six hundred shipwrecks, some from prebiblical times, are lying in one small swath of ocean off Portugal. At least three sunken Egyptian cities thought to be more than two thousand years old have recently been discovered kicking around on the bottom near Alexandria's harbor. When underwater archaeologists began to explore them, they happened upon Napoleon's sunken fleet.

In other words, even in places where the topside is familiar, there are whole new universes and ancient buried worlds swirling around down there, like rooms you didn't know about in your house. I found this thrillingly spooky. For years, I'd had a recurring dream—actually, it hovered on the edge of nightmare territory—in which I floated at night, surrounded by large, unearthly fish. I could never see them clearly, but I knew the water was alive with them, all these hidden creatures, sweeping and circling. When I saw the Farallones on the screen that first time, the memory of these phantoms vaulted out of semiretirement and into my consciousness. This was some *weird* water. What was going on beneath the surface?

FINDING OUT MORE PROVED DIFFICULT. THE BBC PIECE ABOUT THE Farallon sharks was the only one that existed. What articles I could turn up tended to be wonky treatises on seal populations and seabird migration, or terse newspaper stories that raised more questions than they answered. The *Los Angeles Times* called the Farallones "the most forbidding piece of real estate in America, if not the world," but didn't elaborate. A *New York Times* headline from 1858 reported that a fisherman had been "seized by an octopus" at the islands, yet provided no details.

I came across random facts that intrigued: A female skeleton had been found in a sea cave, and to this day her identity remains a mystery . . . a century ago on Southeast Farallon Island there was a town that even had its own school . . . a new kind of jellyfish had been discovered there; it had *arms* instead of tentacles. And the sharks, always the sharks. Commercial divers refused to work anywhere near the place. Government divers were not permitted to enter the surrounding waters for insurance reasons. Great white sharks had even foiled a world-record attempt to water-ski from the Golden Gate Bridge to the Farallones. "That was the stupidest thing I ever did," admitted the skier, who spent hours plowing through bone-jarring fifteen-foot swells, only to have his boat spring a leak when he neared the islands. Swimming beneath the hull to check for damage, he suddenly realized he was not alone: "All I could see was a swarm of sharks." The man leaped back into the boat, whereupon he and his crew hightailed it back to San Francisco, bailing as fast as they could.

Being at the Farallones, it seemed, was like hanging around Mount Olympus as the gods glided by for another round at the buffet. And in this foreboding spot, humans were neither wanted nor needed. The usual rules of civilization did not apply. Here was a place where nothing was fake and nothing was for sale, where cars and credit cards, cell phones and expensive high-heeled shoes got you nowhere, where animals thrived while people died in any number of unlikely ways. This lost outpost, it seemed to me, was more than an unexpected scrap of America, more than a window into an interesting marine world. It was a glimpse into another realm.

As I watched the two men on TV, surrounded by sharks in their little boat, I realized that somewhere between San Francisco and the Farallon Islands, there was a border crossing. On one side of the divide was the world of blacktop and happy hour, and on the other was an uninhabitable place where four-hundred-million-year-old predators still roamed. I wanted to cross that line while it still existed, before civilization reached out and blurred it, then tamed it, then erased it completely. But how? The place was off limits, forbidden in every way. And aside from that, I had no idea how I would get there. But the Farallones had stirred something in the deepest folds of my imagination, and I knew that one way or another I was going. I had to. How often do you have the chance to step inside your own dream?

THE ISLAND

CHAPTER 1

NOVEMBER 16, 2001

The phrase "islands in the Pacific" brings to mind images of lushness and ease; of gently rustling breezes, sunshine, relaxation, and elaborate cocktails. These Pacific islands, however, are not like that. Nothing is easy at the Farallones. Even stepping onto Southeast Farallon Island is a white-knuckle affair requiring physical agility and no fear of heights, because the landing involves being hoisted by crane from a skiff and then winched up a cliff on a metal disk the size of a manhole cover. Or leaping ashore from a bucking Zodiac and scrambling up a rock face while hauling gear, making sure to time the waves just right to avoid getting plucked off like lint and swept out to sea. All of this takes place in a constricted area that allows the boat driver no room for error. To the right, waves and eddies boil over a narrow gulch fringed with toothy rocks. At left, the ocean explodes against a granite outcropping, sending sheets of spray into the air. Above: thousands of dive-bombing seagulls. Below: a ring of great white sharks. Not exactly the perfect infrastructure for receiving company.

Living at the Farallones presents another round of challenges. Sixty-five-acre Southeast Farallon is the only island in the group that is even remotely habitable, thanks to the flat strip of marine terrace that runs along its southern edge. On this stretch of rock, two identical weather-beaten houses, originally built in the 1870s, face the ocean like sentinels. One of them has electricity and running water, the other does not. The sole source of freshwater on the island is a sickly yellow stream that only a desperate person would drink from. In the past, many have. These days, rainwater is collected on concrete catchment pads, then funneled into tanks and run through seven stages of filtration. Hot water is scarce. Food varies in availability, particularly during winter and spring when ferocious storms often prevent supply boats from arriving for weeks on end. Although by law there are never more than eight people living on Southeast Farallon at any one time, privacy's nonexistent—everyone has at least one bunkmate and that person is likely to be a biology intern who hasn't showered in the past eleven days. Oh, and the toilet can't be flushed that often.

Getting an invitation to come here hadn't been easy, either. The year before, when I'd contacted Peter Pyle, introduced myself, and proposed writing a magazine piece about the islands, he had advised me to apply to the U.S. Fish and Wildlife Service for a media day pass. Staying overnight was completely out of the question— nobody but scientists got to do that. And he'd warned me: even day passes were rarely granted.

But Peter is naturally a friendly guy, and our conversation stretched for hours. He'd been one of the Farallones' head biologists for some sixteen years at that point, and along with his shark credentials he was a renowned ornithologist and a one-man encyclopedia of the islands. Talking to him only made my desire to visit stronger, and he ended the call agreeing to help in any way he could. Soon after, I applied for—and received—a one-day permit to write a story for *Time* magazine. Unfortunately, the day I visited, November 17, 2000, turned out to be virtually the only sharkless day that season. It was worth the trip just to see the islands in their creepy beauty, and I liked Peter and Scot on sight, but the hours passed and the only wildlife I encountered were hordes of gulls and piles of seals and sea lions. My disappointment must have been obvious, because as I was leaving Peter offhandedly invited me back during the next year's shark season. To return to the Farallones as a de facto intern.

And, of course, I accepted. Which is how, three years after catching the BBC documentary, I came to be lying on a bunk in the Jane Fonda bedroom, upstairs in the Farallones' main residence. (The room got its name because its door was once decorated by an oil painting of Jane in her *Barbarella* days, wearing nothing but feathers. Someone had since come along and painted it over with a picture of a bird called the common grackle.) The Jane Fonda bedroom's decor spoke of a dorm room gone horribly to seed. Mice scuttled in the corners, ripping and tearing at something in the closet. (Powerbars I'd left in my duffel bag, it turned out.) Threadbare towels thumbtacked over the windows served as makeshift curtains. The mattresses looked like Rorschach tests, the paint was peeling, the plaster was cracking, and the dresser was marked "Property of the U.S. Coast Guard."

Though it was barely daylight, just after six, I heard voices downstairs. I got up and brushed my teeth in the communal bathroom, wearing the same three layers of clothes I had slept in. At this time of the year, early morning temperatures hovered in the forties, and even inside the house the air felt clammy and damp and the linoleum floor gave off a chill. I pulled on a pair of ski socks and made my way down the steep wooden staircase. The lower floor of the house was divided into three main rooms: a living room filled with battered flea market furniture, a workroom ringed by computers of various vintages, and the kitchen, which was the house's main gathering spot.

Scot and Peter were already done with breakfast and had probably been down in the kitchen for at least an hour. Part of Scot's daily ritual was to arise at 3:30 and check the weather for shark potential, then briefly return to bed before reawakening to brew a particular blend of Peet's coffee that he personally imported from the mainland. In contrast to the decrepit state of the bedrooms, the kitchen was warm and homey, with cast-iron pots dangling from the wall and cheerful blue countertops and a tiered stadium of a spice rack crammed with everything from plain old salt to black malabar peppercorns. Dominating the room was a stainless steel, restaurant-grade Wolf range that was probably worth more than the entire house. Scot stood next to it, pouring a cup of coffee. Peter sat behind him in one of the mismatched chairs. He was tilting back, laughing and talking, his dark hair curling out from beneath a sun-bleached San Francisco Giants cap. He was wearing what I now recognized as his trademark outfit: bulletproof Carhartt pants, a heavy canvas workshirt worn soft with use, and a fleece vest. A tidal calendar lay open in front of him.

The two men were in their early forties and of average height, and they both had that authentic glow that self-tanners can't replicate and the easy, confident manner of people at home in their own skins. It was as though they'd stepped from the pages of a Patagonia catalog, where perfectly disheveled and impossibly great-looking men who hadn't shaved in recent memory were pictured doing things like kayaking the Zambezi and hanging from their fingertips off El Capitan. And these guys had the attitudes to match. When I had arrived two days ago aboard a whale-watching boat called *Superfish*, Peter had picked me up in the shark research boat. The seventeen-foot Boston Whaler plunged up and down below the sixty-five-foot *Superfish*, each vessel rising and falling in opposing cadence with the eight-foot swells. My job was to make the jump without falling into the water and being crushed like a bug between the two boats, or snapped at by a curious shark. I managed it but was scared almost speechless, and my legs hadn't quit shaking for an hour. Meanwhile, Peter, cruising through the boat-eating waves, was talking to the *Superfish* crew, greeting people, watching the birds out of the corner of his eye, and helping me aboard, all at the same time.

Both he and Scot seemed completely at home here, and in a way the Farallones were like home to them. Over the years, they had established familiar routines. Scot always slept in a bedroom called the Wind Room (also known as Jane Fonda's Ugly Sister's Room, because it was small and shunted off to the side). Peter always transported his gear in Rubbermaid tubs that kept out the mice and the bird lice and the damp air. Scot dealt with the Shark Project equipment; Peter handled the island logistics. Scot brought the coffee and the beer; Peter brought the Two-Buck Chuck. Both men liked to drink Jack Daniel's, knew how to read the ocean, and could fix things. They had this place down to a science, insofar as such a thing was even possible.

They coordinated their schedules so that during shark season, at least one of them was always present. Peter loved to spend the bulk of the fall here not only because of the sharks but also because it was a major birding season. Scot preferred to come out only when the weather was conducive to his work. When the winds swept in or the fog came down and, as he put it, "someone turned out the lights," he often tried to hitch a ride on a fishing boat back to Inverness, the laid-back town near Point Reyes where he lived with his girlfriend. During the other nine months of the year, Scot worked as a park ranger at the Point Reyes National Seashore, and as a parttime naturalist for the Oceanic Society. Peter also lived in Inverness, with his wife and two children; when shark season ended at the Farallones, he took it up on the mainland, fund-raising for the project, answering its mail and phone calls, organizing the research, writing reports, and turning the other part of his attention to the bird world.

We were all somewhat puffy-eyed this morning, on account of the several bottles of wine that had been part of last night's dinner, and I grabbed a mug and poured myself a coffee too. I sat down next to Peter. "Good morning," he said. "Are you ready to run?" In other words, was I properly dressed for a shark attack, should one suddenly break out, without any additional coiffing or wardrobe adjustments. Hell, yes. Last night I had carefully placed my jacket, my binoculars, my sunglasses, my camera, and my boots right by the front door, within easy snatching range.

Adam Brown and his wife, Natalia Collier, known to everyone as Brown and Nat, came into the kitchen and began to make toast, rifling around in the two refrigerators for slices of homemade bread and the last remaining chunk of butter. Brown, twenty-nine, was the third—and newest—researcher on the Shark Project; in fact, he was the only addition that Scot and Peter had ever made. He was a strong-featured guy, tall and lanky, with a blond ponytail. Nat was a biologist too. She was in her late twenties and effortlessly pretty, with thick coppery hair and not the slightest hint of makeup. She had a resoluteness that seemed unusual for someone her age. You could absolutely tell that Nat was going to save a species or two before she was done.

For most of the year, the Browns traveled a peripatetic circuit on which the Farallones were only one stop. They'd spent several months on the island of St. Martin in the Caribbean before arriving here, monitoring bird populations and setting up their own environmental nonprofit. Unlike the majority of twenty-something couples, these two had decided that their ideal life did not involve corporations, minivans, or suburbia. They had no fixed address. During the lulls between jobs, they surfed.

The couple had been here since August and, Nat had told me, would be staying until early December. Only three days remained in the official shark season, however. To date it had been a so-so year. There were fewer seals around, and it seemed likely that the sharks were still hungry. Last week, apparently, the weather had been unusually cooperative, the water had been clear, and things were just going off. Shredded carcasses were popping up left and right, with bunches of sharks cruising around and surfacing to feed and Scot, Peter, and Brown floating in the middle of everything in their research boat. But the run of action seemed to have ended. The conditions had turned foggy, windy, and nasty. Typical Farallon weather, but not so great for seeing sharks. During the two days I'd been on the island, the temperature had barely risen above fifty degrees, the sea had gone from ultramarine blue to gunmetal gray, and we'd been socked in the entire time.

I had spent my hours on the island exploring, wandering on the flat parts, scaling the ankle-breaking path to the old lighthouse, climbing the sides of scree-strewn hills, and ripping up fistfuls of New Zealand spinach, an invasive plant that had quickly colonized the island after its seeds hitched a ride on the bottom of somebody's shoes in 1975. (Peter had outlined the mission, all-out war against the exotic species: search and destroy the leafy green scourge whenever possible.) Yesterday, Scot had shown me a spot called the Emperor's Bathtub, a dramatic, sheltered cove filled with seals and sea lions lounging and capering, snorting and belching, as the water eddied around them in a crystalline Jacuzzi. Walking farther down the dribble of a path, we rounded a corner and dead-ended at the North Landing and Fisherman's Bay. It was a view that made you grab for your camera, a spooky semicircle of rock spears surrounding an unquiet cove that had no lee whatsoever. One of these farallones, Arch Rock, had a bungalow-sized hole pierced through its center, like the eye of a needle. Another was larger, though less showy; it was called Sugarloaf, and it rose in full-moon grandeur at the northwestern edge of the bay, separated slightly from the rest of the group.

Even without sharks, it was exhilarating. I could have happily spent a year or two exploring all the fabulously named spots—like Drunk Uncle's Islet or Funky Arch or Jewel Cave—taking in the seals and rocks and birds and waves and the unpredictable, mercurial sky. But there were less than forty-eight hours left in my visit, and I was feeling more than a little preoccupied by the fact that I had not, as yet, seen a shark. Whiffing for the second time in two years was inconceivable.

"Tomorrow's the day," Peter had assured me last night. "We're overdue for a big, bloody attack."

"THE TRUE BIOLOGIST DEALS WITH LIFE, WITH TEEMING BOISTEROUS life, and learns something from it, learns that the first rule of life is living," John Steinbeck wrote in *The Log from the Sea of Cortez*. Upon his graduation from college in 1979, Peter Pyle set out to prove him right. A twenty-year-old bird savant with big hair, a seventies-issue mustache, and a fresh zoology degree from Swarthmore, he hit the road with the express purpose of seeing as many birds as he could, from the jungly forests of Hawaii (where there were few birds, it turned out, but plenty of opportunities to make some cash tending marijuana plants), to Europe, and on to Asia. Along the way, Peter met another ornithologist who mentioned that the real bird action was taking place in Bolinas, California, under the auspices of a group called PRBO, the Point Reyes Bird Observatory. It was an organization of genius and irreverence, dedicated to conserving ecosystems, wetlands, marine environments—anyplace, basically, where birds lived. "You belong there," Peter was told.

And so, on New Year's Eve in 1979, he pulled into Bolinas in the beat-up navy-blue VW Bug that had occasionally served as his home as well as his car. After volunteering for several months at Palomarin, PRBO's field station set against the rugged West Marin coastline, he was offered an eight-week internship at Southeast Farallon Island, which PRBO monitored in a partnership with the U.S. Fish and Wildlife Service.

When Peter stepped onto the East Landing for the first time, he took it all in: the masses of birds, the stark landscape, the furious weather, the perfect isolation, the cute female interns. Everything he wanted was right in front of him, all rolled up into one improbable package. *This is it,* he thought to himself. *This is my place.* By 1985, he had secured a staff biologist position at the Farallones, which enabled him to spend as much as half the year living on the island.

In the early days there wasn't much awareness of the resident sharks. However, as sightings of giant dorsal fins and slashed-up seals increased throughout the eighties, so did the biologists' curiosity. Whenever Peter witnessed an attack from the island, he would jot down his observations, but that was about all he could do. Everyone was riveted when the sharks showed themselves, awed by their size and the large pools of blood just offshore, but there was no research program devoted to great white sharks, no resources to study them, and no one on this island of ornithologists with the time or the inclination to do so, anyway. An intrepid marine scientist named Peter Klimley, who had already distinguished himself with his cutting-edge shark studies, got the ball rolling, arriving in 1985 at the invitation of the Farallones' head biologist, David Ainley. Ainley, by all accounts a sort of biological visionary, wanted to create a research program devoted to great whites. He and Klimley, assisted by Peter, began to set up systems for collecting data and tried for several seasons to entice the sharks into gobbling sheep carcasses that contained transmitters. The idea of having sharks swallow tracking devices was innovative and promising (and was later continued at the island by a scientist named Ken Goldman), but Ainley had his hands full running the place, supervising every bit of research that was going on, and Klimley had other shark projects in Baja and elsewhere that demanded his attention, and could not devote an entire season to the island. The Farallones was, above all, a field post and required someone to be there at all times, watching.

Which, in 1987, is exactly where Scot came in. He had grown up, appropriately, in Tiburon (Spanish for "shark"), a bayside town in Marin County. While other kids were taping Farrah Fawcett and Rolling Stones posters to their bedroom walls, Scot had been putting up great white shark pictures. He knew about the Farallones. And as someone who had spent his whole life around this stretch of ocean, he'd heard every last legend and big fish story about the sharks. In the seventies and eighties, though, even the insiders didn't know very much. Local fishermen reported that there were great whites out there, plenty of them, but that was it.

Scot wasn't the only person interested in researching great white sharks at the Farallones, but without a doubt he was the most determined. He systematically made his way to the islands over the course of several years, cultivating colleagues who could help him get there, and learning to band birds, a complicated and technical process, so that he could qualify for an internship. When he finally arrived, he made himself indispensable by doing everything with extreme competence—from cooking a mean lasagna to fixing the roof. Whatever it took.

But most important, it soon became obvious that he could see things about the sharks that no one else could. He had a sixth sense for knowing where to look at just the right moment, and eyesight one could fairly describe as bionic. Shortly after Scot's arrival, the fall biologist at the time, a seabird specialist named Phil Henderson, appointed him to a newly created post: principal great white shark researcher. Peter was the only person whom Scot could convince to motor out to a mangled carcass, the only other scientist who was as drawn by the sharks as he was. And Peter, with his ability to tell a LeConte's sparrow from a Henslow's sparrow at a hundred yards, shared Scot's gift of vision. The partnership turned out to be ideal.

And so, together, in 1988, with the joint backing of PRBO and the U.S. Fish and Wildlife Service, they created the Farallon Islands White Shark Project, the only long-term study of individual great white sharks—or white sharks, as scientists prefer to call them—in existence. When they said "individual," they meant it literally. Using underwater video and topside observation, Scot and Peter had identified more than a hundred white sharks, cataloged their whereabouts around the island, even named them. (While naming the animals might come across as a sweet, neighborly thing to do, it had an essential scientific purpose: This was the easiest way to keep track of them in the field.)

One of the first things they learned was that these great whites were the alphas among alphas. Fifteen feet was an average-size Farallon shark, eighteen was large, and twenty was rare but not unheard of. In other great white hubs—South Africa, Australia, Mexico's Guadalupe Island—the sharks were generally eight- to twelve-foot juveniles, which is certainly no small fish. But at the Farallones, a twelve-foot white shark came across like a runty teenager trying to get into a bar.

With their project, Scot and Peter had a coup: to study a *neighborhood* of great white sharks doing their great white shark thing, year in and year out. As a result, the duo had been the first to document the great white's natural feeding habits, its instinctive behavior around other sharks, and its innate hunting strategies. While these observations might seem mundane, in the biology world it was like winning the trifecta. The unique setup at the Farallones—the lighthouse viewing post, the convenient living quarters, the abundance of sharks and seals and throngs of gulls to point the way to the attacks—enabled them to rewrite entire chapters of the book on great white sharks. Which is fortunate because, as it turns out, most of the conventional wisdom was wrong. Scientists thought great whites hunted at night; they hunt by day. They thought these sharks had poor vision and stalked by smell; they're visual predators. People thought these animals were insensate killing machines, but in truth they go after their prey with caution and a plan.

These days, Peter and Scot had zero hesitation about getting next to a feeding great white shark. In the beginning, though, things were scarier. They wanted to observe the sharks at close range, but their boat was only eleven feet long. They called it the "Dink Boat" or the "Dinner Plate."

Powering up the Dinner Plate and approaching a shark in the aftermath of an attack required a leap of faith—they had no idea what the animals would do. It wasn't the kind of thing you could look up in a reference manual: Procedures for Operating a Tiny Boat Next to a Feeding Great White Shark. Everyone was still under the dark influence of *Jaws*. Both men suspected that the sharks wanted to eat them. Why *wouldn't* they rock the boat and try to tip them out?

Certainly, white sharks had a reputation for biting, ramming, attacking, and even sinking small boats. Captains worldwide told stories of them butting sport-fishing crafts, as if making a territorial statement, and from time to time their teeth were found embedded in the hulls. At Cape Breton in Nova Scotia, a twelve-foot great white smashed a hole through the bottom of a dory. In South Africa, a fishing boat came to an abrupt stop despite the fact that the engine was still running. When the fishermen peered over the edge at their outboard motor, they discovered that a great white shark had locked its jaws around the propeller. Breaching great whites had been known to accidentally land on top of small vessels, killing people, crushing pelvises, and, in at least one case, chewing on the upholstery.

As they settled in that first year, the two men crept closer and closer to the attacks and whenever anything scared them, their response was always the same: gun the motor and rocket out of there. Which was exactly what they did on their third time out to an attack, a clear-water day off the western tip of the island, a spot called Indian Head, when a shark approximately twice as big as the boat came up to nose around. And she wasn't alone. It was the first time they'd encountered two sharks simultaneously. When they could track one shark circling beneath them they felt reasonably secure, but the idea of the second one sneaking up from behind while they were watching the first was too unnerving at that point. They hit the gas. After hovering fifty yards away for a few minutes, watching the fins pirouetting around the carcass, curiosity won out and they inched their way back to the feeding sharks. And the sharks eyeballed them, but kept right on tearing at the seal. "We realized that we could go out there, look at the attacks, and not die," Scot recalled. "That was a big deal."

PETER'S WEATHER PREDICTION HELD. AS THE LIGHT CAME UP AND I stepped outside I saw that the fog had dissolved, the ocean was unveiled, and the jagged contours of another farallon, Saddle Rock, were crisply in focus for the first time since my arrival. Saddle Rock reared out of the water only two hundred yards southeast of the main island, and from certain angles it looked exactly like a dorsal fin. Cormorants bunched along its edges, forming an elegant black picket fence. It marked the divide between Mirounga Bay (where the Rat Pack hunted) and Shubrick Point (where the Sisterhood reigned). Many an elephant seal head had been lost in its shadow.

Scot and Peter and I drank our coffee on the front steps, looking out at the water glimmering in the early light. There was a feathery wind and a handful of scudding clouds. The morning was hardly tranquil, though. The gulls screeched at top volume, as always. Surf boomed onto the rocks and the air was hazy with spray. Seabirds flew formation passes over the water, and every time they seemed to favor a particular spot I felt a little flash of hope—was there a carcass out there? Peter seemed to have other things on his mind; he was eyeing a perfect eight-foot barrel wave that rolled along an area known as "Shark Alley." The wave, unsurprisingly, had never been ridden.

Not for lack of surfboards, though. There was a quiver in the supply shed at all times—Scot used them as decoys to lure sharks to the surface for photo IDs. To a shark, apparently, a nice little six-foot swallowtail does a near-perfect imitation of a seal. When retrieved, the decoys were often missing hubcap-sized chunks from their sides, and surfers had taken to sending Scot their castoffs, hoping to repossess them after the sharks had paid a visit. Along with their research value, the strafed boards made for great conversation pieces.

According to Scot and Peter, the Queen Annihilator of Surfboards was a shark named Stumpy. Stumpy was nineteen feet long and weighed five thousand pounds, and when she was in residence, she ruled the Farallones. "She was the only shark that I think understood who we were, what we were trying to do," Peter recalled. "And she didn't care for it. When Scot was first putting out the decoys Stumpy would just come up and destroy them, more because she didn't like them than because she was fooled by their silhouettes." He turned to Scot. "Hey, it's an odd-numbered year. Stumpy could be here."

"If she was, we'd know it," Scot said.

Stumpy patrolled a swath of sea along the east side of the island near the main boat launching spot at East Landing. For prey, this was not an advisable route onto shore. "No seal gets by her," Peter said. And while other sharks would take twenty minutes or more to consume their kills, Stumpy could polish off a five-hundred-pound elephant seal in three minutes flat. Though the distinctively cropped tail fin that earned Stumpy her name hadn't been spotted for several years, Scot and Peter still talked about her with a respect that bordered on awe. "Stumpy was a goddess, there's no other way to put it," Peter said, lowering his voice in reverence. One time, Scot rigged a video camera on the underside of a surfboard to determine which angle the sharks were coming from when they attacked. He set the video board adrift off East Landing. Right on cue, like some battle-hardened test pilot, Stumpy gave it everything she had. The resulting footage was stunning, all teeth and whitewater and violent smashing noises that brought to mind a subaquatic train wreck. It was the first time anyone had successfully filmed great white sharks underwater in California.

Stumpy made her movie debut in the BBC documentary I had seen, and won Scot an Emmy for cinematography. During the first furious hit the board snapped in two and shot into the air, and as the camera dispassionately recorded the wreckage, Stumpy resurfaced and gave the bobbling pieces a fierce backhand with her tail, before swimming off grumpily in search of real food.

None of this seemed like the best testimonial for the sport of surfing.

And yet everyone involved with the Shark Project surfed. In fact, Brown had actually been attacked by a shark while riding waves in Palm Beach last November. "Yup, I'm a statistic," he admitted the night before when I asked for details. "I wouldn't say I was *attacked*, though. It's more like I was bitten." By seventy-six teeth, to be exact. Waiting for a set, Brown had felt some pressure on his foot and looked down. All around him the water was red. *Holy shit! Look at all that blood,* he thought, not quite realizing it was his own. He never saw the shark, but after examining his wounds he concluded that it was a sand tiger, a spooky-looking, snaggletoothed shark that eats fish. And in the turbid Florida water, flashing white feet can look an awful lot like fish.

Peter grew up as a surf rat on the beaches of Oahu. Every day after school he'd run to grab his board, a hulking ten-footer that he'd bought for four dollars at a garage sale. (The deal might've had something to do with the board's sky-blue patina of lead-based paint, which would chip off and lodge under Peter's toenails.) Even as surfing gear improved and evolved over the years and his friends began to do flamboyant tricks on the new shortboards, Peter always preferred the big logs. Longboarding was more soulful, he felt, more in tune with the ocean. Whether other surfers agreed with these esoterics or not, there was at least one advantage to a larger board: It didn't look quite as much like a seal. (Boogie boards, apparently, were the worst.)

"I know exactly how I'd do it," Peter said now, gesturing toward the wave. "But to get into the water here . . ." His voice trailed off.

"Well, *maybe* you could try it in April," Scot said. Shark attacks in the spring were rare. Even so, he didn't sound too convinced. He had only recently taken up surfing, and was openly cautious about wave selection. With good reason. While the Farallones provided a convenient drive-thru for seal-hunting sharks, it was certainly not the only place around here where you'd think twice about getting on a surfboard. All of Northern California is sharky, so sharky that the area extending from Tomales Bay in West Marin County to the Farallones to Monterey is known as the "Red Triangle." More attacks by great whites had taken place in this pocket region than in all the other shark hot spots of the world—combined. Close to home near Inverness, there were a handful of surf spots that Scot wouldn't even consider.

"North Beach and South Beach," he said. "I won't go there." These beaches were just north of the Point Reyes Lighthouse and featured nearby elephant seal colonies. Both areas had strong undertows and rogue riptides and wonderful ambush potential and, of course, seals, all of which add up to precisely the type of arrangement that great white sharks like. There was also an ominous place near the mouth of Tomales Bay called Shark Pit, where surfers had recently encountered three white sharks in a single day. Concerned, one of them asked Scot, What's going on? Had there been a sudden influx of seals? Was it the full moon? The red tide? The new yellow wetsuit someone was wearing?

"Nah, they're usually there," he told them. "You guys just saw 'em."

"I don't surf where there are sharks," he emphasized to me now.

"You surf in Bolinas!" Peter said, with a snort. Bolinas was a tiny beach town, also in West Marin, that was only eighteen miles by boat from the Farallones. Sightings of healthy-size white sharks in the town's channel were not uncommon. Recently, a boogie boarder had been attacked there. In other words, Bolinas had plenty of sharks.

"Yeah, but I'm in water that's only up to my chest," Scot replied, laughing. "And I always have a buffer zone of about fifteen kids around me."

All this shark talk was making me impatient. Where *were* they? As if reading my mind, Scot suddenly stood up. "There's something going on down there," he said, pointing toward the wave. Even without binoculars I could see the black dorsal fin, it was that close to shore; any closer and the shark would be joining us for coffee. We watched for a moment as the fin carved a few tight circles like a figure skater diligently practicing and then disappeared into the surf.

"There's no carcass," Peter said.

"Yeaahhh, that's just one of them being weird," Scot said.

"Well, it could be a sea lion, though." Sea lion carcasses don't float like elephant seal carcasses. Thus, attacks on sea lions were much harder to spot. It was decided that we'd launch the whaler and take a look; even if there was nothing going on in Mirounga Bay, we'd be out on the water, that much closer to the action.

WE WALKED THE QUARTER MILE TO EAST LANDING, WHERE SCOT grabbed a surfboard from a storage shed that had the words *Shark*

Shack stenciled on its door above a black-and-white painting of a shark. (Scot was always drawing sharks; the logbooks were covered with his sketches.) The three-foot-wide path from the houses to the landing, paved a century ago, had built-in rails and a rail cart that rode along them. The pavement was crumbling now, but the rails still worked, and the cart was useful when things like propane canisters or solar panels or three months' worth of groceries had to be trundled back and forth. At the edge of the cliff, the whaler rested beneath the king-sized blue boom that would lift it up, swing it over the side, and lower it into the water.

Brown was radioed down to operate the crane. Peter, Scot, and I piled into the boat, now laden with surfboards and video cameras and life jackets. Using a giant carabiner, Peter clipped the whaler's harness to the boom. The crane roared to life, and for a moment the shark boat hung suspended in the air like something out of a James Bond movie, and then we ratcheted down. I was comforted by the fact that Peter had done more landings, in every possible condition, than anyone else. He could read the waves, maneuvering the whaler in the surge channel with one hand while unhooking it from the boom with the other. Anticipating the next set's arrival was key—if he timed it wrong, the swells would paste the boat against the rocks.

We motored into Mirounga Bay, cutting the engine just west of Saddle Rock, about three hundred yards from shore. Scot tied the surfboard to a fishing line and tossed it off the back, where it drifted, looking rather alone. From where we sat, the land and the water appeared as barren as the moon. In fact, below the surface the area served as a hub for the entire food chain. Along the teetering edge of the continental shelf, life roared from the depths as cold water pushed its way upward, bringing plankton and nutrients that attracted the birds and the krill and the tiny baitfish and the wacky invertebrates such as jellyfish and urchins and octopus and squid, which in turn brought the rockfish and the salmon and the other pelagic creatures that seals and sea lions and mako sharks and blue sharks just loved to snack on; and all these animals made for one big party that the whales couldn't possibly miss: the grays and the humpbacks and the lordly blues and, of course, where there were whales and seals and a selection of midsize fish, there were great white sharks patrolling the joint, making sure that no one felt too immortal.

We drifted in silence. The only noises were the wind chuffing by and the water lightly slapping against the side of the boat. I kept my eyes on the surfboard.

"Shark approaching," Peter said this softly. A shark's presence was always preceded by a boil, the flat surface pattern made by its powerful tail fin right before it broke the surface. Naturally, they saw the boil long before I did. In the next second the shark appeared, knifing toward the boat. Peter and Scot stiffened into high alert, standing with their pole-mounted cameras poised like harpoons. Suddenly the whaler felt ridiculously small and as though it was riding way too low in the water.

The first thing I noticed about the shark was its immense girth. I suppose I had known, intellectually, anyway, that a shark might be as long as the whaler, but I didn't expect it to be as *wide* as the boat too. Here, for context, are some measurements: a twenty-foot shark is eight feet wide and six feet deep. That's wider than a Suburban, as wide as a Mack truck. That's wider than Yao Ming is tall. The outsized tail of a great white looks more like something that might belong to a whale, but while a shark's tail rides vertically in the water like a gigantic rudder, a whale's tail sits horizontally, like the spoiler on a race car.

Another thing about white sharks: They're black. Not inky black like orcas or labradors but a sort of mottled charcoal black that takes on a luminous sheen below the water's surface. And not only that, white sharks suntan, which makes them darker. Only their undersides are white. This two-tone color scheme means that from below great white sharks look as ephemeral as ghosts, while from above they possess the solidity of lead. It's great for camouflage, especially above rocky areas. "Whoever named them must have had one upside down," Peter pointed out.

This particular shark, which looked to be about fifteen feet long, glided under us, then came to the surface and bumped the back of the boat. Its head was scribbled with black scars that looked punctured and deep, as though someone had been playing tic-tac-toe with an icepick. Each shark had a signature set of divots and spots and scars and scratches, or a chink taken out of a fin, but this one looked like it had lost a knife fight. I felt a very old part of my brain, the part that served us so well back on the veld, snap to attention. The shark cruised around us with the insistent, unthreatening curiosity of a cocker spaniel looking for scraps under the dinner table.

"They have split personalities," Scot said. "When they're in attack mode, their dispositions change." He explained that the shark was merely investigating us, using its mouth to explore something that might be food. After all, they don't have hands. And being savvy hunters, they aren't about to launch themselves full tilt at something that might hurt them. Not that even a preliminary looksee by a food-seeking great white is a desirable thing if you're in the water. But these two distinct modes of behavior are the reason why so many people who encounter a white shark will live, if they manage to survive the initial bite.

Now there were three sharks circling us. Their presence was tentative and—as unlikely as it sounds—almost gentle. They kept their distance from each other but they were all working from the same playbook, looping from every possible angle, swimming about six feet below the surface so their fins stayed submerged, trying to figure out whether the whaler represented food. At this shallow depth they were clearly visible, and their dark bodies gave off a kind of glow, as though spotlighted from within. If a shark decided to surface, its tail would pop up first, then its dorsal fin, and then its head. The three animals were in no particular hurry, checking us out like low riders trolling the strip on a Saturday night. They dove beneath the whaler, bumped it, slapped it with their tails. Looking down over the side, trying to follow their movements, I came face-to-face with a shark arrowing straight up from below; this was how they rushed their prey. I could see its eyes and its crooked, fiendish smile. "Oh my *God,*" I said, lunging back from the edge.

Next to me, Peter plunged his camera in the water. "White sharks have this great grin on their faces when they're coming right at you," he said. "It's cute."

"Aren't they *beautiful?*" Scot said, with the kind of pride that others reserve for their children.

Then, off the bow, I saw a tail that dwarfed the others. It looked more like the tail of a Gulfstream jet than of a fish, and it moved with the languorous swishy motion of a runway model. It was so enormous that even with its back end next to the boat, I couldn't make out the front half of the animal. This shark had a different aura. It could only be a Sister. Her great tail gleamed, and it bore absolutely no scars. She swam with unbelievable power and un-likely grace, a Sherman tank making dressage moves. As she van-ished into the depths, another shark emerged from the darkness, making several quick runs, back and forth, under the whaler. Scot leaned over the edge to get a better look.

"Hey, that's Cuttail!" he shouted.

Cuttail, he told me, was a Rat Packer, back at the Farallones for his thirteenth consecutive year, which was a record. He was a can-tankerous shark but enormously popular because he was one of the "Adopt a Great White Shark" candidates that were part of the project's fund-raising. Little girls who had "adopted" him wrote ar-dent letters to Cuttail with regularity. (Eight-year-old Paige Hulme from England was a typical correspondent: "Dear Cuttail: I am writing to you to say everything really! I love you so much. I want to see you. You know that key ring you gave me, well it's on my pencil case. My friends think you're scary [only being childish like they are]. I love you so much. I will always love you longer than anyone shall live. P.S: Could you please write back?")

The sharks kept coming and coming. At least five of them vis-ited the boat, maybe more. As the afternoon passed I lost track of time, crouched in the whaler's scooped-out bow, bouncing from one railing to the other while the massive fish cruised under us like submarines; I could have kept it up, I think, forever. I was stockpiling questions. Did they recognize the boat? Each other? When they lifted their heads above the water, could they see us? I wanted to know which individuals we'd seen, but often that was hard to tell from above. We'd find out exactly who had stopped by later, when Scot and Peter analyzed their video. Sometimes they would notice more sharks beneath the ones they'd seen from the surface, apparitions that the camera picked up as blurry shadows lurking in the watery twilight. Scot couldn't figure out why we were so popular this afternoon; there was no blood in the water, nothing to explain the sharks' continuous laps. They were acting hungry.

Most of the time when a human encounters a great white shark, it's hunting something; at other times these animals hide with expert slyness. But even when a great white is in quiet reconnaissance mode, stalking on the periphery, its presence is overwhelming. You can *feel* them, a phenomenon acknowledged by researchers, surfers, divers—anyone who's spent enough time on the water to have had a brush with one. The only thing more powerful than a great white's arrival is that prelude instant right before the fin appears because, somehow, you know it's coming. I'd heard surfers refer to this sixth sense as "that sharky feeling" and "the creeps." Peter referred to it as "being in the groove," and it was clear that both he and Scot cultivated the instinct.

With so many sharks converging on the whaler right now, their presence was as palpable as heat. It struck me as surreal to be floating among them, drinking a Diet Coke, only a thirty-mile hop from the Macy's in Union Square.

But there was something even stranger going on two hundred yards away. Smack in the middle of Stumpy's lair, just about the last place you'd ever consider dipping your toe, a boat was anchored, and a man was climbing out of the water. His name was Ron Elliott, Peter said. Ron was the last commercial diver at the Farallones, the only man left who was willing to take his chances here. He picked urchins, working solo from his boat, an immaculate aluminum crabber with a sky-blue shark stenciled on the gunwale. The boat was named *GW,* the letters of which reversed out of the shark in white. I could see a lone figure standing on deck in a hooded wetsuit. "He keeps a real low profile," Scot said. "Doesn't even have a deckhand."

"His boat is spotless," Peter said, shaking his head in admiration. *"Spotless,"* Scot repeated.

Clearly, they were in awe of this guy. And, after seeing firsthand what lived in these waters, so was I. Peter radioed the *GW* to see if we could come over and say hello, the Farallon equivalent of dropping in on your neighbors.

RON ELLIOTT DIDN'T ALWAYS HAVE THE FARALLONES TO HIMSELF. Though the waters here are as cold and dark as a haunted basement, forbidding enough even without the sharks, in the days before people knew better there were numerous divers who worked them—for abalone, for urchins, and even for sport. On Sunday, January 14, 1962, to cite just one incident, more than a hundred divers arrived at Southeast Farallon Island to participate in a spearfishing competition.

At about 10:30 in the morning, a spearfisherman named Floyd Pair had just surfaced, about one hundred yards from shore, when something hit him from below. Confused, he looked down and saw a fourteen-foot shark with his right leg in its mouth, shaking its head to shear off a hunk of thigh. Pair whacked the shark repeatedly with his spear gun as he yelled for help, and it swam off— toward the other divers. Even after all the spearfishers were safely back on board, and the emergency helicopter had been summoned, the shark remained at the surface, circling. Floyd Pair lived, but he had incurred "serious fang-like lacerations" that missed his femoral artery by less than a centimeter.

Later that same year the Mighty Skin Divers Club of San Francisco anchored at Middle Farallon, a nubbin of rock set off by itself about three miles north of Southeast Farallon. It was November 11, the height of shark season, although no one knew that at the time. The new sport of scuba was becoming popular and the divers were excited to photograph the psychedelically colored rockfish and octopi that lived on the marine shelf next to the islet, maybe spear a few of them while they were at it. The thirty club members were guided by Leroy French and Al Giddings, two extremely experienced divers.

At the end of the first dive Giddings was standing on deck, counting heads to make sure everyone had returned to the boat. There was one diver missing, though—French. At that moment Giddings turned and saw a large shark, at least sixteen feet long, thrashing on the surface. Leroy French was in its mouth. The shark lifted its enormous tail, slammed it down, and, as the scuba club watched in horror, dragged French underwater. Giddings heroically jumped from the boat and swam to the spot where his colleague had gone under. Seconds later French's life jacket inflated and he popped to the surface, screaming and clawing at the water. With the help of another diver named Donald Joslin, Giddings managed to get him back to the boat. French was then airlifted to the Harbor Emergency Hospital in San Francisco, where 480 stitches were required to close his wounds. The shark had bitten him three times, taking chunks out of his forearm, calf, and buttocks. Seven years later, by cruel coincidence, Donald Joslin would also be attacked by a great white shark while diving for abalone off Tomales Point, the apex of the Red Triangle. And he too would live, after hours of surgery and hundreds of stitches.

And so it went through the sixties, the seventies, and the eighties as more and more people discovered the hard way that the Farallon Islands were not an ideal diving locale. Scuba clubs went elsewhere. Spearfishermen followed. The abalone and urchin divers, however, remained for a time. The waters around Southeast Farallon were too rich to ignore, and these men were not easily intimidated. Yet the sharks began to make increasingly frequent appearances as the seal population revived over the decades, and there were several near-fatal attacks and many close calls and as a result everyone carried a 9mm pistol when diving at the Farallones, a specially modified Glock that could fire underwater. Some divers even wore elaborate jungle gym–like cages on their backs in the manner of turtles. But the cages only made it harder to move quickly and almost impossible to climb back onto the boat, and the guns were better in theory than in practice. One by one, the divers lost their nerve.

Soon it was only Ron. At first Peter and Scot thought he was on some kind of suicide mission. They noticed that when selecting his dive sites, Ron had an uncanny knack for anchoring at the scene of the latest shark attack. They worried that any day they would be picking up Ron's body. But the years went by and he kept showing up to dive, often calling on the radio at day's end with valuable observations about shark behavior that only someone who was down there with them would ever see. The three men became friends.

Today the *GW* was anchored off Shubrick Point in front of a dramatic cathedral of a sea cave called Great Murre Cave. The cave's opening was a two-hundred-foot-high vertical slash, cleaved into the island like a lethal wound. This was Sisterhood Country. We tied alongside. Ron stood on deck in his wetsuit, its thick industrial neoprene giving off the dual auras of hard work and tired seal. He was a trim guy, in his early fifties, with an efficient brushcut and eyes that, while kind, definitely didn't miss much. We greeted him, Peter introduced me, and the talk turned immediately to sharks. Scot mentioned the drive-bys we'd had near Saddle Rock.

"Yeah, just saw one myself," Ron said. He spoke slowly, with a California drawl. I asked him how many times he'd seen sharks while diving in the Farallones. He thought for a minute, scratched the side of his neck. "Well, I don't really count, but, ahhhh, at least . . . three, four hundred."

Over time I would come to understand Ron's attitude toward the sharks. Emotion didn't enter into it. In his mind they were simply doing their job, same as him. And if, to do his job, Ron occasionally had to get away from the sharks by hiding under rocks, fending them off with his urchin basket, or staring them down— well, that was just another day at the office.

Only the week before, in fact, he had jumped into the water at Shubrick Point and practically landed on one of the Sisters. She swam away and then turned, mouth wide open, and barreled toward him with unmistakable intent. "She tried to give me a little love bite," Ron said. "I shoved my urchin basket in her nose and then she flipped around and attacked the basket, shook it over my head, bent my arm, you know, sent me sailing." In the scuffle, Ron's wetsuit hood was ripped from his head, his mask jammed down around his neck, his nose bloodied. Then the shark turned and thwhacked him with its tail. "I thought she broke my face," he said. "She kept circling me, following me around. She wasn't one of those ones you could bluff out."

The sharks knew exactly what they were looking at when they ran into him down below, of this Ron was certain. Often, a shark would make several passes, from different directions, trying to figure out the craftiest means of approach. Ron could sense their presence, however, even when they were behind him. And sneaking up from the rear was their specialty.

There were the stinging jellyfish and sea anemones to contend with as well, and the sea lions that cruised in marauding gangs, occasionally pausing to sink their teeth into the back of his neck. But Ron didn't mind the danger involved in diving here. In fact, he preferred it—the diciness meant that everyone else stayed away. He'd started out diving for urchins in Southern California in the seventies, and when he and his wife, Carol, moved north to Point Reyes, he looked out at the Farallones, only a two-hour boat ride away, and realized that urchin-wise, it was the place to go. He had to dive there. And the first time he did, in 1989, he encountered a seventeen-foot shark.

As he carefully coiled his air hose, I asked how Carol felt about his job site. "She's okay with it," he said, and then paused. "Wellll, maybe she's getting a *little* tired of it. But she knows that if something happens, I'd rather have it happen out here than, you know, in a *car*."

It was dusk; it was time to leave. We had been on the water for five hours. The light had slowly thickened and the ocean looked as black as tar. As we pushed off from the *GW*, I turned to Scot and Peter, the question clear on my face. How could anyone possibly do this for a living? "Ron's all about competence," Peter said. Scot agreed, and marveled at Ron's fearlessness. "People cry on the evening news if they see a dorsal fin in the surf," he said. "And here's a guy who's around them all day long and doesn't want to tell anyone."

It was hard to imagine that all the competence in the world could keep a diver safe in a place where a floating surfboard can draw a great white shark to the surface within minutes, sometimes even seconds. How long could Ron's mix of skill, sangfroid, and luck possibly hold out? Launching into the water here with no backup seemed like Russian roulette with reverse odds. Now I understood Peter's and Scot's awe. It was tinged with fear. No one wanted to witness the day when things went wrong.

As we drove back to East Landing, I pointed at everything—gulls, shadows on the water, nothing in particular—thinking it was a shark. "You've got sharks on the brain," Scot said. "That happens. You just can't be close to a creature like this and not be affected. How big they are, how they glide around you." He cast a glance at the darkening ocean. "You see their eyes, and you know they're looking at you."

SCOT WAS SCHEDULED TO COOK DINNER, AND WHEN WE GOT BACK TO the house he disappeared into the kitchen. Peter went outside with Brown and Nat to do something bird related, and I sprawled on the living room couch with the kind of deep fatigue that comes from gunning your adrenaline glands all day. The room was cluttered, strikingly decorated in a critter motif. There were many skulls. One particularly large skull, don't ask me what kind, was wearing a jaunty gold crown. There were shark books and shark teeth and shark photographs and a box of Motorola radios in various states of disrepair. There were stuffed birds and weather gauges and whale bones and an old guitar. Next to the window, an old Mexican blanket covered the back of an armchair that had seen better days. A marine radio sat on a wooden desk, spitting out weather reports and bursts of static. Above the radio, displayed like artwork, hung the remnants of an inflatable Zodiac that was bitten and partially sunk by a shark named the Cadillac. Hanging in a place of honor, the scrap of rubber displayed a set of tooth marks that could only have been made by a two-foot-wide set of jaws.

I was drifting off when Peter opened the front door and shouted, "Come out here—you have to see the Green Flash!" I wasn't sure what the Green Flash was, but I got up anyway. The entire human population of the Farallones, all five of us, gathered on the front steps. The sun was going down. It hung heavy on the horizon, like a drop of water about to fall, then vanished in the next instant. And in that millisecond, there it was—a small, crescent-shaped emerald that flared up like demented lightning. Blink, and you'd miss ten of them. Later I learned that the Green Flash is so seldom glimpsed it's often considered a myth or a hoax, even though it's a readily explainable illusion (if you happen to have a degree in optical physics, that is, and can readily explain principles like refraction and dispersion). To provide even the dimmest hope of a sighting, a checklist of conditions must be met at the instant of sunset or sunrise: a perfectly flat horizon, clear air at a precise temperature relative to the water, and a long span of sky with nothing impeding the view, not even a single cloud.

Everyone applauded the Green Flash before heading back inside to escape the sudden chill wind. Dinner was an improvisational masterpiece Scot had whisked together from the dwindling supply of canned tomatoes and half-finished boxes of spaghetti, and the kitchen took on a celebratory air. I had finally seen the sharks. (Also, Kabul had just fallen, with the Taliban sent scurrying, though no one on Southeast Farallon Island was aware of that quite yet. War, terrorism—those were the concerns of another planet.) Scot made it clear that our afternoon sightings were nothing compared to a full-on attack, but I was still flying from the experience and wouldn't have traded it.

"Shall we?" Peter asked, reaching into the bookshelf behind the kitchen table for two thick binders. These were the island journals in which, from 1968 on, every last thing that happened at the Farallones had been carefully documented—from the bloodiest shark attack down to a previously unseen species of fly. At year's end these logs would be taken ashore and bound into hardcovers. Then they'd be returned to the house, where they would remain. And at some future date, when someone needed to know whether a rare brown shrike really did touch down on September 20, 1984, or what the barometer read on New Year's Eve, 1973, or on which days, exactly, a Sister named Whiteslash had killed five seals during the 2000 shark season, they would be able to find out. The journal was recorded every night after dinner, and it was the closest thing the islands had to a native religion.

Nat, Brown, and Scot all pulled yellow field notebooks out of their pockets. Peter ran through the birds first. "Loons and grebes? Swallows, nuthatches, creepers, and wrens? Pipits, waxwings, shrikes, starlings? Vireos and warblers?" Birds went on for some time. And then: "Whales? Dolphins? Mice? Bats? Butterflies? Sharks?"

"Well we have the one sighting in the morning," Scot said. "And then several up to the boat this afternoon. Including Cuttail. All in Mirounga Bay." Peter wrote this down and added a few notes of his own. His journal entries, I had noticed, were longer, more poetic, and more carefully written than anybody else's. Reading the logs I was aware of a wide range of styles and disparity in quality. Some people would write, "Krill event, east side." Peter, meanwhile, would write something like "Red highway of krill in eight-foot seas lured humpbacks to the island, and we watched them breaching under a rising moon."

THAT NIGHT THE WATER DREAM RETURNED, BUT THIS TIME THE IMAGE was clearer. I recognized the sharks gliding by: Stumpy, Cuttail, and the unknown Sister with her monstrous tail. For once, though, the dream didn't strike me as strange. Out here shark dreams were so common and so vivid there was a section in the logbook devoted to recounting them; Scot had confessed that he still had them every night. In my dream it was dark, and I was alone, drifting in a small boat. Once again I looked down as shadowy creatures swam beneath me, just barely visible by moonlight. And all night, majestic and terrible fish cruised through the Jane Fonda Bedroom in otherworldly silence.

CHAPTER 2

We are no longer alone.

—FARALLON ISLAND LOGBOOK, SEPTEMBER 10, 1994
(FIRST DAY OF SHARK SEASON)

NOVEMBER 17, 2001

The old tower stands at the highest spot in all the Farallones, a precipitous perch that goes by the misleadingly gentle name of Lighthouse Hill. When the Farallon light blinked on in 1855, it had a first-order Fresnel lens, an optical jewel shipped from France, and a crew of devoted operators. An indentured mule named Jack hauled its fuel—drums of sperm whale oil—up the zigzag path. (Even by mule standards this was no picnic; when Jack retired twenty years later, his fur had turned completely white.) In 1972, the eighteen-foot-high lens was replaced by a pair of automated beacons, and the last lighthouse keeper sailed off on a coast guard cutter.

These days the lighthouse is a wreck, colonized by mice, smeared with guano, and sprouting neon-green lichen. But if you're up here to scout shark attacks, it's nature's luxury box. On a clear morning the observer has ten miles of visibility and can make a 360-degree sweep of the south islands: gazing west into Maintop Bay; looking straight down on Fisherman's Bay and Sugarloaf to the north; Tower Point, Shubrick Point, East Landing, and

Saddle Rock to the east; and Mirounga Bay rolled out like a carpet to the south. Seven miles off in the westerly distance, the North Farallones jut up, and three miles northwest, Middle Farallon pokes out of the ocean like a speed bump. The lighthouse tower itself, a two-story concrete cylinder with a small rectangular entranceway, provides little shelter from the inevitable howling wind, and walking around the deck requires one hand on the railing at all times.

This was the obvious place for Sharkwatch, which Scot created in 1987. During every daylight hour of shark season, someone was stationed up here—Scot, Peter, Brown, Nat, or one of the interns who completed the crew—scanning the water for attacks through a powerful scope. Right from the start, Scot had claimed the first slot: for the past fourteen years, every September, October, and November morning, whenever he was on the island, he had switchbacked his way up 348 vertical feet to man his eight o'clock shift.

When Scot was watching, no nuance on the water would go undetected. Not that a shark attack at the Farallones was typically a subtle event. Elephant seal blood is a brilliant scarlet due to its high oxygen content, and it left a big slick on the blue water that was hard to miss. The most obvious clue, though, appeared in the sky. The site of a kill was instantly engulfed in a Hitchcockian swirl of gulls, all fighting to scavenge a snack. Sometimes the aerial view provided even more detail: the Sisterhood's lair lay directly below, to the east, and when one of the Big Girls ventured out in the late afternoon light, you could see it all: the blood, the seal, the outline of the shark.

Sharkwatch had a simple set of rules: If Scot spotted a slick or a bird rally on the water, he would radio Peter, chart the position of the ruckus using a surveying instrument called a theodolite, and then sprint down the hill to meet everyone at East Landing. The idea was to launch the whaler as quickly as possible and get out there to video. Later, every last detail of the encounter would be noted in a field report, including an identification of the shark and a diagram of which parts of the seal were missing.

Hurtling down Lighthouse Hill in a big hurry to go see a shark attack, however, was an easy way to die. Not only was it treacher-
ously steep, ranging from a thirty- to a fifty-degree incline, but the
ground was unstable. The path was a loose carpet of granite chips,
decomposing bird corpses, and skittery stones, and your feet tended
to whip out from under you as if you were roller-skating on ball
bearings. Recently, Scot had acquired a girl's banana-seat bike to
speed his descent. The bike was sized for someone about three and
a half feet tall, and it had a glittery pink seat, purple streamers, and
knobby tires.

At the moment I was more concerned with the ascent; despite
my two-hour-a-day training schedule in the pool, I'd stopped
twice along the way. When I eventually joined Scot, breathless
from the last pitch to the top, he had been studying the ocean for
an hour. He stood in cinematic relief on the narrow concrete
apron that encircled the tower, his arms crossed against the pum-
meling winds. Classical music wafted from a boom box. There
was a dizzying amount of sky up here and the sea pressed in on all
sides. At the horizon's far edge, you could trace the curve of the
earth.

I had been up to the lighthouse before, but only in the haze, and
the expanse of the view startled me and brought on an unexpected
sadness. The raw grandeur was almost too much to take in, a reminder of trifling human scale. It felt terribly lonely.

Scot turned and gave me a half wave as I summited, glancing
over for a nanosecond before returning to his ocean surveillance. I
asked if he'd seen anything that looked potentially sharky. "Nothing yet," he said. "But it's almost high tide." Most shark attacks
took place during high tide; this was another piece of the great
white puzzle that the Farallones had supplied to the world.
Because—think about it—unless the sharks were watched all the
time, and from a fixed position, how would anyone ever figure
this out? You needed the continuity. It was one thing to spot a
great white, note its location, track its behavior for half an hour.
Maybe, if a researcher were especially lucky, he would be able to

determine its sex, which requires getting a good look at the shark's underside—the males have two long claspers. (As one might guess, this is not an easy thing to do.) But things got far more interesting if you actually *knew* the shark. For instance, if you happened to know that a particular shark was Spotty, a large Rat Packer with a lopsided grin, and you kept track of his appearances over the seasons, you could draw the following conclusion: Spotty had been coming to the Farallones for eleven consecutive years, almost always in the company of Cuttail. And then you might take it one step farther: Did they travel together all the time? Or were they simply sharing some turf? Scot and Peter were hoping to put satellite tags on both sharks next season to find out. Such a discovery would be huge. If these two had been hanging out together for a decade, how could anyone go on thinking of white sharks as rogue assassins, the ocean's killing machines? Rather, they'd be animals with intelligence enough to choose their friends, and to keep them close by.

Prying secrets from the great white shark wasn't a job for dilettantes; it required a rigorous system that extended all the way down to a dress code. The Farallones were hard on a person's wardrobe. Clothes got covered in mud and blood and bird shit, whipped with salt water, fog, and rain. Everyone on the island wore heavy work pants and the kind of footwear one might select for hacking through the Congolese jungle; to this Scot added a jacket, a hoodie that he kept cinched around his head whenever he was outside, and polarized sunglasses that covered half of his face. Underneath the sunglasses, Scot's eyes were ice blue, with the intensity of lasers.

I looked down over the backside of the peak. A misstep in any direction would result in substantial air time before landing on the spiky granite below. The island seemed to be made of six-dimensional rock, striated by a million tiny crevices and fissures casting disco ball shadows in every direction. It was rock as imagined by a cubist on peyote, a mad jumble of stone veined by seawater and runneled with elemental abuse. The whole place was pocked with caves and holes and long twisted passages that led to other long twisted passages. During big storms the island actually vibrated and hummed, making what frightened visitors often described as a "moaning noise."

DURING THE FIRST FEW YEARS HE WAS UP HERE, SCOT'S SHARKWATCH shift often lasted for twelve hours straight. He bought a heap of photo equipment for the project, paying for it himself, and the lighthouse bristled with telephoto lenses. Launching the Dinner Plate was dicey when the water was rough, and the water was almost always rough, so until 1992, when they got a bigger boat (fourteen feet!), the lighthouse was the best place for viewing the attacks. Spending whole days at the light—standing on concrete, at the mercy of the weather—was hard on his legs, and sometimes on his psyche, but the vigil had its rewards.

During the long waits between shark attacks there was always something amazing to see—a pod of dolphins cruising by, or a squadron of whales breaching and spouting. Sometimes a fantastically rare bird would put in an appearance, wildly off course in its migration. The Farallones were famous for these sightings, and they happened regularly, especially during the fall. Birds that ought to be at the North Pole or winging over the Serengeti would instead blunder their way down to the lighthouse or land on one of the three small trees on the island. Red-flanked bluetails and Eurasian wigeons and Xantus' murrelets—they all showed up here eventually. Once, Scot watched as an African pink-backed pelican touched down in the middle of a flock of standard-issue brown pelicans, looking like an exotic stuffed toy that had fallen from the sky.

The solitude, the long, dramatic views, the challenge of the task—it all suited him. Scot was not a big talker. He appreciated routines. And though he got along well with people, he also liked to be alone. In Scot's ideal life, all of the hustle and commerce, frantic movement and paperwork stayed so far off his personal horizon that he would never even have to see it, much less become caught in its tentacles.

As a kid, he was crazy about fish. Scot would watch people angling off the Tiburon seawall for hours, hoping for a glimpse of whatever they caught. There was something about seeing a fish flashing through the water that seemed magical, like finding a piece of hidden treasure. One day he was out on a fishing boat when someone landed a small leopard shark. The creature was burnished bronze and silver with a catlike face, perfectly symmetrical spots, and a sinuous elegance. Scot was instantly struck by its beauty. The leopard shark didn't flop around in a panic; it moved straight across the deck like an alligator, with an air of self-possession. That image never left his mind.

He knew then that what he really wanted to do was to study sharks. But more important, he wanted to study them in their element. That, he thought, was the only way you could ever understand them. Forget about sitting at a desk writing grant applications or leaning over the computer plotting numbers on a graph. Trying to figure out the life of an animal by staring at a screen struck him as futile. For a time he worked as a deckhand on local fishing boats, a job that was great for viewing marine life but not so great for getting his foot in the door as a biologist. Scot realized quickly that advanced shark access required at least one college degree, but he had struggled with school in the past and worried that he was dyslexic. Eventually, he found a school called World College West that wasn't afraid to try things differently. Scot supplemented its new age approach with marine biology courses at the nearby College of Marin, where he hooked up with a gifted teacher named Gordon Chan and realized, for the first time, that he actually loved to learn.

His education extended to a bird census in Alaska, the Tsukiji fish market in Tokyo, and six months in Kathmandu, where he lived with a Nepali family and learned to speak the language.

Back in Marin, his homework included intercepting the flatbed trucks of fishermen as they cruised the streets of Point Reyes, proudly hauling the bodies of great white sharks that had died in their halibut nets. When the sharks were butchered, he asked for—and received—the surplus parts, and then he and Gordon Chan would dissect them, trying to figure out how it all fit together.

In the field, Scot's curiosity, dexterity, and unorthodox science background sparked innovations like the decoys, the pole cameras, and the video surfboard. He was determined to come up with newer, more effective ways to spy on this community of sharks. Other great white shark researchers had come and gone at the Farallones, doing interesting work, just not staying very long. And not everyone is suited to life on an isolated set of rocks in the Pacific. In order to make it on this island, a researcher had to be hearty, adaptable, and emotionally together, with a deep sense of respect. Scot was all that. And more than anyone else, he seemed able to think like a shark.

Even the Cousteaus couldn't hack it. In October 1986, Jean Michel Cousteau and his crew steamed into the Farallones aboard a 103-foot-long boat called the *Alcyone* and promptly began to shower the place with blood and guts to chum for sharks. They anchored off East Landing for several days. Peter had received instructions from the U.S. Fish and Wildlife Service to accommodate them in any possible way, and he stood by on Southeast Farallon for their call. They never radioed the island. On their third day, he watched from shore as two big, bloody killfests took place less than one hundred yards from the *Alcyone*'s bow. He decided to launch the Dinner Plate, to go out and tell them that they were missing the action. Pulling alongside the ship, he hollered a greeting, but no one responded. He couldn't see a soul from the water, so he drove around to the stern and peered onto the deck. It was a bright autumn day, and the entire Cousteau crew was sunbathing, clad in bikini briefs. They looked up from their sun reflectors with irritation. One man waved him away, saying, "Yes, yes. We will call you later."

Afterward, in a book titled *Cousteau's Great White Shark,* Jean Michel bitterly recounted his time at the islands: "We were equipped with cameras and an antishark cage . . . but we did not see even a single dorsal fin. When gallons of fish and animal blood failed to lure great whites during the Farallon expedition, the Cousteau team began to question the abundance of sharks in the area."

Cousteau's empire aside, no matter how many dorsal fins ring these islands, the world of professional shark research remained brutally competitive. There weren't enough jobs. There wasn't enough funding or enough credit. And clearly there weren't enough study subjects to go around. Scot had visited the great white shark hubs at South Africa's Seal Island and Guadalupe Island off Baja, and both areas had their disadvantages when compared with the Farallones. The waters surrounding Seal Island were heavily trafficked by white sharks, but the animals were dispersed over a much larger area, making them harder to study. Also, behemoth Sisters were unheard of. Likewise, at Mexico's Guadalupe Island, many of the sharks ran small. More problematic for research, though, was the fact that Guadalupe was a wild free-for-all involving freeways of chum and no limit to the number of operators that can dunk a cage in the water. These sharks, in Scot's view, were so tourist-addled that they swam toward the boats in anticipation of food the moment they heard the anchors being lowered. And in Australia, a location previously synonymous with great whites, the populations were fading quickly, despite the animal's protected status.

You could run your finger across a map of the world, stopping at every location where white sharks are found, and you'd never come close to the kind of perfect research arrangement provided by the Farallones. Scot and Peter had the ultimate spot, and they were proprietary about it with good reason. They were the ones who'd put in the time.

Standing at the lighthouse being blasted by wind and grit, I doubted that I could spend the equivalent of several years of my life up here. Sharkwatch was demanding, and to me, a twelve-hour shift exceeded the bounds of duty—it was an act of devotion. I said as much to Scot. He nodded. "White sharks require patience," he said, scoping the water. "Pete and I are very patient." Suddenly, his eyes turned glacial. He clicked on his radio. "The man has arrived," he announced, in a voice an octave lower than his regular tone. For a second I thought he was talking about a shark, but then I followed his gaze, east toward San Francisco, and I saw a boat emerging over the horizon, heading directly for us. It was still only a speck. I could barely make out a handful of figures dotting its deck through my binoculars, but Scot knew exactly who it was. It was the outside world, pressing in.

"ATTENTION ADRENALINE JUNKIES! THE WORLD'S BEST SPOT FOR SHARK diving is just minutes from Fisherman's Wharf," trumpeted the October 2002 headline in *Men's Journal* magazine. It was only a matter of time before someone tried to make money on the Farallon sharks. That person was Lawrence Groth, thirty-six, the founder and president of Great White Adventures, a company specializing in great white shark encounters. As his website pointed out, Groth "pioneered the world's first cage-diving operation at the Farallones that manages an 86-percent rate without the use of chum!" Every morning during shark season, weather permitting, Great White Adventures arrived with six divers, each of whom was paying $775 to be there.

The economic incentive was clear. To me, what was surprising wasn't that Groth's operation was here, but rather that there weren't ten Groths plowing their way out every morning, one after the other, in successively larger boats. But there are good reasons why cage diving hasn't caught on at the Farallones. The weather, as mentioned, is often nasty; the water temperature hovers around fifty-two degrees. Underwater visibility is a scant fifteen feet—and that's on a good day. This is a far cry from the warm, clear waters off Baja or Cape Town. Generally, the divers get tossed around like dice in a cup.

Over the years, numerous other cage-diving outfits had tried—and failed—to make it. In fact, none of them lasted longer than a week or two. Groth, a compact, sturdily built guy with a lavish mustache, was more persistent and had deeper pockets than any of his predecessors. Growing up in Hayward, California, he'd heard tales about the sharky Farallones since childhood. When he finally made it out to see for himself, in 1998, a shark breached so close to his boat that everyone on board got drenched. He was hooked.

Groth started his business in 1999, and he started it big—purchasing a thirty-two-foot dive boat called the *Patriot*, state-of-the-art aluminum cages, and hiring an experienced crew. When asked by a newspaper reporter why he'd invested more than a hundred thousand dollars to set up another cage-diving operation in the spot where so many before him had given up, he answered, "I wanted to see great whites. And I think other people should see them, too. It's an incredible creature, and it's right here in our backyard."

He had been ramping up his operation ever since, upgrading his boat, increasing the number of trips he made, advertising in places like *Shark Diver* magazine, investing in an elaborate website, and promoting Great White Adventures in the press. Demand appeared to be strong, and he wasn't having trouble finding a clientele who wanted to take their chances in these turbulent conditions. People were coming from as far away as Japan.

Nature didn't always cooperate with the plan, however. There were days when the cage divers would witness something truly memorable, like multiple sharks feeding or a breach near their boat. But these were the exception, and on a typical day, a client paying the better part of a g-note might see the blurry outline of a shark pass by the cage—if there wasn't too much plankton clogging up the visibility. And then there were the days when they struck out entirely, when the sharks stayed hidden and all the shivering divers saw from their cage was a murky emerald void.

The *Patriot* usually chose to anchor in Mirounga Bay or off East Landing. Though these areas were undeniably hot spots, from either position at least two-thirds of the water around Southeast Farallon was effectively invisible to them. A whole conga line of sharks could be cavorting on the northwest side of the island, off Sugarloaf or Indian Head or Fisherman's Bay or West End or Maintop, and they'd never know it. As a result, Groth wanted badly to "work with" Scot and Peter; having close ties to them would mean hearing the lighthouse radio down the attacks, among other things. Clearly, this would be an advantageous relationship for the cage divers.

There was only one problem: Scot and Peter didn't want anything to do with them. The relationship between the Shark Project and Great White Adventures started off badly and deteriorated from there. The first time Peter encountered the *Patriot*, Groth was chumming, trailing a slick of mashed-up fish parts and blood. Chumming at the Farallones was heavily frowned upon; on a scale of bad behavior it ranked up there with chain-smoking in someone's emphysema tent. Peter launched the whaler and drove out to put a stop to it. In response, Groth handed him a letter written by a lawyer in Washington, D.C., asserting their legal right to chum in the island waters.

Shortly thereafter, Groth did stop chumming. Although he acknowledged that the practice was unpopular with the biologists, there may have been another reason for his sudden change of heart. "It didn't work," he noted in a September 2000 interview with the *San Francisco Chronicle*. By that time, Groth and his partner had made Peter and Scot an offer: In exchange for providing information on the whereabouts of the sharks, the *Patriot* would "protect" them from other, less sensitive cage-diving operations. To Scot and Peter's way of thinking, it was extortion. They declined.

For the rest of the 2000 shark season, things were frosty on the water. When the *Patriot* began towing seal-shaped decoys around the island, the biologists accused Groth of building them out of heavy lumber that could break the sharks' teeth. In return, Groth accused Scot and Peter of selling access to the island, and of ramming into feeding sharks with the whaler, sending a videotape that allegedly recorded this to a local television reporter.

The politics became ugly. With the Point Reyes Bird Observatory's backing, Peter lobbied for rules to limit recreational activities in the area. As things stood, there was nothing on the books to prevent a fleet of pleasure boats from motoring out to the islands on any given day with a six-pack and a surfboard, trying to tease the sharks into an appearance. "Before the shark watching business gets out of control at the Farallones as it has in Australia and South Africa (completely ruining studies at other research sites), we wish to petition the sanctuary for regulatory amendments protecting the sharks and allowing for the continuation of our research," Peter wrote in a brief to the director of the Gulf of the Farallones National Marine Sanctuary.

Furious, Groth argued that this represented "restraint of trade" and "tortious business interference." There was talk of lawsuits, accusations of libel. In September 2001 Groth offered "the olive branch one last time," urging the biologists to accept his partnership deal.

"They're bad news," Scot said in a May 2001 newspaper interview. During the 2000 season, he felt, the cage divers had completely disrupted the Shark Project's work; in one run of seven feeding events, they'd driven away the sharks at three of them. Groth saw things differently. He envisioned the *Patriot* as a satellite observation base that could contribute additional data, claiming to have constructed a remote-operated video platform that could film the sharks feeding from afar. This device, which he'd named the GEO (Groth Eco Observer), had, to his mind, "positive research applications."

Now more than a decade into their long-term study, the biologists did not find the prospect of collaborating with Groth very appealing. For outfitters, coupling research (real or pseudo) with commercial cage diving had become a popular way to lend gravitas to what could easily devolve into one big yee-hah. And it no doubt relaxed clients to think they were in the presence of someone who knew something about these animals. But what was best for research—or for the sharks—was not necessarily what was best for business.

Scot was especially concerned that drifting decoys all day, every day, would desensitize the sharks. They are, after all, nature's most exquisitely adapted predators. How long could one reasonably expect them to go on being dupes, snapping away at fiberglass? In his study Scot had always carefully varied the location, the time, and the shape of the objects he floated, and after a shark investigated a decoy, he would remove it for at least three hours. Then he'd sneak another one out there, but this time he would use an entirely different shape. To avoid influencing the sharks' natural hunting behavior, he limited his decoy use to fewer than twenty hours per season. During the fall of 2000, the *Patriot* floated and towed decoys for almost one hundred hours. By mid-November, Scot could see that their effectiveness had plummeted. The boards continued to be investigated, but they were no longer attacked. It had taken less than two months for the sharks to become wise to the whole deal.

Nonetheless, 2000 was a fantastic shark year, the best on record. On some days there had been as many as four feeding events. Groth's success rate was high and, far from throwing in the towel, he was more encouraged than ever. Ecotourism had arrived at the Farallones, and it wasn't going away anytime soon. People yearned to see these animals; they always had. And to that end, Groth's endeavors actually represented progress: before cage diving was available, seeing a great white shark had usually involved killing one.

. . .

THE WORLD'S AQUARIUMS ARE FILLED WITH SHARKS—SOUPFIN SHARKS, sevengill sharks, hammerheads, tigers, oceanic whitetips, nurse sharks, reef sharks, angel sharks, zebra sharks, sawfish sharks, horn sharks, leopard sharks, a rare albino Port Jackson shark—the list goes on. Great white sharks have been conspicuously absent. This is not for lack of trying.

Before it was widely understood that *Carcharodon carcharias* is one of the few warm-blooded shark species and therefore suited to cooler water, several white sharks were parboiled in tropical fish exhibits. Most refused to eat. And then there were the transportation challenges. It wasn't easy to cart around a live, two-thousand-pound fish with a mouthful of razors. White sharks must keep water flowing over their gills to stay alive; when forced to remain still, they eventually drown. Often, when a shark arrived at an aquarium it was already half-dead, having been tangled and asphyxiated in a fisherman's net. And how exactly was a twelve-foot shark supposed to move through the water while it was on the back of a flatbed truck rolling down Highway One en route to Marineland of the Pacific? The whole enterprise was outlandishly complicated.

But in the wake of *Jaws*, in the seventies and eighties, the cash potential of having a real live "monster" on display made marketers salivate. Aquariums kept trying in the hope that one day, one of these animals might make it. At least thirty-seven great white sharks expired in the process; SeaWorld San Diego alone went through five in a dogged series of attempts between 1976 and 1980. Most of the sharks lasted less than twenty-four hours, but in the continuum SeaWorld also managed to set a longevity record by keeping one alive for sixteen days. That record should come with an asterisk, though. In 1968, an eight-foot male white shark exhibited at the Manly Marine World in Sydney, Australia, had shown signs of thriving in captivity—and suffered a very public death because of it.

The Manly Marine World shark defied all the odds. He'd been caught on a hook and line and had fought for hours before he was landed. When the aquarium arrived to get him, he was dragged onto a beach, dumped into an unfiltered tank on the back of a pickup truck, driven over bumpy roads for forty-five minutes, taken out of water, and hauled by stretcher up several flights of stairs, only to be deposited in a shabbily constructed exhibit crammed with turtles, nurse sharks, and assorted fish. By which time most other sharks that had endured such treatment would have already died.

Not only did this one survive, he swam easily around the tank showing no signs of disorientation. On day three he began to feed, with enthusiasm. Unfortunately, rather than eating the dead fish proffered by the aquarium's divers, he chose to dine on his tank-mates. For a week, the divers watched uneasily as he worked his way through the snappers. Then he began to show interest in the divers themselves. After a particularly close call, it was decided that the shark had to go.

But how? Manly Marine World was ill-equipped to have a great white shark in the first place, and it had no easy way to extract him. Its solution: the shark would be shot at point-blank range. And—why waste the opportunity!—tickets would be sold. This was the environmentally unaware sixties, after all. The house was packed when, ten days after the shark's arrival, a group of divers entered the tank armed with underwater guns called "bang sticks." It took seven bullets to kill the feisty little shark, and several minutes before he sank to the bottom of the exhibit, presumably to the cheers of the crowd. "The White Pointer was Mad . . . It Had to Die Before It Emptied the Aquarium," read the headline in the *Australian Post*.

Despite the barbaric finale, this incident proved that the right great white shark, held in the right conditions, could possibly make it. And if you were an aquarium director in the United States, you knew that California was the place to get your hands on one. Before gill nets were banned, fishermen regularly caught white sharks all along the shoreline in West Marin County, sometimes hauling out several in a single day. SeaWorld San Diego wasn't the only local outfit in the hunt. San Francisco's Steinhart Aquarium badly wanted a great white as well. Competition between the two aquariums was intense, and a bidding war began for a healthy, smallish shark. Local fishermen who called the Steinhart to report possession of a viable specimen were answered by a SWAT force—the "Steinhart White Acquisition Team." SeaWorld, for its part, maintained cargo trucks in the Bay Area, ready at a moment's notice to ship a shark down the coast in temperature-controlled containers replete with tranquilizing chemicals in the water and oxygenated jets that would keep the liquid gently coursing over the animal's gills. Not to be outdone, the Steinhart created a vehicle it called the "Elasmosarcophagus," an elaborate rolling fish tank. SeaWorld responded by upping the bounty: five thousand dollars for a healthy great white shark.

Mike McHenry was a local fisherman who knew exactly where to find a great white shark. He also knew how to catch one. He'd fished for salmon and black cod at the Farallones since the fifties, and often, as he hauled in his lines, the sharks materialized to shear off the fish. One day, a colossal Sister approached his boat. He figured she had to weigh two and a half tons, like nothing he'd ever seen before. She was so scary, even to a man who'd been on the receiving end of just about every frightening thing the ocean could dish up, that McHenry immediately shot her in the head. As he watched the enormous fish sink, he felt regret: "Goddamn, that was a stupid thing to do!" When you considered the going price of the jaws, lucrative ticket sales from exhibiting the beast: "That thing was probably worth *forty thousand dollars*." Years later, in 1982, McHenry captured four white sharks—three males, one female—in a single day while anchored off East Landing, using only baited hooks on a half-inch line. (Some people speculated that the bait had been a freshly shot sea lion, an accusation McHenry denied.) He was amazed at how easy it was to catch the sharks; only the female put up any kind of a fight. "We'd have to take a half turn on the stern cleat to slow them down," he recounted. "But after that we could pretty well pull them alongside, where I'd kill them with a round of double-aught buckshot."

So when he heard about the bounty for a captive shark, McHenry turned to his deckhand and said, "Well, let's go get one." And he did—another female. He caught her on the lee side of Saddle Rock. This one was fifteen feet: small for a Sister, but still far too big for any aquarium tank. Steinhart's director, John McCosker, rejected McHenry's shark for exhibit, but after the animal died he placed it at the California Academy of Sciences so that it could be studied. "I guess this means I don't get my money," McHenry complained, as the shark was taken away.

It turned out that a perfect, tank-sized shark was ultimately captured in Bodega Bay. That was Sandy, a seven-foot female, accidentally netted by a fisherman, Al Wilson, who named the shark after his girlfriend. Wilson sold Sandy to the Steinhart Aquarium for one thousand dollars. (In hopes of an even higher payout, he had first tried to contact the SeaWorld scouts who were encamped in the area, but no one answered the phone at their hotel. The entire staff had gone out to do their laundry.)

On August 12, 1980, Sandy made her public debut in the Roundabout, Steinhart's brand-new, hundred-thousand-gallon, donut-shaped tank. Forty thousand people lined up to see her over four days, with thousands more turned away. Walter Cronkite proclaimed Sandy "the Darling of San Francisco" on national news. *Life* magazine devoted a spread to her. John McCosker was pictured in the tank with the shark, accompanied by a caption that read, "His swimming companion is a four-month-old, seven-foot, 300-pound great white shark, a species better known . . . for dismembering women and gulping down small children."

Scot, who was twenty-four years old at that time, rushed to the aquarium. A queue of people snaked out the front door, spilling onto the street. He stood in the line for an hour, slowly making his way into the Roundabout where Sandy swam against the current, surrounded by yellowfin tuna, barracuda, and rays. Viewers were allotted ten minutes to watch her before they were shuttled out and the next group ushered in. It was Scot's first encounter with a live great white, and he was struck by how substantial she was compared with the other sharks he'd seen. Sandy was disoriented in the tank, but there was nothing tentative about her movements. She was just a baby, but you could already discern her power.

Still, this was hardly the invincible killer that people expected. She avoided food, even delicacies like skinned sturgeon. She seemed afraid of the dark, so lights were left on around the clock. And, most troubling, a minute electrical current from the tank's power system drove her to bang her body repeatedly against the wall. Even as the stunned animal thrilled the shark-crazy public, McCosker felt heartsick about the consequences. "We were at a loss about what to do," he wrote later. "But if we did nothing at all, she would probably be dead in a week."

The decision was made quickly. On August 17, five days after her arrival, Sandy was removed from the Steinhart and once again loaded into the tricked-out Elasmosarcophagus. She crossed the Golden Gate Bridge with a full police escort. When the entourage arrived at the Sausalito Harbor, Sandy was carefully placed in a sling that hung alongside the boat that was to lead her out to the Farallones. The trip was an especially drawn out ordeal as the boat churned through heavy seas at the glacial pace necessary to keep the shark alive and in the sling. Members of the press, who'd clamored to document the release, suffered through hours of ferocious seasickness. But it was the right thing to do. When Sandy was released, she bolted away with a vitality she'd never shown in the tank.

MEANWHILE, AN URCHIN DIVER BY THE NAME OF JOE BURKE HAD HIS own solution to the problem of keeping a great white alive in captivity: He'd exhibit a dead one. Burke had been diving at the Farallones since the eighties and had seen sharks with regularity. Mostly they just cruised him, swimming by slowly and taking a good long look. Being sized up by great white sharks is never a calming experience, and Burke (unlike Ron Elliott) was always rattled by the encounters. But the red-hot Japanese market made harvesting urchins akin to, as Burke described it, "swimming around picking up hundred-dollar bills." The untouched reefs and ledges of the Farallones' seafloor were covered with money, and the only thing standing between a diver and his urchin bonanza was a fleet of Brinks trucks with teeth.

One day while he was harvesting his cash, Burke met a shark, a huge female, who was different from the others. Her size alone made him gasp into his mouthpiece, but this one had a chip on her shoulder, to boot. She kept circling him, coming closer and sharply flicking her tail. At that point, Burke thought it might be a good idea to tuck himself underneath some rocks. The shark vanished for a moment and Burke took the opportunity to flee. But the second he moved away from his shelter, the shark reappeared, and he had to retreat. This went on and on—Burke trying alternately to hide and escape, the shark harassing him like a cat toying with a mouse. Finally, in desperation, Burke climbed inside his urchin basket and signaled for his deckhand, Donald, to winch him up. As he rose to the surface, curled in the wire netting like the catch of the day, the shark continued to circle menacingly, as though trying to figure out the best angle of attack. Getting out of the water in one piece seemed like a miracle.

Burke could not forget the encounter. He was stunned by the shark's distinctive personality and her relentless aggression. There was more to these animals than anybody realized, he thought. And he set out to do something about it.

He hatched a plan to tow a dead great white shark around in a tank and charge people to take a look. But unlike the aquariums, Burke wasn't after a manageable-sized white shark—he wanted a full-on Sister, a spectacle of nature, a leviathan. To be specific, he wanted the mad shark that had chased him out of the water. He wanted everyone to understand the true measure of her length, and her impossible girth. He wanted them to be able to look into her black, all-seeing eyes.

The troubles with Burke's scheme began immediately. If the shark was not preserved in liquid, it would quickly rot. But a portable glass tank big enough to hold an eighteen-foot Sister would collapse under the weight of the liquid required to encase the animal. His fallback plan, to build a metal tank with portholes, didn't work, either. Such a tank would cost an ungodly sum and require an 18-wheeler for transport.

And then there was the shark. Quietly plucking urchins off the bottom and fishing topside for a two-ton specimen were pursuits with about as much in common as tai chi and football. Burke and Donald fumbled around at East Landing with only the vaguest ideas about how to catch a Sister. They made attempt after attempt, littering the Farallon waters with everything from sheep carcasses to several hundred frozen chickens. On one hot October day, Scot and Peter watched from the island as the duo hauled two large cardboard canisters onto the deck of their boat, which was called *Under Pressure*. The canisters held a new, particularly rich type of chum: sheep entrails and sludgy cow viscera, slopped up from the slaughterhouse floor. And it had been simmering, fermenting, *festering* below deck in the afternoon heat. When Donald stabbed a knife into one of the canisters to open it, there was a large explosion and, for a full second or two, a bloody shower of cow. The two men, covered in the stuff, both began to scream at once. Within seconds the air was saturated with a stench so putrid it made the twenty-five thousand western gulls smell like perfume.

Burke never managed to catch a shark at the Farallones. After advertising widely to fishermen along the California coast, he paid ten thousand dollars for a seventeen-foot female that had been killed in a swordfish net. But when the shark arrived, Burke was dismayed to see that she had an aesthetically unpleasing smirk on her face and the appearance of buckteeth. And once the jaw sets after death, it can't be realigned. He began to hate his shark.

Loathed the way she looked. In the end, Burke took a chain saw to the carcass, gave up on his exhibition plans, and moved his family to New Zealand.

But the boats kept coming. Through the seventies and eighties, even the early nineties, regulations protecting the Farallon sharks were weak. Safely protected as a wildlife refuge, the islands themselves were untouchable by law, but right offshore, anything went. Fishermen shot at seals with high-powered rifles. Boats set longlines all over Mirounga Bay, each hoping to land a great white. Some sportfishing outfitters offered one-thousand-dollar rewards to any client who managed it.

The biologists could do nothing but watch. The island logs express their frustration, and their painful compromise: "October 7, 1988: Quarterflash out all day baiting in Mirounga Bay without apparent action. They are now being buffeted by 25+ knot winds. Ahh, gee." Later the same week: "Los Hermanos y Hermanas is anchored at East Landing again, slowly pumping 50 gallons of horse blood over the side to attract sharks." And on September 7, 1990, the log read: "The two sharker boats of yesterday were at it again today without success. . . . We went out and talked with the captain of the Mayflower who was bitten by a shark last year. We traded stories and we convinced/asked them to just take one shark, if any. They said they would, and would allow us to examine and photograph any sharks they caught. They seemed very interested in our work."

By this point, the biologists had begun to know these animals, which made the hunting that much harder to watch. They were particularly concerned about one shark, a Rat Packer named Half Fin. Half Fin was happy-go-lucky, somewhat goofy, perhaps not the smartest shark out there. He was easily recognizable because his dorsal fin was half gone, lopped horizontally through the middle. And he was always around. Anytime a surfboard was dropped into the water, Half Fin would be right on it, like a retriever bounding after a stick. Scot and Peter were amazed that he never caught on that the decoy wasn't food, the way the others did. It seemed likely that the long-liners were going to catch him, that if any shark was going to end up stuffed into someone's glass case, it would be Half Fin.

And at what point would the hunting stop? When all the sharks were gone? There certainly wasn't an endless supply. Nature doesn't dole out apex predators at the same rate that it provides us with, say, pigeons. White sharks, like tigers and lions, reproduce slowly, giving birth to live young. Their gestation period has not been precisely determined, but it's thought to be close to eighteen months and result in only a handful of pups. In recent months, great white sharks have earned a spot on the World Wildlife Federation's "Most Wanted Species" list—the ten animals most likely to go extinct, "based on threats of unsustainable trade and consumer demand."

So in March 1993, PRBO, the Center for Marine Conservation, the Natural Resources Defense Council, Defenders of Wildlife, Earth Island Institute, Surfrider, and at least a dozen other environmental groups in California proposed a bill to protect the state's great white sharks. They had an unexpected advocate: Mike McHenry had decided that it wasn't right to kill these animals. "After a while, I started feeling sorry for them," he said, recalling the old days. "They're big and they're intimidating I guess, but you could wipe 'em out in two days if you wanted to." At the bill's hearing, he stood up on behalf of the fishermen and supported the motion. "We don't need to kill any more of them."

It wasn't an entirely selfless stance. Fishermen were beginning to wake up to the fact that the ocean wasn't infinite after all. Much of their livelihood was simply gone, wiped out by bad management. For certain species like Atlantic cod and sturgeon, the destruction was so quick and so thorough that it was almost as though the industries had put their heads together to figure out how best to annihilate the planet's marine life. And monkeying around with the balance of nature is the ultimate fool's game: Strip away the top of the food chain and the bottom is likely to sprawl, with opportunistic animals (fish-devouring sea lions, for example) dominating and breeding unchecked, worms, viruses, parasites, and their ilk having a high old time. Oceans without sharks would be pest-filled affairs, and that's only the most obvious side effect. Given the paltry state of knowledge about the aquatic environment, no one really has a clue what would happen if the ecosystem were to be upended in such a drastic way. One thing's for sure: It's not likely to be good for the catch.

After provisions were made for continuing attempts to exhibit great whites (to appease aquariums), Bill 522 passed unanimously, and was made permanent in 1999. White sharks could no longer be killed in California. Not deliberately, anyway.

THE FINAL MORNING OF THE 2001 SHARK SEASON CAME UP SURLY AND gray. And I was leaving. Both things depressed me. I had that sinking party's-over feeling and a gut hollowness that seemed a little bit like heartbreak. I'd completed my reporting; Scot and Peter had answered all of my questions, and then some. I'd met Ron. At this point, an article would practically write itself, and yet it all felt incomplete. Basically, I'd been handed a ticket to a private showing of the secrets nature guarded most possessively—you don't just walk out on that, on the shark visitations and the Green Flash and the probability that something even grander will reveal itself tomorrow. I felt seduced by all the animals I hadn't seen yet. The island wasn't a place that allowed for the detached, casual, drop-in guest: I wanted to stay here, and in a bad way. Of course I knew this was impossible, but it felt equally impossible to turn around and go back to a sharkless urban life. And that was what I dreaded, really, returning to the ordinary.

While we were watching a meteor shower the night before, Peter had warned me about the difficulty of what he called "reentry," adding that it often took him weeks to get used to being back in the civilized world. The first time he had come off the island, after eight weeks, he had been a zombie, completely unable to deal with even the basics of mainland life, things like traffic, or returning a phone call, or maneuvering through a crowded store.

After breakfast, everyone ran off to do various chores and I sat in the kitchen by myself, soaking up the warm, communal vibe of the house. It seemed wrong to stay indoors though, so I clipped a radio to my jacket, went outside, and roamed the marine terrace looking for seal stones—rocks that had arrived at the Farallones in the bellies of fur seals. I'd noticed several of these stones, known as gastroliths, displayed in the living room. There were only a handful of fur seals on the island now, so the stones were scarce, but occasionally you could still find them. The seal stones stood out from the island's flaky granite; they were round and smooth, like they'd been through a polisher, and they had a dense quality, as though a much larger rock had been condensed into a pebble. No one knew exactly why the seals ate stones, but maybe, some thought, it was for ballast. Or to help digestion. Or to stave off hunger. Or, as Brown had written in the journal, "maybe they're just weird." Sometimes a single seal would ingest ten pounds of rocks.

It suddenly seemed like the most important thing in the world to find a seal stone, a piece of this place I could take back with me. I walked with my eyes fixed on the ground, and the wind scoured my skin with tiny pieces of grit. Every so often a gull would come barreling over, flapping its wings and screeching in fury. At the shoreline I looked down into the finger gulleys, where dozens of elephant seals loafed in lumpen gatherings. When I came closer, they hissed like cats.

In two weeks the winter crew was arriving. Winter was the most tempestuous and solitary season at the Farallones, devoted to monitoring elephant seal breeding and surviving wave after wave of vicious weather. Shark attacks would continue sporadically for the next six weeks, but by January they'd gradually taper off. Attacks in winter or spring or the early summer months were not unheard of, but they were uncommon. Most of the sharks simply disappeared; once December rolled around they blew out of here like socialites fleeing to St. Barts. Although no one had any idea where the sharks went.

At least not yet, they didn't. During the past two seasons, using long harpoonlike poles, Peter and Scot had tagged a dozen sharks, mostly Rat Packers, with a sophisticated new type of satellite transmitter that collected information about their travels. At a preset interval, anywhere from two weeks to nine months, the tag would release from its position just below the shark's dorsal fin and beam a torrent of data to the Argos satellite system. The information would then be used to plot the longitudes and latitudes of the animal's route, the depths at which it was swimming, its daily schedule. The tags were a technological marvel that promised to shed light on some of the knottier white shark mysteries, and there was a push to get more of them in the water. But each tag, essentially a miniature computer, cost $3,500. And given that the Shark Project ran on a shoestring budget of about ten thousand dollars per season, personally subsidized by Peter and Scot, cost was an issue. One of Peter's off-season tasks was to recruit sponsors for next year's tags. Raising this kind of money would require a new, more ambitious strategy. Lining up a few more kids to adopt Cuttail wasn't going to do it.

Peter detested fund-raising, all its cocktail-party schmoozing and time spent away from the field, but the tagging effort was important. Knowing where the sharks roamed was key to protecting them, especially if they were cruising around in the open ocean, that vast and lawless no-man's-land of international waters where factory-fishing fleets the size of small cities trawled with giant nets and dragged longlines studded with millions upon millions of hooks. These operations were ruthlessly efficient strip miners; a decade-long study by Dalhousie University found that *90 percent* of the global sea's large, predatory fish had been wiped out in the last fifty years. As if that wasn't bad enough, sharks had taken an extra hit from the odious and illegal practice of "finning," whereby their fins were sliced off and their still-live bodies dumped back overboard. The dried shark fins joined the rhino horns (sawed off and ground up as so-called aphrodisiacs), tiger penises (ditto), elk antlers (yet again), and bear gall bladder bile (worth more per ounce than cocaine) in Asian markets, where they are prized as the thickening ingredient in shark fin soup.

Peter came walking down the path and signaled that we had to leave. It was 11:30, time to gather my stuff and ship out. He'd made arrangements for me to return to San Francisco via *Superfish,* the same boat I'd come out on. Its captain, Mick Mengioz, was a friend and didn't mind interrupting his whale-watching tour to pick up a hitchhiker. The boat was expected around noon. After ferrying me out, Peter would pick up Scot and drive the whaler to Bolinas, where it would remain in the harbor until next summer.

I walked back to the house and said goodbye to Brown, who was fishing a golden-crowned sparrow out of a mist net so that it could be banded, and Nat, who was headed up to the lighthouse to relieve Scot. As Peter and I hauled our gear onto the front steps, I noticed that the *Patriot* had returned and was idling in Mirounga Bay. It was quite close to shore, and I could make out two people in hooded wetsuits being helped into the cage by a deckhand. A man wearing a fire engine–red parka and a baseball cap, I supposed it was Groth, stood at the captain's console on the upper deck next to another well-swaddled figure who was holding a beer. The *Patriot* dropped anchor on the spot where, two days ago, all the sharks had surrounded us.

Peter's radio trilled. It was Mick; he was ten minutes away. We set off down the cart path to East Landing, where we were joined by Scot on his toy bike. I lifted my pack into the whaler. Next to the boat, a life-size, human-shaped neoprene decoy named Buoyhead Bob lay jackknifed on the landing. Much of Bob's stomach had been ripped out. The sight of him, mangled as a well-loved dog toy, was a graphic reminder of what I'd be missing. I said good-bye to Scot, and then he craned us over the edge.

Superfish hovered in front of Shubrick Point, waiting. This time I was going to have to vault *up* and bridge a six-foot gap between the two bucking vessels. Mick leaned over the side, ready to help me aboard. He was tall, sandy-haired, and rugged with heartthrob good looks and the buoyant personality of someone who regularly dealt with the public for money. His passengers were crowded around him.

"This is one of the shark guys!" Mick announced, pointing at Peter. "He's out here running around after all the sharks!" Fifty curious faces peered out from under layers of Gore-Tex. This was Peter's cue to say a few words about the Shark Project and give credence to the notion that, likely, there were great white sharks stalking around below us at this very moment. He and Scot tended to avoid situations like this, but with Mick, they made an effort. He was always ready to help them in any way, constantly ferrying out people and gear, and in general behaving with admirable cool around the sharks. And make no mistake: When the likes of Scarhead or Kyra or Mr. T put in an appearance near *Superfish*, they were very good for business.

As the crowd gaped, Peter reeled off a Cliff Notes version of the research, passing my gear up to Mick as he spoke. *No one gets to do this*, I thought, conscious of all the whale-watching eyes following our movements. *And now it's over.* The boats were pitching angrily in the waves and it was time for me to make the jump. Peter hugged me like we were old friends, and then I stood on the railing of the whaler, took a deep breath, and grabbed Mick's hand. As he yanked me up, I pushed off and, for a brief instant, hung in the air between the boats. But then I landed firmly on the *Superfish* and stood there for a moment, trying not to look as disoriented as I felt. The crowd examined me as if I'd just dropped in from another planet. And I suppose I had.

SUPERFISH CRUISED OFFSHORE, SPENDING A FULL THIRTY MINUTES IN Mirounga Bay so that everyone could get a good look at the jagged, arched rocks and the twisted old buildings and the shadowy mounds of seals perched along the edge. I stared hard at Saddle Rock as we motored by, trying to cast it into a permanent memory that I could summon back at will, replete with smells and sounds and images of sharks unfurling like frightening ideas in slow-motion technicolor. As Peter, Scot, and Brown moved around on shore packing up decoys and camera equipment, loading gear and garbage to be shipped off, *Superfish* completed a loop of the four south islands—Southeast Farallon, Sugarloaf, West End, and Saddle Rock—and set off toward the North Farallones, seven miles away, in search of whales. Leaning against the stern, I watched as Peter and Scot launched from East Landing and turned toward Bolinas in the shark boat, standing at the console, side by side.

The whale watchers were full of questions about life on the island. "Was it really boring?" "Do you get television stations there?" "What do you eat?" I didn't feel up to answering any of them, and retreated into the cabin. Several people were bunched around a table, looking cold. One stout woman, who had obviously misunderstood some basic information about the trip, was wearing shorts, a cotton T-shirt, and flip-flops. A bearded man sat in the corner next to his frizzy-haired female companion. The pair wore matching foul-weather coveralls and had an array of Ziploc-bagged snacks spread in front of them. Clearly, this was meant to be a romantic outing because his hands worked overtime, pawing at her and tossing back fistfuls of mixed nuts. Watching him knead her thigh and inhaling the thick sweet peanut smell while the boat buffaloed through fourteen-foot swells was a sure recipe for seasickness, and the cabin slowly emptied out. Luckily I'd taken a Dramamine, my daily vitamin at the Farallones. Others weren't so fortunate. A half-dozen people clustered along the back railing, their sheet-white faces drooping with misery. Several more were buckled over the side. But then we arrived at the northern islands, and even the sickest passenger had to lift his head in amazement.

The North Farallones were a knife-edged set of spires that made the South Farallones look downright inviting. They erupted out of nowhere, five sheer rock pinnacles ranging in a tight circle, like a clawed hand. Fierce surge channels poured between them. Seals and sea lions had scaled their steep sides and they sat lodged in the gloom, barking like a Cerebus choir. Sharks had also been seen in these parts, divers menaced and attacked. Few people came here though, and it was easy to understand why. When I had asked Peter about the North Farallones, he'd described them as "wicked scary." Even Ron admitted that the diving up here was challenging; the currents were odd and strong and the islets dropped off sharply into underwater caverns filled with eerie deepwater critters like wolf eels and ratfish and giant octopi. He didn't care much for it, mainly because the urchins were low quality. "The southeast island is the mother structure," he'd declared. For some reason that made me think of the movie *Alien,* and as *Superfish* approached the North Farallones, I tightened my grip on the rail.

We rounded the islands and then traveled a few miles farther west, until we were straddling the edge of the continental shelf. On one side of *Superfish* was a relatively easy-to-envision one-hundred-foot depth of ocean; on the other, a long and vertiginous drop of two miles. It was probably a good thing that the seasick people didn't realize this. The wind had whipped the ocean into towering swells, and I became chilled and went into the wheelhouse to sit with Mick. Even this far out, hanging over the shelf, there were no whales to be watched. Mainly because, he confided to me, whale season had been over for two weeks. The onboard naturalist, an overenthusiastic woman who made people clap when a lone dolphin passed by, was reduced to walking around the deck holding a plastic model of a humpback.

On the trip back to San Francisco the water became even snarlier, and by the time *Superfish* hit the Potato Patch, a shallow spot in the channel where outgoing currents collide with incoming swells, the waves were cranky mountains. Mick had to pull the throttle way back so he didn't bury the bow. When we finally pulled into the marina at Fort Mason, it was almost dark and nearly everyone was huddled in the cabin.

The marina was crammed and congested, filled with people in a hurry and the din of civilization: traffic humming, metallic machine noise, the constant background buzz of human voices. Ringing cell phones. Slamming doors. An endless line of cars trolled impatiently for nonexistent parking spots. Looking across four lanes of frantic road at a bustling shopping center, I wondered how a place as primitive as the Farallones could possibly survive sharing a zip code with seven million people. I was afraid that it couldn't.

BACK IN MANHATTAN THERE WAS NO SUCH THING AS ORDINARY LIFE. September 11 was barely two months old, and the city was still in shock. A pall hung over everything, and a numbness, and it wasn't uncommon to see people walking on the street with tears streaming down their faces. My office in Rockefeller Center was bristling with guards, soldiers carrying automatic weapons patrolled the subways, and almost every day Fifth Avenue traffic was halted for memorial services at St. Patrick's Cathedral. The city had turned inward to heal its wounds, life seemed darker and more fragile than anyone could bear, and I couldn't stop thinking about the day when all the sharks came up to us in the whaler, like chiaroscuro visitors from another planet.

CHAPTER 3

I have never seen an inhabited spot which seemed so utterly
desolate, so entirely separated from the world, whose people
appeared to me to have such a slender hold on mankind.

—CHARLES NORDHOFF, "THE FARALLON ISLANDS,"
HARPER'S NEW MONTHLY MAGAZINE, 1874

JANUARY 10, 2003

Point Reyes smelled like leather and eucalyptus and moss and
wood and smoke when I pulled onto the main street in my rental
car, looking for a diner called the Station House. I knew it wouldn't
be hard to find—there were only about a dozen buildings in the entire commercial district. This was a rugged, Northern California
beach town, a place of woodstoves, balky plumbing, and artisan
cheese, nestled into folds of low coastal hills and edged by a finger
of ocean called Tomales Bay. Tomales Point, at its mouth, was a popular place for surfing, kayaking, and abalone diving, despite the fact
that more people had been attacked by great white sharks there than
anywhere else in the world. From the point, it was only twenty
miles to the Farallones.

The 2002 shark season had just wrapped up, and I was here for
a recap. Though I'd intended to make a day trip or two to the
island with Ron this past fall, magazine work had kept me pinned
to Manhattan. I had no idea how the year had played out in terms

of sharks: who'd been back and who was AWOL; how many tags had been deployed; what fresh discoveries had been made. In emails, Peter had offered hints of difficulties, with tensions from the cage-diving feud affecting everything they did. I wanted to hear about all of it. I still, as Scot would say, had sharks on the brain.

By now I was a sort of cocktail-party expert on great whites and could hold forth about them for any amount of time. I often found myself thinking about the Farallon sharks during long sets at swim practice, and they continued to populate my dreams, sometimes even waking me at night. Unlike most memories, soon relegated to the brain's discard pile (even the sentimental favorites) the sharks occupied prime real estate in my head. And as the months passed, my intrigue about the islands themselves intensified, too. Whenever I had a spare moment between deadlines, I'd dig deeper into my Farallon research. My apartment filled with nineteenth-century newspaper clippings set in metal-and-wood type, with headlines like "Marooned on the Farallones" and "Frisco's Strange Outpost," melancholy sepia-toned pictures of people who had lived—and died—on the islands, buildings that no longer existed, and the two houses that remained, their facades morphing unhappily over the decades. A few leads paid off, and each clip of information became a clue that pulled me to the next source. As the pieces fell into place, I began to see the outlines of a haunting story that dated back to the sixteenth century. Bit by bit, the islands' lost history became clearer. And stranger and stranger and stranger.

FROM THE BEGINNING THE FARALLON ISLANDS HAVE HAD AN IMAGE problem. Sailors referred to them as "the devil's teeth," in testament to both the nautical dangers they posed and their sublime appearance. In a nineteenth-century magazine article, the islands were compared, unfavorably, to prison. "God has done less for it than any other place," griped one early visitor.

In 1579, Sir Francis Drake became the first European to set foot on the islands, visiting just long enough to stock up on seal and seabird meat. He christened the Farallones the "Islands of St. James," but the name didn't stick. I could see why; it was indefensibly fancy, like naming California "Sussex" or Colorado "Devonshire." Or saddling rugged Point Reyes with the precious name "New Albion." (Which Drake also did. That didn't catch on either.) Seventeenth-century coastal Miwok Indians called them the "Islands of the Dead," considering the place a kind of offshore hell: "An island in the bitter, salt sea, an island naked, barren and desolate, covered only with brine-spattered stones, and with glistening salt, which crunches under the tread, and swept with cursed winds. . . . On this abhorred island bad Indians are condemned to live forever."

Or rapacious fortune hunters. The first wholesale effort to convert the islands' abundant wildlife into cash took root in 1807 when a Yankee fur trader named Jonathan Winship, captain of the Boston-based trading vessel *O'Cain,* noted "a vast number of fur and hair seal" on Southeast Farallon. Three years later the *O'Cain* returned, and over the course of two years managed to kill seventy-three thousand animals. At the time, Winship was involved in a joint venture with a group of Russians, who'd been doing a brisk business trading seal and sea otter pelts with China, hunting their way across the Bering Strait and then down from Alaska, eventually establishing their southernmost base at Fort Ross, one hundred miles north of San Francisco. The Russian American Fur Company's hunters were Kodiak, Aleut, and Pomo Indians, some of whom were slaves condemned to this duty on murder charges. This operation remained on the Farallones for nearly thirty years, cleaning the place out of everything from seabird feathers, eggs, and meat; to sea lion oil and meat; to seal skins; to the ultimate prize—sea otter pelts.

To run your fingers through a sea otter pelt, with its millions of hairs per square inch, is to viscerally sense its doom. This is one plush animal, richer than ermine, silkier than mink. Even back in the preinflationary early 1800s, a single hide fetched forty dollars in China. Fur seals had coarser coats and were far more common.

They sold for only two dollars per skin. But there were few otters at the Farallones, and furthermore, the seals were easy to catch. While crack teams of Aleut hunters were imported to snag sea otters from the water, zipping around in small, agile kayaks called *bidarkas,* when it came to the seals, skill was not required—anyone with a club could do it.

Living conditions were beyond wretched: there was little shelter from the elements, plenty of disease, no freshwater, no way of getting back and forth to the mainland. The relentless damp brought on skin rashes and sores that quickly became infected. Ships dropped off provisions at long and random intervals, but most of the time there was nothing to eat but sea lion meat, abalone, and seabird eggs. Deaths were numerous. In his euphemistically titled book *Adventures in California, 1818–1828,* a Russian teenager named Zakahar Tchitchinoff recounted his time on Southeast Farallon:

> About a month afterward the scurvy broke out among us and in a short time we were all sick except myself. My father and two others were all that kept at work and they were growing weaker every day. Two of the Aleuts died a month after the disease broke out. All the next winter we passed there in great misery and when the spring came the men were too weak to kill sea-lions, and all we could do was to crawl around the cliffs, and gather some sea-birds eggs and suck them raw. On the first day of June of that year (1820) my father lost his balance while trying to reach out for an egg and fell into the water and as he was too weak to swim the short distance to shore he was drowned. His body was not washed ashore on the island and I never saw it again.

By the late 1830s, even the Russians had decided that conditions were too harsh. Plus, there were no more seals. Within thirty years, the number taken per season had dropped from forty thousand to fifty-four. In December 1841, the Russians packed up Fort Ross and left California for good.

And then came the literal gold diggers. Within a year of the monumental 1848 discovery in the gravelly sand of the American River, San Francisco's population had swelled from eight hundred to forty thousand, with four thousand newcomers surging in every month, relegated to tents and shacks. As the population exploded, so did the anarchy. Infrastructure was nonexistent and justice was administered, often brutally, by vigilante groups. The general idea was this: Lay claim to anything you could get your hands on and then keep it by means of force. And during the early, scrambling days of the new metropolis, there wasn't enough of anything to go around.

Women and food were in particularly short supply. While an enterprising businesswoman named Eliza Farnham attempted to import females from the East aboard the jauntily named *Eliza Farnham's Bride Ship*—all a woman needed was $250, a character reference from her clergyman, and nothing to lose—an arrival from Maine named Doc Robinson noticed that there were not many chickens in California. Therefore, no eggs. And without eggs there could be no cakes, no pies, no breakfast rolls, no omelette brunches. Robinson had heard rumors of an island just outside the Golden Gate, home to an enormous population of common murre, a duck-sized seabird with tuxedo markings like a penguin and the sleek head of a loon, that laid eggs every bit as edible as a hen's. What's more, a murre egg was the size of a softball.

So in spring of 1849, Robinson and his brother-in-law, Orrin Dorman, chartered a boat and sailed to the Farallones. Immediately they realized that, if anything, the estimate of how many murres were on this island was wildly understated. There was nothing *but* birds here, jammed shoulder-to-shoulder, packed onto the rocks in unfathomable numbers. Trying to count the birds on Southeast Farallon Island was like counting grains of sand on the beach or blades of grass in a field. It simply couldn't be done.

And everywhere they looked—eggs. Hundreds of thousands of murre eggs lay on the rocks, out in plain sight rather than tucked away in nests. The eggs had leathery, speckled shells that ranged in color from pale taupe to ivory to soft green or turquoise. They were covered in black scribbles, like writing in a secret murre language. Tapered on one end, the eggs were well designed for the terrain; they wobbled in circles on ledges rather than rolling off the side.

For baking, everyone agreed, this was a perfectly fine substitute. When cooked straight up, however, the seabird eggs were less appealing. A fried murre egg had a bloodred yolk, clear whites, and a fishy aftertaste. And if you ate a bad one, it was rumored to take three months to get the taste out of your mouth.

Robinson and Dorman loaded their boat with eggs and headed back to San Francisco, coming up against a nasty storm and dumping half their cargo into the ocean just to stay upright. Nonetheless, they sold the remaining eggs for a dollar a dozen and pocketed three thousand dollars, serious money in those days. Robinson opened his own burlesque hall—another big growth segment of the fledgling California economy—and neither man ever went back to the Farallones. But others did. Within a week of the successful egg sale, Southeast Farallon was swarming with "eggers."

In keeping with the land-grabbing ethos, six men immediately staked their claim, declaring that the islands belonged to them exclusively due to "rights of possession," and incorporating as the Farallon Egg Company. Egging, though lucrative, proved a tough way to make a living. The season spanned eight flurried weeks between May and July, during which time it was man against murre, and both parties against the gulls. Climbing near-vertical rises of crumbling granite, the eggers carried clubs in their free hands to fend off the attacking birds, at the same time stuffing the eggs into specially designed "egg shirts"—giant gunnysacks with multiple pockets. Scalp wounds were common.

By day's end, the shirts were filled with as many as eighteen dozen eggs, and the eggers would be staggering under the bulk like a troupe of drunken, lumpy Santas. The rocks were slick from guano and fog, and it was ridiculously easy to fall. While the eggers wore rope-soled shoes studded with railroad spikes for traction, injury and death were only a slipped foot or a loose rock away. During the gathering season there were approximately twenty-five men on the Egg Company's crew and sometimes, at the end of the day, an egger was simply entered into the logbook as "missing."

MEANWHILE, IN 1851, THE YEAR THE FARALLON EGG COMPANY PLANTED its flag on the islands, there was not a single lighthouse on the Pacific Coast. Ship traffic was on the rise, and captains from all over the world complained about America's untended western edge. Realizing the dangers of two thousand miles of unknown, unmarked coastline, the federal government set out on a massive project to build sixteen lighthouses from San Diego to Seattle. And, given that the Farallones posed the most notorious obstacle out there, it was one of the first lighthouses to be commissioned.

The Farallon light flashed across the water for the first time in December 1855. It would have been operational two years earlier except the architects' measurements were off, and the lens didn't fit into the lighthouse tower. It cannot have been a happy moment when the error was discovered—the entire structure had to be knocked down and rebuilt. As with all Farallon things, this wasn't easy. The heavy construction supplies couldn't be landed, and the stone for both tower building attempts had to be quarried from the island itself. Workmen were forced to crawl up the side of Lighthouse Hill carrying the bricks on their backs, a handful at a time. After a few days of this, there was a quiet but firm mutiny and a mule was delivered.

Bad blood arose immediately, it seems, between the Egg Company and the lighthouse building crew. The government, which did not recognize the company's claim to the Farallones, had deeper concerns than who got to rob the murres, and let it continue its business so long as it didn't get out of hand. But the Egg Company owners believed that they—and not the government—owned these islands, and they were almost always out of hand. So began thirty years of a bitter marriage.

Four men were stationed permanently at the lighthouse. A spartan stone house with a sleeping loft was built at the base of Lighthouse Hill for their residence, companion to the two Egg Company dwellings that had been erected in the 1850s. Even during the months when they weren't sharing the island with mafioso eggers, the job of Farallon lighthouse keeper amounted to an exercise in hardship. Theirs was an isolated, lonely existence, and the weather made it worse, pounding them with storms and shrouding them in fog. And each year, the egging season itself became increasingly traumatic. There were nonstop dustups as rival gangs battled the company for the rights to harvest the eggs; on more than one occasion, soldiers were summoned to calm things down. The battles often lasted for weeks, involving threats, fistfights, barricades, and small arms, and during those interludes San Franciscans would go eggless once again.

Sometimes the ejected gangs would hide in sea caves instead of sailing back to San Francisco, waiting for the authorities to leave so they could take another run at the eggs. One tenacious group steered their boat inside Great Murre Cave and remained there for two days, during which they were drizzled nonstop with guano. The ammonia buildup inside the cave killed several men. And the dangers didn't stop once the cargo was collected; boats running eggs to the mainland were hijacked with regularity.

It was a larcenous, piratical world—and the four lighthouse keepers were stuck in the crossfire. On top of everything else, the pay was lousy. It occurred to the keepers that *they* should be the ones to profit from the egging. All along they'd dabbled in it, picking small batches of eggs, and taking kickbacks for discouraging outsiders from trying to land. But until 1858, when a new head keeper named Amos Clift arrived, none of the tenders had ever tried to make the Egg Company answer to them.

From the beginning of his tenure, Clift made it clear that he was only tolerating the Farallones so he could have at the eggs. He was an avid letter writer and corresponded to his brother Horace in a very fancy hand, with swirly *S*'s and florid *P*'s and calligraphic sweeps of a fountain pen. These letters are archived at the San

Francisco Public Library, and as I read them I could see Clift in my mind's eye, sitting at the lighthouse as the wind rattled against the door, bent over a sheet of paper with a long pen and an inkwell.

And a bottle of something 100-proof. In almost all of his letters, which tended to run several pages, Clift's elegant penmanship starts off impressively and then morphs into a scrawling mess. As the handwriting degenerates, the complaints about his post become increasingly bitter, and his plans for total egg dominance grow larger in scale. In a letter to Horace, written on November 30, 1859, he outlined the situation: "Before I came here this Egg Company used to have things all their own way . . . but since I have been here things have taken a turn. And they have ascertained that I am not as easily bluffed. . . . I think it will now be settled and the Egg Company driven off the island. I shall not abate my efforts in the least. And if I succeed I may perhaps reap the benefits." To Clift, this meant a chance at more cash than he would likely ever see again: "The egg season is the months of May and June, and the profits of the Company after all expenses are paid, is every year from five to six thousand dollars. Quite an item. And if this Island is Government property, I have a right to these eggs and I am bound to try and get it." And after his fortune had been made, Clift added, "the Government might 'kiss my foot' and so up along."

That same month, an article in San Francisco's *Daily Alta* newspaper reported that the Egg Company was rampaging around Southeast Farallon, "breaking up the government roads" and that it had "drawn lines and pasted up notices warning the keepers not to pass them on pain of death." As spring rolled around and the murres got down to business, the three other lighthouse keepers found themselves on the wrong side of a brutal power struggle. "We are now in the midst of the egg season," Clift wrote, on June 14, 1860. "And the Egg Company and the Light Keepers are *at war.*" This was his last letter on record. Shortly thereafter, the *Daily Alta* reported that an armed group of eggers had tried to force the lighthouse keepers to leave the island. And then, in July, an assistant keeper was assaulted. U.S. Lighthouse Service records for that summer reveal that Amos Clift was removed from his post for "the undue . . . assumption to monopolize . . . the valuable privilege of collecting eggs."

Even after Clift's departure, the fighting continued. The ugly climax came on June 4, 1863, when three boats carrying a total of twenty-seven armed Italian fishermen sailed into Fisherman's Bay and weighed anchor. The two egging parties spent the night drinking and yelling threats across the water at each other, and at daybreak the Italians got into rowboats and made for shore. As they neared North Landing, the Egg Company workers opened fire. After twenty minutes of shooting, an Egg Company man named Edward Perkins lay dead, several others had been hit with musket balls, and at least five in the rowboats were seriously wounded. The Italians retreated. "The Farallones War—Arrests for Murder," read the *Daily Alta*'s headline two days later.

The government, realizing that official sanction was needed to bring to an end what was now referred to, wearily, as "the annual egg controversy," finally granted the Egg Company the monopoly it had always sought. Egging, presumably more peaceable egging, continued until May 1881. But there was a more intractable problem: the eggs were becoming scarce. By now, some ten million eggs had been plucked and, after all, murres, like most seabirds, lay only one or two per year. No thought had ever been given to conserving the resource, and as a result the murre population was in free fall. By 1875, the seasonal haul had dropped from about a million eggs to less than a quarter that number. The price had dropped as well, down to twenty-six cents per dozen and falling fast, as chickens caught up to the rest of the mainland population.

In a characteristic burst of arrogance and hubris, the Egg Company diversified its operations at the Farallones, selling the rights to seal and sea lion rendering in 1879. The process of turning blubber into oil was a noxious one, involving furnaces and giant kettles and stinking piles of flayed carcasses. The stench overwhelmed the island dwellers; the billowing smoke was so sooty and greasy that it obscured the lighthouse beam. Once again, tensions between the company and the lighthouse staff flared. When eggers pushed a keeper named Henry Hess over an embankment and demanded that the lighthouse staff pay for any eggs they ate, government authorities decided they'd had enough.

On May 23, 1881, the cutter *Manzanita* sailed to the Farallones with a U.S. marshal and twenty-one soldiers and forcibly removed every last egger from the island. Only one man protested; he'd been the caretaker there for fourteen straight years and considered it his primary residence. The others were thrilled. As one of them wrote: "We steamed away from the windy rocks, the howling caverns, the seething waves, the frightful chasms. . . . Joyfully we bounded over the glassy waves, that grew beautiful as the Farallones faded in the misty distance, and, having been courteously escorted to the city dock, we were bidden farewell, and left to the diversions of the hour. Thus ended the last siege of the egg pickers of 'Frisco.'"

WITH THE EGGERS BANISHED, THE LIGHTHOUSE KEEPERS FACED ANother, equally daunting challenge: establishing a society of their own at this remote outpost. The merciless elements—wind, fog, corrosive seawater—conspired against anything man-made, and the humans on the island struggled to keep their toehold. Maintenance—and survival—was a full-time job. It hardly seemed like a place for families, but near the end of the nineteenth century, the Lighthouse Service began to encourage the keepers to bring out their wives and children. Perhaps it was simply too lonely for the men without them, or maybe, I thought, in the wake of Amos Clift, this was an attempt to keep the testosterone in check.

To accommodate family life, two identical houses—the two that stand today—were built on the marine terrace. They were duplexes, designed to hold a pair of families apiece. And so the women and children came, accepting an existence apart from the mainstream—no entertainment, no society, none of the conveniences or comforts of the city that lay only twenty-seven miles away. Their big excitement arrived every three months, weather permitting, when a supply boat called the *Madrono* pulled into Fisherman's Bay to deliver mail, news, food, oil, supplies, medicine, the occasional toy.

By 1887, there were seventeen children living on Southeast Farallon. The four lighthouse families pooled what little money they had and set out to create a school. They outfitted the stone house, where the first lighthouse keepers had lived, with desks, books, and a blackboard. All that remained was to convince some young schoolteacher to ship out from happening San Francisco for less-than-competitive wages and settle into lunar isolation. The newspaper *San Francisco Call* pronounced the Farallones "the strangest school district in America." Helpfully, the paper outlined a job description of sorts: "A teacher is wanted in this queer school district. . . . Here is a chance for anyone who can appreciate the ever abiding majesty of the ocean and who covets a quiet place in which to read and reflect." At least four teachers gave the situation a try—three women, one man—but an unfortunate pattern emerged. After their first shore leaves, the teachers all refused to return to the island, requesting that their belongings be sent back to San Francisco on the *Madrono*'s next trip.

For the keepers and their wives, providing an elementary-school education was the least of their worries. Where the conditions were hard for adults, they sometimes proved fatal for children. In 1890, a child died after falling into the frigid water at North Landing while being transferred to a boat. Two years later, a supply vessel capsized in the same place, nearly killing lighthouse keeper Thomas Winther's wife and two children. And, on October 2, 1897, a six-year-old boy named Cecil Cain was washed off the landing and drowned. Cecil was just one of three Cain children who did not survive the Farallones; two brothers would succumb to diphtheria in 1901, as would a third island child. Several others barely escaped the same fate, and for weeks they lay in an improvised sick ward in the parlor of the easternmost house. While the lightkeepers blasted distress signals in the hope that a passing ship would provide medical assistance, brutal weather kept all traffic far from the islands. And when the supply ship finally arrived on its scheduled run and the diphtheria epidemic was made known to its crew, they refused to land, returning to San Francisco instead and dispatching a doctor and nurse.

The Cains' cousins, the Beemans, suffered an even more dramatic and public tragedy. Royal Beeman, the eleven-year-old son of lighthouse keeper William Beeman, became gravely ill on Christmas Day, 1898. A southern storm was lashing the island—it simply wouldn't let up. Days went by. Roy got worse. No ship had any hope of landing; none were expected. By December 29, with the weather still howling, the Beemans knew that if they didn't get the boy to a hospital immediately, he was going to die.

They had one long-shot chance—there was a boat on the island. It wasn't much, a fourteen-foot dory used for fishing and puttering around on the calmest days. Having seen how the water rages at the Farallones, even in fair conditions, I was astonished as I studied the old newspaper clippings to read how William Beeman, his wife, Wilhemina (Minnie), and assistant keeper Louis Engelbrecht laid Royal on a mattress in the bottom of the boat, wrapped him in oilskins, jury-rigged a sail, and set off into the storm in a desperate gamble to reach the San Francisco lightship, a floating beacon stationed at the Golden Gate's entrance. This would mean crossing fourteen miles of open ocean, through one of the most daunting passages known to sailors, without navigational equipment or even a radio, in an overloaded rowboat, in a gale. Also along on the journey was Isabel Beeman, aged two months. She was still breastfeeding; for this reason Minnie felt she could not leave her behind.

Miraculously, eight hours after they set out, the lightship's pilot boat rushed Royal to San Francisco. Mainlanders were captivated by the dramatic story, and Minnie Beeman became a local hero. On December 31, 1898, the *San Francisco Examiner* ran a frontpage feature titled "She Proved That There's No Love Like a Mother's Love." "There are two kinds of American women," the story read. "The fluffy kind that frivols its way from the cradle to the grave, and the other kind, and Mrs. Beeman is one of the other kind. . . . She is strong and straight and active and clear-skinned, thanks to the sea air, and she has the calm eyes and earnest, sweet face that peace and quiet and contentment bring. She is the reverse of chatty, and very quietly and modestly she told the story of how with a two-months-old baby in her arms and the sick boy to watch over she put to sea in a fourteen-foot rowboat to save her boy's life."

Four days later, a smaller piece tucked into a corner of the *Examiner* delivered the sad epilogue: "Death Claims Royal Beeman: A Mother's Love All Unavailing Against the Grim Reaper." "The little colonel of the Farallon Islands is dead," the paper reported. "All that medical skill could devise was done for the boy but the angel of death carried him off." Once again, the paper emphasized the perils of the crossing. "I didn't give much thought to the danger," Minnie was quoted as saying. "Of course I knew it was dangerous—but we had to do it." The way she and her husband saw it, there was never a choice: "He could die a dozen times before a vessel came to us."

THE MILITARY ARRIVED NEXT. IN 1905, THE NAVAL RADIO HEADQUARTERS was erected near East Landing; during World War I, the Farallon signal would be among the most powerful in the Pacific. A plan was hatched, in 1916, to turn the islands into a battlement that would become the first point of defense in the event of an enemy attack on San Francisco. "Mighty Guns on Islands to Sweep the Ocean for Miles Around," announced the *Examiner*. A government report enthused over the possibilities for what could be done with Southeast Farallon: "Leveled off for military purposes it would provide a serviceable area of more than a hundred acres; in other words, ample space for an aviation field and for all the needs and equipments of a modern fortress." And this makeover needn't be confined to land: "The indented coastline invites the construction of harbors for submarines and torpedo craft." I imagined the scene: bazooka rocket launchers tucked behind the cormorant blind; armed personnel carriers lumbering up Lighthouse Hill. The report ended with the recommendation that the entire place be ringed with sixteen-inch guns.

Luckily, the Farallones never got leveled, paved, or armed. (They also narrowly dodged other absurd fates, such as becoming the new home of the Alcatraz prison or a gas station for passing oil tankers.) But the military continued to keep an interest in the island. More war devices were erected: transmitters and transponders and a forest of antennae and a secret radar beacon that no one was supposed to know about. By 1942, there were more than twenty buildings on this small patch of rock, and a town of nearly one hundred people, referred to by its inhabitants as Farallon City. Life was a little easier for this crew—the supply boat now arrived every week—and they actually managed to have some fun, holding movie nights and dances and cocktail parties, even publishing an island newspaper, the *Farallon Foghorn*. After the war, the population, not surprisingly, thinned; when the lighthouse was finally automated, the coast guard sent the last lighthouse keeper back to the mainland.

In 1969, nature finally had its turn. The islands were collectively designated a National Wildlife Refuge, and the Point Reyes Bird Observatory was contracted by the government to repair the damage. Where to start? There was so much to tackle. By the sixties, only six thousand murres nested on the islands (down from a half million), and other seabird populations had taken similar drubbings. Fur seals were a distant memory, the global elephant seal population had been reduced to about twenty animals, Steller's sea lions were gone entirely, harbor seals glimpsed only rarely. No doubt the sharks were there, prowling the waters, but without seals they wouldn't have stayed around for long. (You don't get to be four hundred million years old by failing to adapt.)

As for the environment itself, past ignorance was augmented by present stupidity, and the place was limping. Oil tankers made a practice of pumping their ballast tanks near the islands, killing seabirds by the thousands. Four times, military planes opened fire on Middle Farallon with rockets, presumably for target practice. Gill nets killed indiscriminately, strangling seabirds and snaring every animal in their paths. Fishermen deployed explosives to catch fish, and boats journeyed out to shoot up the wildlife along the shoreline with high-powered rifles.

What little infrastructure still existed on Southeast Farallon was outmoded, corroded, and neglected. Garbage lay everywhere; cats and rabbits terrorized the birds; heaps of rusty refrigerators and washing machines and assorted pipes blocked the East Landing. The place, to put it plainly, was a wreck. But if any group was up to the task, it was PRBO. Undaunted, they sent out waves of all-star biologists, led by David Ainley. Slowly, the island was reclaimed by the wild. Buildings were dismantled, concrete areas were torn up and replaced by nesting terrain for auklets and petrels. Whole stretches of land became completely off limits to burrow-crushing, flock-spooking humans. Eventually, the only remaining signs of civilization were the two houses, the crane at East Landing, some water tanks, a couple of small buildings used for storage, and a crumbling stone foundation near the North Landing, known as the old eggers' house. And, of course, the lighthouse tower itself.

Elephant seals, fur seals, harbor seals, and Steller's sea lions began to reappear on the shores, first as individuals and then, over the years, in colonies. Murres, cormorants, guillemots, petrels, auklets, puffins, shearwaters, fulmars, grebes, scoters, pelicans, terns, loons, and even the odd albatross—they all trickled back. As the twenty-first century began, there were one hundred thousand murres in residence. The gulls, to no one's surprise, made a particularly strong comeback.

THE STATION HOUSE WAS A FRIENDLY LOOKING RESTAURANT WITH A western feel, painted dusty red, with a funky, hand-lettered sign. I pulled into a parking spot out front, alongside two silky hunting dogs in the back of a pickup truck. It was 6:00 p.m. and already dark. As I stepped out of the rental car, I took a deep breath—the air had that cool, tangy ocean smell. The street was deserted. Toby's Feed Barn was shut down tight next door, as was the Point Reyes Whale of a Deli on the corner, and there wasn't a soul walking around. Glancing in the windows of the Station House, I discovered why: What appeared to be the entire town was crowded into the dining room. As I opened the door a wall of noise hit me, and a waitress swept by with a dozen Anchor Steam beers balanced precariously on a tray. A single table was available in the corner of the bar, and I grabbed it.

Peter showed up in his Toyota truck minutes later, followed almost immediately by Scot in his VW van. Fourteen months had passed since we'd seen each other, but little had changed in their appearances: Peter had a few new flecks of gray in his hair, and Scot had shaved his beard, but the net effect was still of two outdoorsmen, inadvertently hip in their perfectly distressed clothing, with a laid-back confidence that turned people's heads.

As the waitress handed us our menus, I asked them about a story I'd just read in the local paper but hadn't quite believed. This past October, apparently, a well-meaning boatload of people who'd nursed a pair of injured sea lions back to health, naming them Swissy and eDog in the process, had decided that the Farallones would be the perfect place to release them. They'd motored out from San Francisco and pulled up to the East Landing buoy. After weeks of rehabilitation and care, the sea lions were petted one last time and lovingly decanted into their new home. They swam around playfully while their rescuers snapped pictures for, oh, thirty seconds.

Swissy was on his second circumnavigation of the boat when a shark seized him, literally biting him in half. Everyone on board screamed; one woman burst into tears. There was some splashing, and the shark dove, taking Swissy's hindquarters with it. The tiny head had bobbed for an instant and then disappeared. I needed confirmation: Was this really true? Peter nodded slowly. Scot winced. "It was *awful.*"

"What were they thinking?" I asked. It was like taking someone with a broken leg, carefully nursing the leg back to health, and then pushing the patient off the side of a cliff. A week afterward, back on the mainland, one of the would-be samaritans sent Peter some pictures of the sea lion's demise. By blind luck the shutter had gone off at the exact moment of the hit, and as far as attack photos went they were the best he'd ever seen.

(Later I saw the pictures myself and it's true, they are spectacular. A two-ton, sixteen-foot male shark named Gouge is heaving himself out of the water only a few feet away from the camera. Gouge got his name because when he first showed up at the Farallones he had three propeller wounds on his head, deep, and so pulpy they looked like raw hamburger meat. In one image, a tiny flipper can be seen hanging out of the left side of Gouge's mouth.)

Over the roar of the restaurant, they recapped the past year for me. Scot was back at his park ranger job, tending hiking trails at the national seashore, and Peter was consumed with a new bird book he was writing, a detailed treatise on the subject of plumages and molt. The sharks were never truly out of mind, though: Seventeen scientific papers were currently on the drawing board.

The 2002 shark season had been mediocre; fifty-six attacks were observed between September and November, approximately the same number as the previous year, but down from the season high of seventy-seven in 2000. Things on the surface were buzzing, however. The *Patriot* had been a constant presence, with cage-diving tours all but sold out. Over the course of three months, their decoy use had topped two hundred hours. Six other boats had shown up, attempting to lure the sharks with surfboards and, in two cases, chum. The shark-tourism situation only promised to get worse, so the push was on to enforce new, more muscular restrictions including a ban on towing decoys and a 150-foot no-approach zone around feeding great whites. Predictably, the cage divers were opposed to this, and an ugly battle loomed this winter. The intensity of the conflict made everybody nervous. Peter had been spending much of his time dealing with the fallout, attending committee meetings, smoothing ruffled bureaucratic feathers, doing his best to ensure that the Shark Project didn't become a political casualty. As he and Scot described the tense atmosphere, I noted a weariness in their voices. They were tired of this, I could see, and longed to return to the days when the island and its sharks were their only focus.

Well, what about the sharks?

"Okay, let's see," Scot said. "So Betty was back, and Emma. Cal Ripfin was back. Our old buddy Bitehead was back; he's got some new bites on his head. Spotty was back, he showed up with Cuttail, late again." He turned to Peter. "That's something we need to look at. As they get older do they arrive later? Could be."

Peter nodded. "Or they learn to come in during the elephant seal peak."

"Or maybe they're spending more time breeding."

I was beginning to realize that studying great white sharks was not really about the rush of seeing them. Instant gratification was beside the point. Decades passed before patterns became visible, before hunches could be proven, before the jigsaw puzzle came together, if it ever did. Science, by definition, was altruistic. You might be the one who benefited from the information you'd collected over the years, you might not. You might be dead, even. And someone else using your data might go on to win the Nobel Prize.

But there had been one major breakthrough this season: The satellite tags had begun to pay off with reams of new information. The Farallon sharks, it seemed, spent most of their lives roving the open ocean rather than sticking close to the coast, as had been supposed. And when they moved away from the islands and over the lip of the continental shelf, they began diving to depths greater than seven hundred meters. That, too, was unheard-of behavior from an animal that hunted its prey on the surface. And the sharks were *booking*, logging as many as sixty miles per day with purposeful efficiency. It was as though they were late for an appointment somewhere and hustling to keep it. A Rat Packer named Tipfin, tagged by Peter in October 2000 (and again in October 2001), was discovered to have cruised 2,300 miles to Hawaii in thirty-seven days. He remained near Maui for at least four months, and then turned around and returned to the Farallones in October. No one had any inkling that great white sharks were such globe-trotters. "It was like seeing owls leave the forests and head out over the open plains," Scot said.

Tipfin was the only tagged shark, however, who went that far west. When the other satellite-tagged sharks left the Farallones, they all swam southwest, to a patch of ocean located approximately 1,500 miles off the coast of Ensenada, Mexico. They remained there for as long as eight months, indicating that this remote place is where they spend much of their lives. Though the gathering spot lacks seamounts or islands or any other notable features, its significance is surely anything but random, and not just among the Farallon set. White sharks tagged at Guadalupe Island and elsewhere in California headed straight to the same area. Scot had long suspected that something unusual was going on when they weren't at the Farallones; he'd noticed that by the time the sharks disappeared in December they had managed to fatten themselves up, but when they returned the following autumn they were much thinner, sometimes unrecognizably so. Often they were trailing remoras, small pilot fish that are found in more southerly waters. The epic trip described by the tags explained the *where,* but not the big mystery: *why?* "So the question is," Scot said, leaning in and raising his eyebrows dramatically. "What the hell are they doing out there?"

Clearly the sharks weren't wasting energy heading out into the wild blue yonder for no good reason. Feeding? Pupping? Perhaps, but neither of those theories quite fit. Chasing down seals in the open ocean didn't make sense in terms of energy expenditure; and the likelihood that the region served as a kind of nursery for baby white sharks was diminished by the presence of so many males. Scot and Peter had the beginnings of an idea, one that couldn't be proved yet but was captivating nonetheless: that this gathering spot might be the great white's ancestral mating ground, a destination with ancient significance that is roadmapped into the sharks' DNA.

Whatever the reason for this hot spot, the tags had done their work. Identifying the region was the first step to protecting it. Findings from the tagged sharks had recently been published in the prestigious journal *Nature,* with Peter and Scot among the authors. Central to the discoveries was a marine scientist named Barbara Block. Block, a MacArthur fellow and by reputation a force of nature herself, had helped pioneer the pop-off satellite tags and planned to affix four thousand of these and other devices not only to sharks but also to sea turtles, squid, albatross, elephant seals, and whales, as well as tuna and other predatory fish. She was one of the leaders on a project known as TOPP (Tagging of Pacific Pelagics), a twenty-million-dollar study aimed at discovering how marine animals journeyed through the Pacific, where they traveled to eat and mate and breed. These creatures spent their lives jetting through the sea, across routes and byways and submarine plains that only they knew about, and for the most part, the only time they were glimpsed was when they ventured close to shore.

TOPP, in turn, was part of a billion-dollar study known as the Census of Marine Life that aimed to spend the next decade determining what actually lived in the world's seas, and what kinds of animals were likely to live there in the future, given the way things were going. The census was massively ambitious, breathtakingly difficult—and long overdue. "We haven't spent enough time exploring our own planet," Block pointed out on her website.

High-powered, well-funded, politically connected, and world-renowned, Block and her team were dream collaborators for the Shark Project. She was encouraged by the fact that twenty-two great whites had been tagged in only four seasons at the Farallones and that, in most cases, the animal's history (and gender) was known. Next September, she intended to send out at least two dozen tags. A major goal for the 2003 season was to tag some Sisters; to date all but two of the jewelry-wearing sharks were Rat Packers.

I could see that Scot and Peter were excited at the prospect of tagging so many sharks, but a little worried about how they'd manage to do it. Especially now. Everyone, it seemed, wanted a piece of the Farallones; requests for access were flooding in from the media. The latest one proposed that Brad Pitt, rumored to be fascinated by great white sharks, come out to host a wildlife special. (Fish and Wildlife authorities vetoed the idea immediately.)

As our plates were being cleared, the bartender emerged from behind the bar and walked over to our table. He was a dark-haired bear of a guy in an apron, holding a bottle of pinot noir, and he must have caught the BBC documentary that had entranced me. Pointing to Scot, he said, "You're the guy with Stumpy!"

Scot nodded. He was used to this. "Yeah, I'm that guy." He gestured toward Peter: "He's the other guy."

"How *is* Stumpy?" the bartender asked, pouring us a round on the house.

"Ah, we haven't seen her in a while," Scot said. "It's sad." I wondered what he hated more: the unexplained absence of his favorite shark, or having to admit she was gone to people like the bartender, for whom Stumpy was merely a myth, a folk hero disguised as a fish.

The bartender, it turned out, had a shark story of his own. He was a surfer, he explained, and he'd recently had an encounter with "the man in the gray suit" near the Bolinas channel. "I was out there by myself in the morning. All the birds disappeared. It got deathly quiet. I started looking around, and all of a sudden this *submarine* came by me."

Scot smiled knowingly. "So you got out . . ."

"I was outta there so fast. I hit the sand and I was *still* paddling."

Peter had a different perspective. "I actually want to see one when I'm surfing. I'd want to know who it was, though." I envisioned him sitting on his board trying to make out the shark's scar pattern—Was it ZZ Top? Or Two Scratches?—while around him other surfers fled the scene.

Scot shook his head and laughed. He leaned toward me and stage-whispered: "Peter's *crazy*." He paused. At one of the tables in the dining room, a drunken chorus of "Happy Birthday" broke out.

"Sure would be nice to see the old stump-tailed girl again," he added, staring at the bottom of his glass.

That feeling of longing—for a person, a place, or, in this case, a shark—was something I understood. It could smack you, wavelike, delivering actual, physical, pain. It could sneak up on you as a tiny catch somewhere near the middle of your throat. Or it could tug at you with the force of gravity, like a magnetic attraction that was impossible to shake off. Right now, after a few hours of Farallon news and shark updates and big plans for next season, after hearing about all the action while being far removed from it, I wanted to be closer. This was undeniably greedy; I'd already been out there twice, which was two more times than anyone else got to go. Why couldn't I just be happy with that?

Perhaps it was as simple as this: At the Farallones, encounters with the rare and the unusual—and even the miraculous—were common. You had the sense that every possibility was still open, even the ones that were unreasonable to hope for. Anything could happen. It was an upside-down place where every normal assumption was challenged, a parallel universe where Peter, Scot, and Stumpy became celebrities and Brad Pitt was told to stay home.

Somewhere along the line, my desire to return had become a need. And although I didn't fully understand it, I was surprised by the force of the urge. I wasn't ready to ask just yet, but sitting in the Station House bar, a docket of Scot's shark photographs on my lap, I vowed to myself: *I'm going back.*

CHAPTER 4

Rest assured that this gull asks only two questions of any living thing: First, "Am I hungry?" (Answer: yes.) Second, "Can I get away with it?" (Answer: I'll try.)

—WILLIAM LEON DAWSON, *BIRDS OF CALIFORNIA*, 1923

AUGUST 3–7, 2003

Kingfish was a handsome boat, and I loved her on sight. She floated in the glassy dawn water of the Sausalito Harbor, all fresh green paint and buffed decks and gleaming brass—thirty-seven feet of immaculate systems, bobbing peaceably in her slip. Tony Badger, the skipper, tall, silver-haired, and natty in a black beret, and his petite brunette wife, Margaret, stood on deck to welcome me as I walked down the dock pushing a wheelbarrowful of groceries. I knew there was a precise nautical term for the type of boat *Kingfish* was, but I couldn't think of it. Whatever. In about five hours I would be back at the Farallones.

This time it was official. I'd proposed to write a series of longer articles about the islands and had spoken at length with Joelle Buffa, the U.S. Fish and Wildlife's manager of the refuge. Buffa is whip smart and a devoted guardian of the place, as well as a working biologist specializing in birds. When the generator exploded and the power went out and the plumbing needed to be replaced entirely and the coast guard suddenly decided that, after forty years, they were not going to deliver water anymore—Buffa was the one who got the call and had to figure out a way to fix the problem. Entertaining visitors was not high on her priority list. And considering the mugging that the wildlife took for so long at human hands, it was both defensible and easy for her to turn every applicant down cold. But she didn't give me a flat-out no when I first approached her, so I had flown in for a meeting at her office near Palo Alto. She was small, sharply pretty, and all business in a crisp U.S. Fish and Wildlife uniform, and she had an amazing set of eyes: jade-colored with hazel starbursts in the irises. As Buffa looked me over with the x-ray stare of a customs interrogator, I pled my case. I wheedled and cajoled. I practically begged. And in the end, she granted me one of the only weeklong permits that had ever been awarded; it came, not surprisingly, with many conditions attached. Condition number one: I was to choose a week that did not fall during shark season.

I had expected this. As a result of the power struggles and regulatory wrangling of these past two years, the Shark Project had attracted a surfeit of press attention, not all of it positive. In print and on TV, Groth had accused Peter and Scot of treating the island waters as a "private playground," and of attempting to bar public access. Never mind that this wasn't true—anyone could visit the Farallones simply by booking a day trip on *Superfish*. They just wouldn't get to tramp all over the island, and there was certainly no guarantee that they'd encounter a shark during their one-hour loop. But it *sounded* outrageous: Who were these arrogant scientists to stiff-arm the American taxpayer, to think they could hog the great white sharks all to themselves? As the feud flared, more requests from the media poured in. Buffa's only possible response was a blanket rejection: sorry. The few day permits allotted during shark season had been scotched; there were no exceptions.

Peter's hands were tied. Unofficial visits were out of the question. Great white research at the Farallones was on probation. My choice was this: I could write about the mating habits of cassin's auklets, or I could stay in New York.

I opted for the birds.

With characteristic optimism Peter had explained that I'd see another side to Southeast Farallon: with all of the breeding seabirds in residence, a couple hundred thousand in the space of a few city blocks, it was an entirely different place. He would be out for a few days during my trip; there was prep work to be done for the fall and he, too, was missing the sharks. The night before, we had met up for drinks in Bolinas. "We'll go out," he said. "Drive around. There've been some huge, bloody attacks in August." He took a long pull on his beer and shot me a sly look. "We'll see someone."

THE BADGERS WERE MEMBERS OF THE FARALLON PATROL, A THIRTY-strong flotilla that had been delivering people, supplies, and groceries to and from the island since 1972. This support fleet included powerboats and sailboats of various styles and vintages, all of them spacious enough to accommodate overnight trips. Every two weeks one of the boats would make a run—their role was as critical as the *Madrono*'s had been in the lighthouse era. Even so, there was no pay involved. Farallon skippers joined the patrol out of a desire for adventure, and for the prestige of association. (Since only badass sailors could really handle the trip, this was an elite crew.) The captains all felt a kinship with the islands.

When one of them, Ed Kelly, lost his wife to cancer in 2001, he'd spread her ashes in the surrounding waters while making a supply run. Shortly after he'd done this, Peter spotted a shark attack off Shubrick and convinced Kelly to jump into the whaler with him to take a closer look. The shark was a gargantuan Sister with a quarter-moon-shaped scar on her head, and she passed directly under the boat, dwarfing it, like a visitation, like a creature you could only half believe, giving new meaning to the word *grace*.

Peter knew he would recognize this shark if he saw her again. He named her Jane, after Ed Kelly's wife.

Peter had coordinated my trip with the Badgers, which was also serving as a supply run of food, mail, and propane. The logistics of shuttling people and supplies to and from the Farallones were devilishly complicated and always involved a chess game with the weather gods. Figuring out who went where, and when, and with whom, and who would buy the groceries and who would be dealing with the garbage coming off the island and who was going to courier the new generator part to the Emeryville Marina at 5 a.m. and hundreds of other details was like trying to untangle something heavily knotted and three-dimensional. Peter seemed to manage it with ease. And the job was crucial: You didn't want someone who'd been stuck on an island for thirteen weeks left standing in the marina parking lot with five duffel bags of gear, an urgent need for a shower, and no means of transportation. You didn't want to forget to send groceries to a group of people who'd been down to rice and lettuce for the last several days.

I shook hands with Tony and Margaret and was introduced to Tony's sailing partner, John Boyes, who appeared on the dock. John was fit and energetic, clean-cut and square-jawed and shipshape. He, too, wore a black beret cocked on the side of the head. It must be a sailor thing, I figured. Also making the trip were the Badgers' son-in-law, Pelle, and a PRBO intern named Parvenah, who was riding along so that she could see the islands for the first time. One of the perks of being a patrol captain was permission to come ashore if time and weather permitted, but *Kingfish* frequently sailed in the roughest conditions, and in all their trips to the Farallones, the Badgers had never made a landing. This morning, however, the weather was placid, and disembarking seemed like a possibility.

Tony and John hustled around, checking gauges and doing complicated things with ropes. As we pulled out of the marina, Tony delivered a tough-love lecture about what never to do while on *Kingfish*: where never to stand, how never to walk along the railing, which buttons never to lean against. He spoke in a drill sergeant's voice, with John occasionally adding his own stern directive. Clearly, this was not their first rodeo. In fact, Tony told me, he had raised his two daughters on a boat this size, and they had sailed the world like a seagoing Swiss Family Robinson.

Both men stressed that it was critical to watch out for ship traffic as we pulled under the Golden Gate. "If we're going to hit a boat this is where it will happen," Tony said grimly, as if this was something that occurred on most days. I could see what he was getting at. A marine layer of fog clung to the water, and even this early there were fishing boats of all sizes buzzing around in every direction, most of them without radar. Thousands of container ships the size of three football fields hauled in and out of this port every year, and they moved at deceptively fast speeds, materializing out of the mist without warning, bearing down on smaller boats like blind locomotives.

"The San Francisco Bar is the most dangerous stretch of water on the West Coast," John announced. He explained that the channel was only fifty feet deep in places, the tides inhaled and exhaled at a brisk six knots, and a series of crazy currents cut through it all, running as fast and wild as rivers. When you threw in some swells, the effect was like dipping a spoon into a shallow bowl and whipping it around for a bit. The waves bashed and tumbled over one another, bouncing off the bottom to create a trampoline effect on the surface, and in general making things unpleasant and quite dangerous.

"They lose about three boats a year in here," Tony added. I looked out at the water as we passed under the bridge. Gone was the harbor calm of twenty minutes earlier. In its place was a black and roiled ocean, pocked with sudden whitecaps and foam-swept crests.

It wasn't just the twenty-seven miles to the Farallones that had kept people away. It was *these* twenty-seven miles. Tony was right to be vigilant. Others had taken the crossing less seriously, and paid for it. Countless accidents had occurred en route, even more upon arrival. Flipped boats, crushed boats, abandoned boats, swamped boats, boats bashed to slivers by rock—there had been more lost boats at the Farallon Islands than anyone could count. Tricky seas conspired with sudden, poleaxing weather changes to create instant emergencies, and even the most experienced skippers could find themselves caught out. During a two-man race around the islands in the eighties, a catamaran radioed Mayday; during its last transmission someone was heard to scream, "A wave just came through the cabin!" The crew was never found.

Over the years the coast guard had called often on the marine radio, asking the biologists to be on the alert for missing vessels. On more than one occasion, rescues had been made. One blustery November morning at around 6 a.m., Peter had just come downstairs when he heard a knock at the front door. Since everyone else on the island was upstairs, asleep, this was interesting. On the front stoop two Vietnamese men stood in street clothes, gesticulating wildly. "Boat! Boat! Boat!" was all they could manage in English, but they were clearly upset and they led Peter to Fisherman's Bay, where a snarling southeaster was pounding their twenty-four-foot skiff to matchsticks on Aulon Rock, also known as the Tit because of its nipple-shaped peak. At the top of the Tit, two other men crouched in a small lee; one of them, an elderly fellow, was clad in an orange bathrobe.

Another time, a twenty-foot runabout showed up with no one aboard; originally it had been manned by a family of five from Sacramento, out for a day of fishing. Not one of them was ever found, though for days the biologists were instructed to walk the island perimeter, searching for bodies.

Incidents like these were most frequent during the fall, when conditions looked promising on the mainland and recreational boaters thought nothing of lighting out to the Farallones to catch a few salmon. On a clear day in San Francisco, the islands could even be seen from shore—how hard could it be to motor out there and back? People had no idea what they were in for, and they tended to lack things like compasses and flares and extra water and radios. When the weather snapped its fingers, they found themselves in dire situations.

And you could write an entire book about the commercial vessels that had met these rocks, oceangoing clippers and schooners and freighters. During the pre-LORAN, pre-GPS, pre-EPIRB days there were a dozen major shipwrecks at the Farallones, starting in 1858 when the *Lucas,* a full-rigged ship carrying two hundred people, slammed into Saddle Rock at 2 a.m., and twenty-three passengers died in the icy water of Mirounga Bay, less than fifty yards from shore. From that point on, that scene played itself out every few years with a variety of victims: *Noonday, Morning Light, Annie Sise, Champlain, Franconia, Bremen, American Boy, Louis, The Bardstown Victory.* Ship after ship crashed into the islands, and the main culprit was always the same: weather.

Even now, the ships lay down there like so many cautionary tales. Ron Elliott had told me that he often found large hunks of them embedded in the ocean floor; one time he swam up to an anchor that was nine feet tall. He'd come across old sextants and binnacles, brass chains and bronze bowpieces, masts and hulls, all of them splintered and crumpled and cloaked in sediment. The waters around Southeast Farallon were one of the most notorious boneyards in North America.

Today the water was flat all the way out, and *Kingfish* made it to the Farallones in less than four hours. As the islands came into view I felt a surge of happiness. There were the familiar spires and towers, thrusting out of the black water. Something was different, though. The last time I'd been on Southeast Farallon, the island was brown. Now, it was sort of . . . white. And then, as we got closer, I heard it—an otherworldly echoing din of wailing, screeching, mad cackling. Tiny bird heads popped up from behind rocks; sleek, aerodynamic bodies lined every surface; stray feathers fluttered in the air. It was as though the island itself was heckling us. And then there was the smell: an ammonia-fueled cloud that settled, tentlike, over the boat. The Badgers, who had been visibly excited about going ashore, suddenly looked uncertain.

Biologist Pete Waryzbok came out to meet us. He had been on the island for more than four months at this point, and he sported a russet-colored beard that would've made Grizzly Adams jealous. He was driving the Dinner Plate. This was the first time I'd actually seen it in the water—it was shockingly small. The only thing that set it apart from something a kid might point to in the Neiman Marcus Christmas catalog was its thick coating of gull guano. But this was the only boat the bird biologists had—the shark boat belonged to Peter, and it was at the island only during shark season.

This time, instead of being winched up in the boat, we were hoisted on a contraption known as the "Billy Pugh" (pronounced Billy Poo). No one had any idea if someone named Billy Pugh had created this device, or whether there was a salty anecdote behind the name, or whether the gadget's inventor just had too many martinis one night and thought, *What the hell.* The Pugh was shaped like an enormous badminton birdie with a heavy metal disk at the bottom. (I knew it was heavy because it fell on my leg the first time I tried to climb onto it.) The disk was encircled by rope netting that was gathered at the top and attached to the crane. Two by two, we clambered from the Dinner Plate onto the Pugh, looped our arms through the netting, and clung as we were winched up and swung ashore.

Manning the crane controls was another scientist named Russ Bradley. He was in his late twenties, tall and fit, with curly blond hair and wire-rimmed glasses, handsome even in a full-length slicker streaked from top to bottom with gull shit. In fact, as my ears adjusted to the bird noise and I looked around, I noticed that every last object was extravagantly splattered.

We gathered on the landing while everyone got pughed up. Russ warned that the gulls had a tendency to dive-bomb from above. Hats, therefore, were advisable. And any item of clothing one might ever want to wear again should be taken off or covered up. Or, better yet, left at home. "Part of the gull's defense strategy is to give you an idea of how much they don't want you here," Russ said. "And they have a lot to give." He indicated the drippings running down his jacket.

Something off to the side caught my eye. Three feet away on a flat rock ledge, a dead sea lion lay in a crumpled heap. It was oddly deflated-looking, and its head twisted backward at an unnatural angle. Russ, following my gaze, explained that there were more sea lions than usual at the islands and that some of them were starving. He stated this as a simple fact, in a businesslike voice.

I suppose I had always known that the Farallones was all about living and dying. But during seabird season, the killing, as I would witness, proceeded at a pace that would startle Darwin. It was never more than a few inches away from you, death. And the gulls were master assassins. The entire world population of western gulls totals fifty thousand birds, and from the months of April to August, twenty-five thousand of them congregated here, packed onto this sixty-five-acre island. They pillaged the murres as they always had, plus the cormorants and the auklets and any other bird that came around, and they killed their own too, with cannibal gusto. The adults—always agitated, always screaming—stood side by side with their chicks, which started out in life as spotted fuzzballs the size of a shotglass but within six weeks would grow as large as their parents. The young gulls were identified by their brown color, spotted markings, and odd bit of down. But their time-lapse photography growth spurt was disturbing and mutant-like, as if you had delivered a baby one day, and a week later it was wearing your clothes.

While Pete stayed at the East Landing buoy with *Kingfish*, Russ gave a quick tour of the island. It was already clear that Tony, Margaret, John, and Pelle couldn't wait to hit the road. We were halfway up to the lighthouse, being harassed from above and slipping around on dead bird carcasses when Tony turned to me, his beret knocked askew and splotched with white. Struggling to be heard over the shrieking, he yelled: "You're staying for *how* long?"

• • •

IN ADDITION TO RUSS AND PETE, THERE WERE THREE INTERNS ON THE island: Jen, Meghan, and Melinda. The women were all in their early twenties and all beautiful; despite their lovely appearances, all looked right at home in their work outfits of hard hats and en- crusted coveralls, with flea collars fastened around their ankles to keep the bird vermin from crawling up their legs. They had been out here for more than three months, and today's grocery delivery was a welcome event. Feisty seas had dashed several recent land- ing attempts, and food supplies had run low. Fruit was long gone; all that remained of the vegetables were a few spongy zucchini; milk and cheese were finished; eggs, gone. Last night Melinda had tried to make a quiche and quickly given up. This morning's break- fast had consisted of dry cereal.

Kingfish had also brought their mail and a few recent newspapers, and after they had unpacked the groceries they sat in the kitchen, lost in their reading. The group seemed tightly familial. It was an in- teresting mix, an experiment in unlikely utopia that appeared to have taken. Pete and Russ, like Peter and Scot, knew how to handle this unruly island, and they were seasoned scientists as well. Russ had tracked birds in places even more remote than the Farallones, studying albatross in the far western Hawaiian islands and hacking his way north through British Columbia in search of endangered murrelets. He'd crawled into damp tents and slept on moldy pillows and gone hungry in the field enough to have developed a thorough appreciation for the basics—at least there was a house here. And most of the time, there was plenty of food. When Russ spoke, the words tumbled out in a stream of enthusiasm punctuated with heartfelt inflections—awestruck whispering, yelps of mock outrage, intense emphasis placed on a single word—and every description re- quired a string of superlatives: "It's just an *unbelievably beautiful* bird. I was *incredibly fortunate* to see it. Their wingspan is *sick.*"

Tall, rugged, red-haired Pete was a New Yorker. Like most of his kind he was tough, terse, and skeptical on the surface and then, after he got to know you, he'd suddenly flash a shy smile and reveal his warmth and his wicked sense of humor. Pete was twenty-eight years old and had come to realize that cities weren't his thing; recently he'd experienced a serious bout of claustrophobia when he came off the island. At the end of seabird season, he was heading for Alaska.

The chemistry could so easily have gone wrong. And had in the past. Crack-ups, hookups, breakups, and even, according to Peter, four divorces could all be chalked up to the Farallon crucible. Nervous breakdowns snuck up on people after an eight-week run of bleak weather, a few missed grocery drop-offs, a piggish housemate or two, and days spent watching animals kill and eat each other. Tempers exploded, psyches unraveled. Wind, in particular, could really wreak havoc with people's mood, as could fog. One couple who'd come out together as interns broke up when the woman fell for another biologist and moved into the bedroom across the hall. (The next boat was ten days away.) Another intern threatened lawsuits after tripping on the back steps of the house. Someone's fist went through the wall. On a few occasions people had panicked when they realized they couldn't leave the island at will; one of them ended up chartering a helicopter to get off. And one disgruntled visitor, no one was really sure whom, had spray-painted scarlet graffiti, a mess of streaks and whorls, across the vaulted ceiling of a sea cave.

One recent night Russ and Pete had been sitting in the coast guard house, watching *Survivor*. A contestant was whining. He was freshly shaved and looked chipper, but psychologically he was coming apart at the seams. "It's been twenty-eight days," he moaned. Russ and Pete looked at each other, ungroomed for weeks, facial hair running amok. "It's been *seventy-eight days!*" Russ yelled at the screen.

Even so, the five of them were loving their time here, never mind that they had to work fourteen hours at a stretch to keep up with the birds. Simply put, they were happy. There was no whiff of the driven, anxious, upwardly-mobile-or-die young professional.

They'd made a career choice that had nothing to do with money and everything to do with the fact that they'd never lost the child's sense of amazement about nature. It was as though the "career goal" entry on their résumés read: "To stay as far away from an office cubicle as humanly possible."

In the early evening I sat at a desk by the front window of the living room, flipping through old logbooks. It was dead calm on the water. About ten miles out, on the edge of visibility, I could see breaching humpback whales and freighters heading to Asia, toys rolling across an iron tabletop.

I was making my way through twenty-five years of shark season notations, accounts and stories of great white doings scrawled in a dozen different pens. Scot's entries, set down in his distinctive architectural handwriting, were succinct, and often dryly funny. While some people poured out exclamation-point-studded epics that went on for pages—one enthusiastic writer had broken a shark attack down into minute-by-minute musings—Scot saved his detailed observations for the Shark Project's reports, and his contributions to the island log read like telegrams:

◄ "1 breach, 2 splash & thrash. Half Fin's back."

◄ "Lots of decoy action. They are here and they are hungry."

◄ "2 attacks plus several visits. SA and PP watched an e-seal get nailed by Stumpy at East Landing. Some close-ups gotten."

Auditing the month of August for shark action, I was encouraged by what I found; on average, there seemed to be an attack or two per week. (By October, every day brought reports of spilled blood.) Leafing from one August to the next, I came across an entry that read, "Ron Elliott was aggressively approached by a sixteen-foot female shark." It was accompanied by a cartoon drawing of Ron fighting off a shark and yelling, "Back off Whitey! I've got urchins to pick!" The logbooks made for addictive reading, and when I finally tore myself away from them, hours had passed and everyone else was asleep. On this trip I was bunking with Jen in a large bedroom down the hall from Jane Fonda. This was fine with me. Two nights ago at an Inverness restaurant, Peter and Scot had informed me that the Jane Fonda bedroom was notoriously haunted. "There's a ghost there," Peter said matter-of-factly, after a few beers. "It's a woman."

"In the *house*?" I'm not sure why I found this surprising. If any place deserved to be infested with ghosts, it was the Farallones.

"Around the island. There was a body found in a cave." He went on to explain that a century ago, the well-preserved skeleton of a woman had been found in Rabbit Cave, down by East Landing, close to the site of the original Russian settlement. Most people assumed she was an Aleut slave; it was their custom to entomb their dead. But others believed she was a Caucasian, a claim they insisted could be confirmed by her dental work. The truth is that no one really knows, and there is no record of her death. Her bones remain on the island, buried near the cave's entrance.

In the years since there had been reports of odd, ghostlike encounters: trouble breathing was commonly cited, as were chills, whispering voices, glimpses of shadowy silhouettes moving across the cart path, footsteps and doors slamming in the night. Now, it's one thing for a few people sitting around on heebie-jeebie island to wind themselves up thinking about ghosts. It's another thing altogether for that group to be composed entirely of scientists, most of whom would rather eat dirt than admit to any sort of belief in the paranormal. But at the Farallones some very logical minds had been flummoxed and terrified by unexplainable encounters.

In the mid-eighties, Peter told me, a biologist was walking back to the house in the last, foggy light of day when he noticed a woman with long dark hair standing on the marine terrace in a filmy white dress. Figuring it was one of the two female biologists on the island, albeit in a fairly strange getup, he continued on his way into the house—where he immediately encountered the two women, sitting on the living room couch. He turned on his heel and ran back outside, but the woman in the white dress had vanished, though there was really no place she could have vanished *to*, short of jumping into the ocean. "And he was Mr. Science!" Peter recounted, snickering. "A guy who would do things like rebuild the transmitter. He said it made a believer out of him."

On another occasion a visiting botanist was intercepted sleep-walking out the front door in the middle of the night, screaming, "NO! I'm NOT going up there!" When someone tugged on his arm and woke him, he explained that a dark-haired woman was trying to entice him to climb to the lighthouse with her.

"What about you?" I asked them. "Had any ghost action out there personally?"

They both nodded vigorously.

"Oh, I've had scary experiences," Scot said. "You get the *creeps.* It's the feeling of a presence around you. It usually happens when you're alone. At night."

For Peter, one incident in particular stood out: he awoke to loud, thudding footsteps on the stairs, followed by the front door slamming, an attic trap door in the Jane Fonda bedroom stuttering rapidly, and a chill wind that blew through the house, rattling the windows *from the inside,* after the door shut. At the time he was one of four people on the island, all of whom were cowering together in one bedroom, scared witless. There was no extra set of human feet that could possibly have been pounding up and down the stairs that night—they all knew it, and they all felt it. This had occurred more than a decade ago, and I could see that telling the story still gave him a chill.

"Certain rooms are scarier than others," Scot said, fingering his glass. "That Jane Fonda room . . . the one you stayed in . . ."

"Yeah, that's the one where most things happen," Peter agreed. "I've never liked that room either."

"I stayed there for a while. Man, I couldn't wait to get out of that room."

DURING BIRD SEASON, WALKING WAS RESTRICTED TO CERTAIN PATHWAYS and, even then, extra care was required to make sure no one felt the delicate crushing of fluff beneath one's boots. There were chicks in every crevice, downy balls bunking down in the most unexpected places. They were even wedged into the front steps of the house. Territory meant everything to these animals; it was the difference between survival and death, and every square inch of it was staked.

Along with the twenty-five thousand gulls, there were one hundred thousand murres on the island right now, packed tight as bowling pins on the sea cliffs. There were also about forty thousand cassin's auklets, twenty thousand cormorants, four thousand pigeon guillemots, and assorted other homesteaders in smaller numbers, including 120 tufted puffins. Every bird needed its own little stomping ground, and they arrived in late fall and hunkered down for months before breeding, simply to hold the spot. The smaller seabirds—the petrels and auklets in particular—had evolved strategies to gull-proof their offspring. They were nocturnal, flying only at night, hiding themselves in underground burrows during the day. (And still, the gulls managed to eat a lot of them.)

For everything on the island with two wings, the point was not simply to hatch chicks, but to successfully "fledge" them, get them flying and diving and fending for themselves. The fledging process was especially dramatic for murres. Before they ever learned how to fly, the chicks were walked to the cliff's edge by their parents, and then they tumbled into the sea, sailing away on the currents like cotton puffs and, if they were lucky, figuring out what to do when they hit the water.

By August, plenty of chicks had fledged already, and those that hadn't yet were thinking about it. I walked along with Russ and Jen as they checked their rhinocerous auklet study plots, reaching their hands into burrows to determine if anybody was home, or whether the occupants had decamped until next season. After months of watching specific birds struggle to make it, the biologists felt like they were viewing a soap opera. On many days, the story lacked a happy ending. Tens of thousands of chicks, and even some adults, succumbed to what was noted in the field as "PIH," or "Pecked-in-Head." This was the gulls' signature mode of killing, and it involved rushing at another bird and, as the acronym attested, knifing their beaks into its skull. Any bird could end up PIH; the gulls murdered their kin as exuberantly as they went after other species. When the fledging attempts began in earnest, a sort of PIH-alooza ensued as chicks wobbled around testing their wings, and stumbled onto a mature gull's turf. At present there were PIH casualties strewn everywhere.

I stood on the lighthouse path, poking one of them with my toe. The bird's beak was frozen open, midsquawk, as though it had been hurling insults right up to the moment the lights went out. Above me, pigeon guillemots peered cautiously from their burrows in the craggy hillside clefts. They were sleek, black birds, with ballerina necks, dove-shaped heads, and sexy detailing: each wing had a crescent-shaped white accent like something Coco Chanel had carefully designed, and both their webbed feet and the insides of their mouths were colored a hot lipstick red. Unfortunately, the pi-gus, as they were known, greeted the nose less pleasantly than the eye—they smelled like rotten fish.

Several yards below, Russ deftly pulled a rhinocerous auklet out of a hole in the ground. The rhino was a regal-looking bird with pale, thoughtful eyes and a horned bump on top of its sharp beak. He held it up for me to see. It looked pissed off. "These birds are a combination of beauty and badass," he said, as it bit him hard on the thumb. "They're puffins, basically. And they're tough." I'd caught sight of a tufted puffin earlier in the day, standing on a rock at North Landing, staring out to sea philosophically through red-rimmed eyes. Its vermilion beak was shaped like a pair of wire cutters and could take off your finger with similar ease.

We moved up the path. Russ bent down to pick up a dead bird. The bird was small and entirely black, no markings. Its eyes were gone. He broke off part of a wing and held it to his nose. "Petrel," he said, handing it to me. The feathers smelled musky and heavy and sort of smoky, like the bird had been part of an all-night poker game. Its tiny body was covered in gull regurgitation, leaving little doubt as to how it had died.

A few steps farther up the hill lay another victim, a cassin's auklet, a crush of gray feathers the size of a grapefruit. This one was fresh, staring straight up at the sky, and it looked pristine, until Jen flipped it over. The back of the auklet's head was missing.

As we walked, gulls rushed us. Sometimes it was a bluff, but other times they meant business. "They know when you're not looking, and they'll coldcock you," Russ said. Much of the time, the biologists wore hard hats. But that only seemed to make some of the birds more determined: One kamikaze gull had slammed into a biologist with such force that it died on impact.

The rhino rounds were done and I wanted to see the murres, the beleaguered bird so tied to the history of this place. In order to do so, Russ explained, we'd have to climb a near-vertical rock face to the murre blind, a rickety shack just big enough for two folding chairs. It was there that the biologists perched for hour after hour, studying the colony below. Walking among the murres was forbidden, as it would cause them to flush. Recently, a starving sea lion had charged through the colony, sending the murres off in a panic and gobbling chicks. The gulls followed in his wake, gleefully bolting down the unguarded eggs. Pete, who was in the blind at the time, watched in horror but there was nothing he could do. It wasn't a biologist's job to interfere with nature, only to observe it.

Looking down into the murre colony from the blind was like viewing an enormous protest rally from a helicopter—it was hard to tell where one head stopped and the next one started. In order to make sense of the mass of birds, the area had been divided into manageably sized plots. Russ, who was Canadian, took pride in pointing out the ones that had been named after provinces: "There's Alberta. Oh, and there's British Columbia, over there." Everything about these birds was painstakingly recorded as part of a data set that was thirty-three years old, and counting. Only after cataloging the population for three decades were the scientists beginning to see the patterns emerge. In El Niño years, the warmer

Pacific produced less food and the sea-dwelling animals suffered, breeding in far fewer numbers. Other years, things boomed. As it turned out, seabirds offered a perfect parallel for the overall state of the ocean, and a bellwether for ecosystem troubles. Such long-term research on a single marine habitat had never been compiled before. Just another pioneering bit of natural history going down on these desolate rocks.

ALL DAY THE AIR HAD BEEN DAMP BUT NOT COLD, AND THE SKY WAS A soft gray. This was gentle, mild weather, a Kleenex draped over the island. We were in a tropical depression, apparently, and there wasn't a hint of wind. This calmness, combined with the peak of the waning moon, created an ideal opportunity to go out and catch birds in the dark. So that's what we were planning to do after dinner.

Tonight's mission was to lure the island's stealthiest seabirds, the ashy storm petrels, into a gossamer-fine mist net so they could be counted and banded. During the day the petrels hid in impossible places; despite the fact that the world's largest colony lived on these shores, they were almost never seen. At 10:30 p.m. the six of us headed up to the net, which Pete and Russ had stretched between two posts on the side of Lighthouse Hill.

As we walked, our headlamps bobbing in the bottomless pit of a night, I asked Pete for his opinion about the ghost stories. He told me that he'd not had any encounters himself, but most of the biologists believed the island was haunted, and that a number of them had been scared by footsteps on the stairs, just as Peter had been. One of them, a friend of Pete's, had awaked to a female voice urgently whispering in his ear, speaking in a language that he couldn't understand.

Turning off our headlamps, we sprawled out near the net, pretty much on the exact spot where earlier in the day I had marveled at the carnage. "I smell something dead," Melinda said cheerfully. "I'm probably sitting in it." It would be hard not to. I was beginning to get used to being surrounded by dead birds, I was slowly becoming inured to the waves of PIH victims, but I really did not want to touch maggots, which everyone else seemed to accept here as a matter of course. (I also preferred not to contract bird lice, another seabird job hazard.) No one else seemed squeamish about lying on the ground, however, so I kept quiet and resisted the temptation to turn on my headlamp.

A scratchy cassette recording of petrel mating noises pierced through the darkness. The nocturnal birds all had eerie calls that seemed to come from somewhere deep inside them; this one brought to mind a heavily loaded Styrofoam box being dragged across a linoleum floor. Almost immediately the petrels began to appear. They were the approximate size of a moth on steroids and they came fluttering toward us with erratic, batlike motions, diving into boomerang turns when they got close enough to spot the net. Often, it was too late. When one of the birds snagged itself, whoever was closest jumped up, snapped on his or her headlamp for a second, and carefully extracted it from the mesh. Jen was doing this right now, and after popping the bird into a little sack to weigh it, she handed it to Pete. He pulled out a pair of pliers and affixed an orange metal band to the bird's ankle, then blew on its stomach feathers. If the petrel was breeding, it would have a brood patch, an almost-bare spot of skin that rested directly on its eggs, warming them. This one did. He passed the bird to me. It was chinchilla soft, and its heart whirred in triple time. The petrel looked up at me with alert, obsidian eyes. There was nothing mean about it—no sharp beak, no raking claws. It had a tube nose: a shiny, two-holed appendage on its beak that served as a kind of portable desalination plant, enabling the petrel to stay at sea, drinking salt water and shooting the salt out of its nose afterward. "I'm *so* into petrels," Russ said. "They're just *absolutely incredible birds*. The *true* oceangoing wanderers."

The petrel banding would continue until 2 a.m., but after a couple hours of lying in the bird graveyard, I became cold and decided to head back to house. There was no light beyond my headlamp and the lighthouse beacon sweeping the Pacific. In the utter darkness all sounds seemed amplified: the screaming gulls, the caterwauling nightbirds, the PIH scuffles, the crashing water. Vaguely gull-shaped things whirled in my direction, vying for a crack at my scalp. I began to walk faster, anxious to get indoors and with Alfred Hitchcock to thank for my state of mind. As I passed the coast guard house, solemn and mute next to its lived-in twin, a large white shape flew up into my face. Too big for a gull. I stepped back, frightened, and then froze for a moment. My headlamp illuminated a single, barren spot on the wall, but beyond the edges of its beam shapes of uncertain origin darted around. "There's just no way this place needs ghosts," I thought, resuming my pace. "Ghosts would be total overkill." Now the wind was picking up, shaking things, and the air was fat with moisture. Tendrils of fog spilled across the path, licking my feet. It was moving in fast and low, erasing the edges, creeping onto the island like an animal.

Diving inside the house, I immediately hit all the light switches, before remembering that you weren't supposed to do this; it blew the auklets' cover. When light streamed out the windows, they could easily be seen by the gulls, guaranteeing a massacre. Reluctantly, I turned off every light but the kitchen's, where I sat with a plastic cup of leftover dinner wine, trying to convince myself that I was not scared. It was rare to be alone in the house at night. In fact, it almost never happened. Which, judging by how I felt at the moment, was something to be thankful for.

I went upstairs to my bedroom. It was past one o'clock, but no one had returned yet. Falling asleep to the sound of a quarter-million shrieking birds took some practice, not unlike becoming accustomed to the car alarms and the sirens when you first move to Manhattan. I tossed for a while in my sleeping bag, heard the others come in, and then drifted off.

An hour or two later, I'm not sure exactly what time it was, something struck the side of the house with a heavy thump. I woke with a start. The birds had gone quiet. Jen lay asleep in her bunk across the room. Suddenly, in the still air, I had the feeling of not being able to catch my breath. There was a tight, unyielding pressure on my chest and it was not at all subtle. Breathing took effort; it became something I had to do consciously. Panicking, I sat up and looked over at Jen, who had her back turned. At that moment, she lifted her head, twisted around in her bunk, and stared straight at me, eyes wide open. "I'm cold," she said, in a high-pitched voice. *"I'm so cold."* I could tell she was not really awake, that she wasn't seeing me. Then she lay down again and was silent.

I felt my chest ease up, as if something heavy had been lifted, and I was able to inhale again without having to think about it. I lay with my heart pounding, trying to come up with a logical explanation. Everyone knew Jen talked in her sleep. This was just a weird coincidence. Wasn't it? I wasn't entirely dismissive of ghosts, but I wasn't a wild-eyed believer either. What *was* it that I felt? It had been definite and strange, but not hair-raisingly scary. The vibe was weak, and it was sad. Like a child struggling to breathe. Like one of the lighthouse children who had lain here, perhaps, in the last, fatal stages of diphtheria.

CHAPTER 5

One attack on pelican off Shubrick. The bird died.
—FARALLON ISLAND LOGBOOK, NOVEMBER 27, 1987

AUGUST 8–10, 2003

"What year is it? Hey, it's an odd year. Stumpy could be here!" Peter was standing on the whaler's gunwale, hands in the pockets of his vest, looking hopefully at the bright yellow surfboard that was floating off the stern. Shubrick Point rose in the background. "Or Trail Tail, who used to hang out with Stumpy. She was this unbelievably big female. The first time I saw her it was like a bus went by. Scot tagged her. I'm not even sure she noticed." He took a few nonchalant steps along the whaler's edge in his knee-high rubber boots. It made me nervous when Peter walked around on the rails without a handhold.

He'd arrived in the shark boat earlier this morning with two trophy salmon that he caught en route. On his way from Bolinas the gold morning light had flashed across relatively silky seas and things were just hopping, rockfish flipping around like popcorn and shearwaters swooping off his bow and humpbacks rolling through the channel, and it seemed wrong not to at least dip a pole into the water. A few hours ago, he'd hailed the island on the marine radio so that Russ could come down to crane him up. Everyone gathered at the landing to greet him; for young ornithologists, Peter stopping by was like John Coltrane suddenly walking into a class of saxophone students. Each of them had a well-thumbed copy of his book *Identification Guide to North American Birds,* also known as the bible of bird banding. Peter, of course, would never mention this unless pressed, but in the course of my reporting, I'd discovered gushing reviews and a roster of awards he'd received for the volume.

It hadn't taken us long to relaunch the whaler and make our way out here. After a few days saturated with birds and ghosts, I was itching to get off the island, and Peter thought the water looked "sharky." To me it looked like it usually did: blue-black and sinister. Of course there were sharks in it.

A Stumpy sighting, not only seeing a Sister looming underneath the boat but discovering it to be the queen herself, was a long shot. Yet despite her discouraging hiatus, she was so invincible that no one had really given up hope. As we drifted across her turf, Peter recalled how during the filming of the BBC documentary, he'd been sitting in the Dinner Plate on this very spot, in similarly flat water, with an island intern and the film's director, Paul Atkins. The three men were waiting off to the side while preparations were being made for a shot from another boat. Abruptly, the little boat rose on a foot-high crest of water. And there was Stumpy, looking directly at them with her ink-black eyes. After a moment of scrutiny she dropped back down, circled the boat, and vanished. When Stumpy's fuselage of a noggin lifted up from below, the intern had imagined her to be staring straight at him and he'd panicked, yelling, then hyperventilating. Afterward, he had declared his refusal to go out in the boat ever again. "She was just letting us know that she knew we were there," Peter told the intern, like that was going to reassure him.

No action in Sisterhoodville today. No boils, no outsized tail fins, no curious sharks giving us a once-over. We drove slowly around the island in a counterclockwise direction, heading south past Tower Point, past Sugarloaf, into the sneaky, double-reefed waters of Maintop Bay, and then, approaching the western tip of the island we came up on Indian Head, also known as Rat Pack headquarters. The surfboard followed behind us, stoic and unmolested. "Okay. Now we're in the money spot," Peter said, stopping one hundred yards away from the sharp rock walls.

Here was where Cuttail had lunged six feet out of the water in a tailstand, chasing Peter's pole camera, the underwater casing of which happened to be colored seal-meat red. Here was where Scot was bumped so hard in the Dinner Plate that its stern lifted clean out of the water. Where Ron watched a shark in pursuit of a seal rocket to the surface five inches from his flipper. Where an abalone diver named Mark Tisserand had been shaken by his left ankle for fifteen seconds before the shark released him and he swam seventy feet to the surface with his foot hanging by a lone hank of skin. This was the spot where a six-hundred-pound elephant seal carcass had once drawn, Peter estimated, a dozen individual sharks, where the waters were stained by "the most blood I'd ever seen and ever will again."

Rounding Indian Head, Peter felt hopeful. "I would be very, very surprised if we didn't get a hit here," he said. I watched the board with great concentration, willing a boil to emerge next to it. We dragged the surfboard back and forth several times down Shark Alley, and then we circled Saddle Rock and idled in front of the East Landing for a while longer. But there were no takers.

Because the sharks were so famished when they arrived here at the beginning of the season, they would promptly investigate anything that was dropped in the water. Sometimes, at first, Peter and Scot didn't recognize sharks they knew well because they were so emaciated. Half Fin in particular would arrive looking downright gaunt and acting crazier than usual until he managed to cut himself in on a carcass. As the sharks fattened up throughout the season, sometimes to the point of whalishness, they were less likely to take a run at the trick fiberglass. But right now, in early August, if any Rat Packers were swanning around Indian Head, there was no way they'd be able to resist the decoy.

Peter turned to me with a sad look. "They're not here yet."

No sharks was an empty feeling, a core letdown. Coming into a silent room where you thought there'd be a party. Discovering that your sweetheart had left you and taken the dog too. The Farallones without great white sharks was a movie without a hero, a military campaign with armies and no general. It was boxing without a super heavyweight division. It wasn't the same.

WHY DID I CARE SO MUCH ABOUT THESE FISH? WHY DID WE ALL? THEY were always in my thoughts, even when I was sleeping, and as I'd confided to Peter, not a day had gone by in the two years since I'd encountered the sharks when I didn't think about them. After that experience I knew one thing for sure: Great white sharks are something altogether unknown in the lineup. Any description of them requires tossing aside the usual vocabulary and settling in with a six-pack of hyperbole—the most mysterious creature on Earth, the last untamed beast, the ultimate predator, the most fearsome monster imaginable, absolutely, positively, supremely adapted for its role. They're simply *different*. As the legendary Australian diver and underwater cinematographer Ron Taylor once put it: "My own feeling was that there was a strong intelligent personality behind the black orb. Not evil, but more alien and sinister than that."

Even the word *shark* is sublime, sleek and cutting and without frills, like a stick whittled into a sharp point. Its origins are not known for sure, but one theory traces it to the Mayan word *Xoc,* the name of a demon god that resembled a fish. Another popular theory holds that *shark* is related to the German *schurke,* which means "shifty criminal." The word didn't come into usage until AD 1570, though, so it wasn't available to the ancient Greeks and

Romans when they became aware of the concept that a fish could tear you apart. There were references to oceangoing men chewed down to their ankles, and the odd drawing of someone in the water being bitten in half. But they didn't know much more than that. So they made stuff up.

In Pliny the Elder's thirty-seven-volume natural history, which appeared in AD 78, the Roman scholar speculated that fossilized sharks' teeth, which were then (and are still) found in significant quantities on land, rained from the sky during lunar eclipses. Later, a more sophisticated theory came along: The teeth were the tongues of serpents that had been turned to stone by Saint Paul on the island of Malta. They became known as *glossopetrae* (tongue stones) and were thought to have magical properties, most notably the ability to counteract venom and other toxins. Given that poisoning folks was a favored pastime, the teeth became popular as jewelry and talismans and were often sewn into special pockets in a person's clothing. It wasn't until the mid–seventeenth century that a Danish scientist named Steno deduced their true origin: He'd had the unusual opportunity to dissect the head of a great white shark that was captured off the coast of Italy and brought into the Florentine court, and got what was likely one of the first chances to examine its teeth.

About a century later, the great Swedish naturalist Linnaeus created the scientific nomenclature system, a universal language by which all living creatures are classified. Finally, the great white shark had an official title: *Squalus carcharias*. Later, when more shark species had been identified, this was refined to *Carcharodon carcharias*, which means "ragged tooth."

Certainly, no one could have guessed that the ancestors of these raggedy-toothed animals had survived at least four global mass extinctions and been patrolling the seas since the Devonian period, 400 million years ago. That era, 200 million years before the first dinosaurs put in an appearance and 395 million years before our ancestors clomped into the Great Rift Valley, is now known as the

"Age of Fishes," because there were so many oddities swimming and slithering around, as though nature was previewing various designs. There were eel-like fish and fishlike eels and giant sea scorpions and creatures with armored shields wrapped around their heads, and extravagant dentition for all. Bony fishes had been around for a while (150 million years, give or take a few) when a new line of cartilaginous fishes, or sharks, made their debut in the Devonian. The sharks were bad news for the other fish—perfect predators right out of the box. There was the *Dunkleosteus* (loosely translated: "terrible fish"), over seventeen feet long and sporting protective plating and self-sharpening hatchet jaws; there was the *Cladoselache*, a six-foot-long tube of muscle fronted by a curtain of fangs. Some of the late Devonian fish made it onto land and evolved into four-leggeds.

And the party was just getting started. The Carboniferous period which followed—now referred to as the "Golden Age of Sharks"— featured such unique creatures as *Helicoprion*, a shark with a wheel of teeth that precisely resembled a buzz saw, and *Edestus giganteus*, a twenty-foot-long hyperpredator with teeth that protruded beyond its jaw like a pair of Ginsu pinking shears. But undoubtedly the most impressive set of teeth to have ever graced the Earth belonged to a shark called *Carcharodon megalodon*, which lived between 20 million and 1.5 million years ago—yesterday, basically, when you put it into perspective. Megalodon is best imagined as a great white blown up to parade-float size. Its teeth, which could exceed seven inches in length, are plentiful enough to have become a fixture on eBay (though the most highly preserved specimens sell for lavish amounts of cash among fossil collectors). A large megalodon tooth is the size and weight of a child's liver, and they're broadly triangular, with serrations, just like the white shark's. But there's one significant difference: Chompers this size indicate jaws large enough for a quarter horse to stand in without nicking its head.

It's hard enough to conjure up the true scale of a Sister, a twenty-foot-long, eight-foot-wide, six-foot-deep animal. Consider for a moment a *fifty-foot* version of same. Megalodon is candy to the cryptozoological set, who love to imagine that somewhere in the unexplored Challenger Deep, skulking in the Marianas Trench or some such unfathomable abyss, it still lives. After all, other long-lost and unknown creatures have been retrieved from the depths. When a brand-new shark called the megamouth, a fourteen-foot weirdo with Jaggeresque lips the size of Chevrolet bumpers, was hauled up in 1976, no one had ever seen anything like it. And when a coelacanth, member of a species thought to have been extinct for at least eighty million years, was caught off the South African coast in 1938, people began to wonder what else was still out there.

But sadly for monster lovers, by general consensus megalodon has flatlined. Hiding, even in the pit of the sea, would be tough for a fifty-foot fish, but more important, megalodon never adapted for the deep water. If Meg was still around, she'd be more likely to hang out near pods of whales, her primary food source. Anyway, a piece of good news for surfers: There's not a shred of evidence pointing to megalodon's present-day existence.

And so it has fallen to great white sharks, which appeared in their current form about eleven million years ago, to occupy the bean-shaped niblet of our cerebral cortex reserved for fear of being eaten by something—particularly something that lurks, hidden, in another element, waiting to burst into ours. Great white sharks, emerging out of lightless depths with a maniac smile, neatly encapsulate every fear on our list. And given that they've lived far longer than we have, it seems reasonable to think that in some way these sharks shaped human evolution, that megalodon coming at you like a bullet train was a very good reason for quickly crawling out of the ocean in the first place.

In any case, it's not just me that's a little bit fascinated by them. Throughout cultures sharks have been worshiped as gods and feared as devils without much neutral ground in between.

Pacific islanders considered sharks to be reincarnations of the dead and offered them human sacrifices served up on underwater altars. Religious wars occasionally broke out between tribes when one of them barbecued the species of shark that was another tribe's sacred totem. The Hawaiians were in on this too; they had several shark gods, including Kamohoali'i, whom they credited with the invention of surfing. And when the navy began to construct its base at Pearl Harbor, workers stumbled across underwater remains of pens where, it was discovered, men faced off against sharks in aquatic gladiatorial matches. The largest pen covered approximately four acres and was encircled with lava stones. Given that the shark was in its own element, playing with a full deck of teeth, and the men had to hold their breath and fight with a weapon not unlike a sawed-off broomstick, odds favored the shark.

Which was for the best, perhaps, because pissing off a shark was considered extremely bad juju. Pearl divers in the western Pacific covered themselves with tattoos intended to placate the shark gods and purchased the blessings of a "shark charmer" before entering the water. Samoans specifically worshiped the great white and hung its effigies from trees; Vietnamese fishermen referred extra politely to sharks as *Ca Ong* (Sir Fish). European sailors believed that sharks had the power to foretell disaster; when one was seen trailing a ship, it was cause for alarm. As usual, the ancient Aztecs went farther than anyone. They believed that planet Earth actually *was* a shark named Cipactli.

There are 460 known species of shark swimming around today, and they're almost as preposterous and diverse as they were in the Carboniferous. We've got angel sharks that are flat, like shark bath mats; green lantern sharks the size of goldfish; reclusive Greenland sharks living under ice with their odd, mottled skin and their poisonous flesh; goblin sharks with what looks like a pink letter opener affixed to their heads; sawfish with their chainsaw noses—it's a circus of evolutionary panache, a wild bonanza of fish. We're scared of most of them, though many look more frightening than they really are (thresher, nurse), and it would be silly to fear the likes of a tiny houndshark, which has flat teeth and is thus referred to as a "gummy." Much of the cultural angst centers on the four shark species that have repeatedly ingested humans: the tiger, the bull, the oceanic whitetip, and, of course, the great white.

It's now becoming clear that white sharks are not malevolent, indiscriminate robohunters—in fact, they exhibit certain behaviors more appropriate for mammals than fish. For instance, they can discern shapes. Over the years, Scot had determined that the sharks wouldn't attack a square decoy, nor one designed to look like a mola-mola sunfish, but when a surfboard or the ill-fated Buoyhead Bob or a seal-shaped piece of carpet were set out, these things would at least be investigated, if not, to quote Peter, "whaled on." A great white's vision is obviously far more developed than anybody realized—no other shark lifts its head out of the water as if to size up its surroundings. The ability to see well, on top of their hair-trigger sense for detecting the subtlest electrical impulses, enables white sharks to tweak their hunting strategies on the fly. And then there's the image-defying aura of gentleness they give off when they're not hunting. Everyone who has ever encountered one—except, of course, for those who've been attacked—mentions it with a puzzled shake of the head.

More intriguing still to the biologists was the relationship the Farallon sharks seemed to have with one another. They weren't organized pack hunters, like orcas, but they were definitely keeping an eye on their neighbors and staying in what Scot referred to as "loose aggregations." Thus, when an attack took place, all the sharks in the area knew about it, and they went straight to the scene. Even if there was a bit of a traffic jam at the carcass, they didn't get worked up into a feeding frenzy. Rather, they did something more interesting. They established a firm but polite buffet line according to hierarchy: the larger the shark, the more preferred its position. Oh, there might be attempts to cut the line, with smaller sharks trying to dart in and grab a quick mouthful, but this was a chancy strategy and some of the Rat Packers had missing pieces of fins to prove it. According to the great white shark rules of the road, Sisters had the right-of-way at a kill, with Rat Packers orbiting at a respectful distance, cadging leftovers.

Admittedly, the sharks weren't doing quadratic equations out there and no one was suggesting a snuggle, but every day at the Farallones these animals were demonstrating far more nuance and intelligence than they were supposed to have. Another thing they weren't supposed to have is a personality. And yet one of the most intriguing discoveries of the Shark Project was that they did. There were aggressors and there were clowns; there were mellow sharks and peevish sharks and sharks that meant absolute bloody business. Scot and Peter knew this to be true firsthand, as did Ron; it wasn't some anthropomorphic fantasy born of being whapped in the head one too many times by the gulls. I found the notion of shark character irresistible and raised the subject at every opportunity.

In an Animal Planet show about the Farallon sharks filmed in 1999, Scot admitted to the camera crew that he and Peter were emotionally involved in their study: "It's unexpected to get on a personal level with the sharks," he said, looking a bit sheepish. "It's turned into more than just research. We've actually got a re-lationship with them." Later in the same program, Scot and the South African shark researchers Chris Fallows and Rob Lawrence discussed this subject at some length. "So what do you think of this personalities-in-white-sharks thing?" Scot asked them. "Did you expect to see this? Because it kind of surprised the heck out of us." The two South Africans agreed entirely; every shark was different. They went on to describe one of their study animals, a big Sister named Rasta, as "the sort of shark you want to just jump in and hug. It's the greatest animal on Earth. Whenever it comes to the boat you're just so happy, like a little kid."

Don't look to read an academic paper about this anytime soon, though. Scientists tend to squirm when the question of individual personalities in animals is introduced, even though anyone who owns a dog or a cat knows they can be as different as Caligula and Santa Claus, tightly wound little beasts with long lists of quirks and habits and moods. But *great white sharks?*

Or how about western gulls?

The subject of animal character came up again at dinner that night, probably because I brought it up. As the fajitas were being assembled and the wine was being poured, I asked, "So, do you think the gulls have individual personalities?" Everyone began to talk at once. As it happened, chronicling gull notoriety on Southeast Farallon made for hours of memorable dinner conversation, though perhaps not the kind of thing you'd want to discuss over squab at Le Cirque. Like the sharks, the same gulls returned here annually, and over the years some had become known for sociopathic behavior. Peter, who'd been watching the resident flock for more than twenty years, had seen it all.

There was Manson, who ate his own chicks, and Troll, who exacted a hefty penalty on anyone who passed by. The Silent Stalker was one of the few gulls that didn't scream threats; he would sneak up stealthily and then, without warning, go for the back of a person's head. Each gull had its preferred attack technique. The Nibbler favored a sharp bite to the Achilles tendon, while the Shitmeister would swoop low, unloading his special delivery. And then there was Spike.

In a colony where any shoebox of space was apportioned by vicious thuggery, Spike's territory ranged across the entire front of the house, an area wide enough for half a dozen gull families. He was an auklet serial killer and a relentless PIH heavy, and when the PRBO biologists came in or out the front door they'd inevitably encounter Spike shrieking hysterically, his entire face covered in blood, surrounded by an array of little carcasses. His auklet victims were meant to feed his chicks, but he would regurgitate them whole, so that the meal the baby gulls encountered was a solid, slimy mound approximately their own size. Spike's chicks usually didn't make it.

Even the average gulls demonstrated the same variety of behavioral patterns you'd find in any cross section of humans. There were birds that were conscientious parents and others that seemed wholly unconcerned when their chicks went missing. There were extramarital gull affairs and bitter gull divorces, homosexual gull couplings, gull spinsters and rapists and nerds. There were, of course, countless thieves. Neuroses and insecurities were especially obvious on the concrete helipad near the coast guard house where the single gulls hung out, hoping to bag a mate. Because this was such a lousy place to breed—fully exposed, no nest materials handily available—only the lowliest misanthropes skulked around, hoping to trade up and out at the earliest chance. Peter compared it to the sidelines at a high school prom.

I'd noticed that, while all the biologists had encountered standout characters, they grappled with the notion of the animals as individuals. In large part this seemed like a defense mechanism. So many animals died, inevitably, that caring about them one-on-one—rather than simply noting down the numbers on their tags or the study plots in which they lived—simply hurt too much. But the alternative, adopting an attitude as dry as a six-month-old auklet carcass, made science itself seem callous.

Peter approached the issue with a sort of big-tent philosophy. "They're animals. We're animals," he said. "We have opposable thumbs and a brain but as far as life on Earth goes, no one thing is better or worse than another." He paused to pour a glass of organic merlot. "I hate the word *anthropomorphism*. It should be the other way around. Not how animals are like humans, but how humans are like animals."

MORNING SUN WASHED ACROSS EAST LANDING. I STOOD HOLDING MY paintbrush as Peter opened two cans of a rubbery, barnacle-resistant paint intended specifically for boat hulls. Black had been the only color in stock, and as we began slapping it onto the whaler, covering the sunnier blue that had been there before, the boat underwent a personality change. After a few strokes, Peter stood back and admired the transformation. "Now it looks more like a real workboat and less like a yuppie fishing boat," he said with satisfaction. The word *yuppie* was Peter's deepest insult, synonymous with every cultural wrong, aimed at those who behaved like spoiled, soft-palmed candyasses with misplaced superiority complexes. People who fit that description possessed only a fraction of the character strength of the average working Joe (or selfless biologist), Peter felt; they had their priorities all wrong and wouldn't last a day at a place like the Farallones. It was a harsh generalization, and though I knew that Peter lived simply and had struggled with lack of means in the past, I was struck by the force of his dislike. While chasing birds he had hitchhiked through some of the most desolate places imaginable—Nicaraguan jungles, Indian slums, Samoan fruit bat colonies—but when asked to name the least likable place he'd seen in the world, he instantly pointed to an affluent California suburb: "Walnut Creek. No question."

He lay on his back beneath the whaler, brushing the center of the hull as toxic paint dripped down onto his clothes, hair, and skin. My sunglasses were flecked with black, and I was marveling at my painting ineptitude when, out of nowhere, Peter mentioned that he intended to surf the Farallones this year. During shark season. At some point, apparently, the idea had gone from an unlikely fantasy to a full-on plan. I was shocked by the matter-of-fact way he announced it, but then I remembered a conversation I'd had with another biologist whom I'd called to check some information, a woman who was familiar with Peter's work. She seemed amazed to hear that I actually knew him, and gave the impression that his reputation was larger than life. "He's a wild man!" she'd said. I was beginning to understand this assessment.

"For real?" I asked. He nodded. Under certain circumstances, he'd decided, it would be safe enough to surf in Mirounga Bay. The swell would have to be just so, as would the wind, the visibility, and the tides. If these ideal conditions coincided, a tow-in approach could be attempted. "Because you don't want to be, like, *paddling* out there," he said. "I would jump off the shark boat, catch the wave, and hustle into shore." I must have looked skeptical, because he immediately added, "All I want is one ride."

"Well," I said, slowly. "I'm not saying you *should* do it, but if you *do,* I'd really like to watch." For the most part, I meant this rhetorically. I was well aware that, as far as outsiders went, this place was locked down tighter than Fort Knox. And I believed that policy was for the best—restricted access had saved the Farallones. If things had been more welcoming out here, there would be condos and a great white shark theme park on this island right now.

Even so, even though I knew they were necessary and in this case noble, I'd always hated rules. All too often they were stupid and floutable, and begged to be defied. While I wasn't a complete outlaw, throughout my life I had questioned most rules I'd come up against, and ignored my share of them. I'm not saying that's the way a person should be, but if the opportunity to sneak back onto the island presented itself, I was game. I suspected the offer wasn't forthcoming, however, and didn't want to push the matter.

I wanted to write the story of this place and its resident sharks, but without access this would be difficult. Ron had offered to let me accompany him when he dove here, which was promising, although day visits were no substitute for being on location. And though I happened to know that Peter disliked rules as much as I did, allowing me a closer look during shark season presented a huge throw of the dice. He'd already noted that there would be an awful lot of scrutiny this year. Stowaways would not be looked upon kindly, and he had once mentioned something about "a six-figure fine," when a group of liquored-up boaters were caught giving themselves a sightseeing tour of Southeast Farallon. Even Scot required an annual permit from the U.S. Fish and Wildlife Service. His role was that of a privileged guest, his permit revocable, and it wasn't within his purview to tote me along for the ride. And so, while there were many things I expected to do this fall, sitting in the whaler watching Peter surf Shark Alley wasn't one of them.

"Well, maybe you can."

I looked at him. He appeared to be serious. "*How?*"

There was a lot he had left out of recent emails and conversations. The fight with the cage divers, it seemed, had done some damage. As the biologists tussled with Groth and his partner over attempts to tighten the regulations, certain officials voiced their resentment that the great white shark issues were dominating the agenda. At the same time, higher up the chain of command, the U.S. Fish and Wildlife Service had begun to note the dangers involved in the Shark Project—and the potential liability. Risky-sounding great white research wasn't part of their program; they were responsible only for the island, not for the waters around it. And so, in July, as the 2003 season logistics were being arranged, Peter had received an official letter declaring the sharks "a species that is not a management priority for the refuge." Concerns about use of Farallon facilities and manpower to conduct research on a nonpriority species were raised. Also, the whaler could no longer be winched on and off East Landing due to new, beefed-up safety rules, meaning that Peter and Scot would have to anchor their boat offshore and row out to it whenever there was an attack (which hardly seemed like a "safer" solution, when you thought about it). Permissible dates for this year's research had been curtailed as well, and included a window in October—potentially as long as a month—when the entire project would be suspended. During that time, several daunting heaps of junk and old diesel tanks and abandoned joists and a rubble-pile navy building or two were slated to be airlifted from the island by National Guard Chinook helicopters, supervised by U.S. Fish and Wildlife and Coast Guard crews. Though it was all part of the worthy plan to return the Farallones to the animals, the endeavor would be complicated and messy and, it was implied, sharks would be an even less welcome distraction.

And then the final blow. The letter wrapped up by saying that, as of December 2004, the Shark Project could no longer do "boat-based work" from the island—meaning that attacks could be observed only from land. Bluntly speaking, it was the end.

The timing was harsh. As a result of past triumphs with Tipfin and others, the Farallon sharks had been officially designated part of Barbara Block's TOPP endeavors, and by association, the Census of Marine Life. Twenty satellite tags were slated to be sent out this fall. That meant rounding up at least twenty individual sharks, a veritable herd, almost as many animals as they'd tagged during the last four years combined. Shutting down for a month at the height of the season would be a hardship at best and, at worst, ruin the chances of success.

Peter didn't seem angry, but he was perplexed: How could they continue their work while accommodating all the new restrictions? There had to be a way, he'd reckoned, and had spent the past month mulling over alternate scenarios. Conducting the project from the water, for instance, rather than its current island perch; that could work. They'd still need permission to keep Sharkwatch going—without someone at the lighthouse, the attacks would be far harder to spot, downright impossible in certain conditions. Luckily, keeping a sentinel up there didn't seem to pose a problem. "So I was thinking," he continued. "We could get a boat and anchor it in Fisherman's Bay. Something with three, four bunk spaces that a few people could stay on. The boat would be our research platform. If we can't work from shore, it's the way to go. And because we wouldn't technically be *on* the island, there'd be no restrictions as to who could be out there . . ."

I could see where this was heading, and I liked it an awful lot.

THE NEXT DAY WAS MY LAST ON THE ISLAND. PETER GAVE ME A LIFT TO Bolinas in the whaler, under sunny skies with a light chop on the water. We'd left early so I could catch a noon plane, and as we approached the harbor all was serene. Surfers bobbed in the channel. The air was filled with softer mainland sounds; the twittering of songbirds replaced the harsh gull cries, and the trees rustled gently. Eucalyptus and other land smells wafted by on the breeze.

Bolinas Lagoon was shallow, accessible only at high tide, and Peter drove slowly, the whaler putting quietly past funky shoreline houses that jutted on stilts above the water. The town was still asleep. He dropped me at the main dock and then anchored the whaler a few yards away, wading back over the sandbar in his stalwart rubber boots. After dropping our gear in the back of his truck, we walked down the road to grab some breakfast at the Coast Café, a sunny place with a shark-bitten buoy on the wall and surfboards hanging from the ceiling. As I scanned the menu, I glanced at Peter out of the corner of my eye. Somewhere in the fifty-yard span from the dock to the truck to the restaurant, his mood had changed drastically. He had turned quieter, darker, closed, as though a gate had slammed down, shutting out the light. So this was what reentry was like for him, I thought, this was the curtain of the real world lowering. I felt it too, and we ate our eggs and toast with a minimum of small talk.

After breakfast we retrieved my rental car, which I'd parked on a nearby side street. It sat there, grimy and neglected, but I was delighted that it was still in one piece; Bolinas was infamous for discouraging visitors by ripping down highway signs that pointed the way into town, and I hadn't supposed that rental cars would be embraced with any great neighborliness. A brindle-colored mastiff stood in front of it, regarding us with a proprietary air. Peter nudged the dog aside. He moved slightly, then padded back to his original spot.

"So we're going to find a boat," I confirmed. "I'll look for a rental online." Since yesterday we had been discussing the logistics. Working from the water was the Shark Project's future, it seemed, and the closure period this season was the perfect opportunity for a trial run. We'd find a captain to man the vessel, and I would stay on board for a week or two. That was Peter's version of the plan, anyway. Mine was to get out there and then stay as long as I possibly could.

"If you can't find anything, I could put it out to the Farallon Patrol skippers," Peter said. "They've offered before. Or Scot might know someone who's willing to lend their boat. An old beater would be great. Something we wouldn't have to worry about too much." It seemed the two of us had different images in mind. I was imagining a floating hotel room; Peter was envisioning a lengthy stay in a dumpster. Though it didn't really matter. To visit during shark season, potentially one of the last ever, I'd bunk down on the Dinner Plate if necessary.

We parted, and I drove off, feeling both elated (I was going back!) and discombobulated (not for six weeks). Between now and the start of the season there was much to do. I would need a cat-sitter. I'd have to make a request for a leave of absence from work. I required better binoculars. Most important, though, I had to find a boat. I fumbled in the glove compartment, pulled out my watch, and noticed that I had badly misjudged the time, leaving me eighty minutes to make the two-hour drive to the San Francisco airport. Clearly there would be no stopping for a shower. The weekend traffic didn't help. The entire Bay Area, it seemed, was headed for the beach. I crawled along the shoreline highway in my dusty Taurus, behind an endless stream of kayak- and surfboard-laden Range Rovers and BMWs.

By the time I returned the car and caught the shuttle to the terminal, I was sweating, and hopelessly late. The ticket agent shoved a boarding pass across the counter and told me to run. Headed for the gate, I mistakenly ducked under some ropes, forgetting that the days when you could do such a thing were good and over. Buzzers exploded, sirens went off, policemen, airline personnel, overempowered security guards all came at me. No one was particularly friendly about it, either. A sour-faced luggage screener grabbed my backpack, which was smeared with drippy gull guano, while a stout woman with a billy club hitched to her waist patted me down. I realized that I looked suspicious: unkempt, dirty, almost feral. During a week on the Farallones, it seemed, I'd forgotten the rules back on Earth, misplaced my copy of the social contract. I barely made the plane.

BOOK TWO

SHARK SEASON

CHAPTER 6

I'm scared of sharks. I've always been scared of sharks and I'm still scared of sharks and I imagine I'll continue to be, because I think that anybody who's not frightened of a shark really is a bit out of his mind.

—PETER GIMBEL, DIRECTOR, *BLUE WATER, WHITE DEATH*

SEPTEMBER 21, 2003

A day upon which you are traveling to meet your yacht is a good day by anyone's reckoning, and that's exactly what I was doing at the moment, sitting on a bench in the cabin of a fishing boat called the *Flying Fish,* slamming over the bunker swells of the San Francisco Bar en route to the Farallones. The morning was magnificently wild: gusty and bright with salt spray whipping raucously over the stern and sparkling in the sun. As the Golden Gate Bridge shrank in the distance, I felt myself unwinding. Last week I'd spent marathon hours working around the clock, writing last-minute magazine headlines, eating greasy take-out food for every meal, and drinking gin with my colleagues. During this unhealthy stretch of days, I'd counted the minutes until my escape. And now, on board, it was just me, the *Flying Fish*'s captain, Brian Guiles, his first mate, Dave, and a thousand dollars' worth of groceries.

I'd chartered the *Flying Fish* to take me to the islands, where I would meet up with Peter and a marine biologist named Kevin Weng, a shark-tagging expert from Hopkins Marine Station in Monterey. Scot was due to arrive in two weeks. Today, at Southeast Farallon, Peter, Kevin, and I would rendezvous with a sixty-foot steel-hulled yacht named *Just Imagine,* a Farallon Patrol boat whose captain was dropping it off on the return leg of a two-week trip to Seattle. Sometime early this afternoon we would anchor *Just Imagine* in Fisherman's Bay, its crew would hop aboard the *Flying Fish* and return to Sausalito, and I would settle into my new, floating home. And then, I imagined, we would toast the yacht with champagne and watch sharks frolicking off the bow at sunset. Or something like that.

I didn't know much about the boat, other than that, as mentioned, it was sixty feet long. In the end, it had been found close to home. After weeks of online searching had resulted in exactly zero suitable boats (and revealed that owners of large, live-aboard vessels are not especially eager to rent them), Peter had mentioned the situation to several Farallon Patrol skippers. Four of them instantly offered their boats; the first person to respond had been a man named Tom Camp, captain of the alluringly named *Just Imagine.* As it turned out, though, Tom Camp wasn't available to man his yacht, so I'd happily agreed to be responsible for it, making sure its batteries stayed charged and its hatches stayed battened and it stayed right side up and whatever else. I knew virtually nothing about large boats, but I couldn't imagine that babysitting one would be very difficult. The thing was going to be lying at anchor the entire time it was at the Farallones, somewhere in the neighborhood of five weeks, depending on conditions. When the suckerpunching northwest storms rolled in around November, *Just Imagine* would be whisked back to San Francisco. In the meantime, it would just float, a two-minute boat ride away from the island. Peter and Scot would be sharing the house with Brown and Nat, who were back for the bulk of the fall once again, along with two interns. During the day, the sailboat would serve as the Shark Project base of operations, with the whaler tied alongside for convenient access to attacks.

I was looking forward to the setup. As shark season had drawn nearer, I'd become increasingly excited about being back here, seeing the sharks, catching up with Peter, Scot, and Ron, finally getting a good look at one of the Sisters. What better way to ensure this than to spend all my time on the water?

Arranging a leave of absence from my job had been smooth; the timing was good, and in my business it was standard practice to tear off in pursuit of a story. I couldn't wait to go native again, to abandon the tamer version of my life. The effect was more than psychological. Each time I had visited the Farallones I'd left New York puffy and office-worn and come back glowing and sleek with extra angles and an uncontrollable dusty mane of hair and dirt jammed under my fingernails. And even when I didn't get to shower for a week out there, I always felt sexier than I'd ever felt walking around Manhattan all cleaned up and wearing Gucci heels or La Perla underpants.

Last week I'd had a staticky cell-phone conversation with Tom, a jovial fifty-five-year-old lawyer from Berkeley, who was remarkably enthusiastic about lending his boat to the Shark Project. He'd touted *Just Imagine* in the booming voice of a game show host. "I don't mean to sound like a hotelier Susan, *but you should see my stateroom!*" From the sounds of it we'd hit paydirt, and despite Peter's desire to procure a beater, the opposite had happened. "I'll take care of *Just Imagine* as if she was my own," I promised.

"Well, I'd just like to get her back in the same shape I left her in," he said.

"Tom, you'll get her back in better shape."

"Haaaaannnnggg on!!!" Guiles yelled from the cabin. In the next instant the *Flying Fish* cratered hard into a giant trough, and I was hurled from the bench onto the floor. I could hear the two men laughing up front. Guiles, who had grayish hair and a lean build and looked to be somewhere in his early fifties, was a hard-core fisherman. He didn't think a lot of the Farallones. To him, as to most skippers, the islands weren't much more than a fine opportunity to wreck your boat, a place you passed on your way out to the albacore that schooled along the edge of the shelf.

As I'd arrived at the dock this morning, he'd greeted me with a smirk: "So, had your last shower?" When I replied that I actually enjoyed not having to brush my hair, he'd laughed knowingly. "Yeah, well, that'll be all right for the first couple of days," then added, "Oh and by the way, they've got *a few flies* out there." When he'd noticed that I was carting about five hundred bags of groceries and another several dozen cases of water, beer, wine, and Diet Coke, however, his eyes bugged. "How long are you going to *be* out there, anyway?"

"I don't know. Depends on the weather. Maybe five weeks?"

Guiles let out a snort. "That's what you think. Here's my card. If I'm not booked, I'll come out and get you. You'll be calling me."

Buying groceries for five weeks on a boat had proven surprisingly vexing. Yesterday I'd roamed the aisles of the Mill Valley Whole Foods for several hours, considering the inventory. Tossing things into the cart with abandon wouldn't do; this particular grocery shopping had to be approached strategically. Over the years there had been memorable food tantrums at the Farallones; people had hoarded food, hidden it, fantasized about it, fixated on it, fought over it. Peter had mentioned that an intern once became physically threatening upon being told that the mayonnaise had run out.

I realized that I didn't even know if I could cook on *Just Imagine.* Surely, I figured, there would be a stove of some kind, but I'd forgotten to ask Tom. He had mentioned a large refrigerated compartment that worked like a dream and kept things very cold. Knowing that, I'd stocked up on frozen burritos and other perishables.

As the *Flying Fish* broncoed through the surf, the vast grocery supplies swayed and clinked on the stern deck. I lurched my way up to the wheelhouse, where Guiles and Dave were drinking coffee and talking shop. Earlier, I'd learned that the *Flying Fish* was the boat that released Sandy, the captive shark, back in the eighties. I asked Guiles about the trip.

"That," he said, shaking his head. "It was a big circus." His boat had been jammed with media people and aquarium people and many cases of beer, and Sandy had been so out of it, there was some concern that she was dead. Guiles himself had certainly thought so. "I picked her up right by the head, and we stuffed a bilge pump in her mouth so the water would flow over her gills. Then all of a sudden she tried to bite me. She was plenty alive." When they slid Sandy into the water, she'd dropped like a stone, arrowing straight down in a stupor, and smacking into an underwater cameraman who'd jumped in to document the release, before pulling herself together and shooting away. TV cameras whirred topside. "And then at eleven thirty that night, after the news, my insurance company called." The representative made it exceptionally clear that, in the future, should Captain Guiles decide to host live great white sharks aboard the *Flying Fish,* he could consider himself just slightly less insurable than the space shuttle.

We were approaching the outer waters of the Farallones, an area where white sharks were often encountered swimming lazily along the surface, and where Guiles had once even hit one. He described the time a sixteen-footer had porpoised alongside *Flying Fish* at railing height, at least six feet above the surface, trying to rip salmon off fishing lines and soaking the passengers: "Shark was so close I could've slapped him right in the face." Another time, fishing near Stinson Beach, a popular swimming spot in Marin, he'd seen two white sharks silhouetted in the surf right near the shore, less than ten yards from a group of boogie boarders. Even so, in his opinion, it was the makos who were the true badasses of the shark world. "Extremely aggressive. Nasty as hell. Makes a white shark look silly." He picked up the radio and tuned it to channel 80, the island's working frequency. "Peter, Farallon Island, Peter, Farallon Island, *Flying Fish,* over," he said.

Peter answered immediately. "Roger, *Flying Fish,* Farallones. Good morning."

"You guys order a pizza to go?" Guiles said, cackling. "Well you're gonna have to wait awhile. It's really rolling. We should be there in about an hour."

He clicked off the radio and turned to me. "You know what the most dangerous thing is out here?" he said. "Not the sharks. The weather." He described being caught out on the far side of the islands when thirty-foot swells rose up and barely making it back in one piece, though the weather had been lovely when he'd left the harbor that morning. And by all accounts, this wasn't an unusual experience.

As if on cue, the Farallones rose on the horizon, looking terrible and beautiful. By the time we reached the East Landing buoy, Peter was already waiting in the whaler; there was a shark attack under way over by Saddle Rock. I looked and could see the clutch of gulls. There was no time for my usual anxiety about clambering between boats; I jumped from the *Flying Fish* into the whaler. As we blasted over, I settled into the spot I liked next to the steering console, where it was possible to grip the rails on both sides. Peter grinned at me from under his baseball cap.

We floated in the slick, watching a tattered hunk of elephant seal bob up and down with no apparent takers. It seemed the sharks had come and gone already, although Peter claimed that often, just when you thought an attack was over, the second string moved in to polish off any remains. One time he'd been watching a lone scrap of seal just like this one for twenty minutes, when he'd noticed a tag attached to what was left of its flipper and reached over the side to make the ID. At that exact moment, a shark emerged from below and snatched the seal right out of his hand, its jaws less than a foot away, its eye rolled back and ghostly white.

There were several large boils around the seal but no probing dorsal fins, and then *Just Imagine* arrived from the north and glided toward us, looking somewhat majestic. This was a serious boat. Its long hull was navy blue with a white deck, its sails were furled and smartly secured by marine-blue tarps. On deck, waving, stood a tall, beefy guy with thick glasses and a mat of gray hair, unshaven and blissed out–looking in a worn purple T-shirt, chinos, and a crinkled sun hat. We decided to abandon the carcass and lead *Just Imagine* to its anchorage. Peter yelled directions to Tom and said that we'd meet him over in Fisherman's Bay. In the background I could see the *Flying Fish* idling, waiting to pick up the yacht's crew. Dave was leaning over the stern, spooling out the fishing lines.

In Fisherman's Bay, we pulled up beside the sailboat and said our hellos. Along with Tom there were now two more men on deck, Bob and Brian, who also had gray, desert island hair. Tom said they needed an hour to clean up the cabin and pack their things. They all looked scruffy and contented, and I felt my heart sink a bit at the news that the three of them had been living on the boat for two weeks and had not yet started to clean.

As Peter and I pulled away from *Just Imagine,* intending to cruise around the island while we waited, *Superfish* arrived at the mouth of the bay with Mick at the wheel and a full house of whale watchers gathered at the stern. All the passengers were squeezed along the port-side railing, watching us, and the boat listed dramatically. Kevin, the marine biologist, was on board, and we drove over to pick him up. He was a Stanford Ph.D. candidate who specialized in sharks, especially great whites, and he worked for Dr. Block.

The crowd parted to let Kevin climb over the edge. He passed two hard-sided equipment cases down to Peter, and then jumped lightly from *Superfish* into the whaler with the kind of surefooted ease that suggested he had maybe been born on a boat. He was a striking person, in his early thirties and athletically built, with jet-black hair and dark eyes and a smile that could light up a small midwestern city. As he reached up to grab his duffel bag from Mick, I noticed that all the muscles in his forearm were sharply defined.

We quickly made introductions, and Kevin told Peter that he'd brought six tags and another six were on their way. Kevin had just returned from Alaska, where he'd been tagging salmon sharks, a bulldoggish cousin of the great white that thrived in cold water, razoring its way through schools of salmon. Before that he'd been in Costa Rica, attempting to tag leatherback turtles as they crawled onto the beaches to dig their nests. And he'd spent July in Southern California working with a team from the Monterey Bay Aquarium that was attempting to capture a baby great white shark for possible exhibit. The aquarium had earmarked $1.2 million to accomplish this—the shark was intended to be the institution's "mascot."

According to Kevin, the aquarium was sensitive to the dismal history of captive white sharks and determined not to make any of the same mistakes. The project had been planned with military precision and advised by eminent scientists. Monterey Bay was perhaps the most reputable aquarium in the world, and if any group could successfully present a great white shark to the public, they could. As I thought about it, I realized that I liked the idea of people getting to see one of these fish at close range. Though there's something fierce and romantic in the notion of one last untamed animal, after seeing a great white you could never think that we'd be better off without them. But it would take a combination of skill and luck to pull this off without another dead shark lying at the bottom of a tank. For five weeks Kevin and the rest of the team had cruised around near the Channel Islands, where baby white sharks were known to gather at this time of the year. Three days before the project's end, they'd retrieved a five-foot female who had gotten tangled in a halibut gill net. She was transferred into a five-million-gallon pen in the ocean, where she was tagged and later observed eating some salmon. It all seemed promising, the shark was perfect, but the lease on the tuna pen ran out and they ended up releasing her rather than attempting to move her to Monterey before conditions were right. (The plan had been to keep shrinking the size of the holding area until it approximated the million-gallon aquarium tank.)

Actually, California had been breaking out in white shark hap-

Looking west toward the South Farallon Islands, known to nineteenth-century sailors as the "Devil's Teeth." SUSAN CASEY

The Farallones'
sole inhabitable
building, a
120-year-old,
weather-beaten
house.
SUSAN CASEY

The cart path,
with resident gulls.
SUSAN CASEY

Peter Pyle, with Great Arch in the background. SUSAN CASEY

Scot Anderson
on *Just Imagine*.
SUSAN CASEY

The Shark Shack
at East Landing,
home to various
surfboards and
decoys, including
the ill-fated
Buoyhead Bob.
SUSAN CASEY

Nothing is easy here: Peter launching the whaler, with the help of the East Landing crane. Due to the sharp rocks and cliffs that form the shoreline, there are no docking facilities at the Farallones. SUSAN CASEY

The Dinner Plate sees some action from a shark named Bluntnose. PETER PYLE

A shark roils the surface during an attack. People who encounter a great white shark at the surface are often stunned by the animal's girth, which can measure eight feet. PETER PYLE

Last man diving: Ron Elliott, the only commercial diver with nerve enough to pick urchins at the islands, on the deck of his boat *GW*, just south of Shark Alley.
SUSAN CASEY

A shark attack at the Farallones is not usually a subtle event; a pole camera is used to capture an underwater shot. PETER PYLE

Aerial view, looking west, of the South Farallones. This photograph was taken in 1949. LIBRARY, CALIFORNIA ACADEMY OF SCIENCES

"Wicked scary": an aerial view of the North Farallones, circa 1952. LIBRARY, CALIFORNIA ACADEMY OF SCIENCES

Eggers unloading their plunder at North Landing, with Arch Rock and Sugarloaf in the background. In 1905, a storm ripped the derrick from its platform and it was never replaced. LIBRARY, CALIFORNIA ACADEMY OF SCIENCES

1896 egger, wearing his specially designed "egg shirt," designed to hold eighteen-dozen murre eggs as he scaled the Farallon cliffs.
BOLTON COLLECTION, LIBRARY, CALIFORNIA ACADEMY OF SCIENCES

A northerly view of Southeast Farallon's marine terrace, houses, and Lighthouse Hill, taken from Mirounga Bay. PETER PYLE

An act of devotion: Scot Anderson on Sharkwatch, which he created in 1987. Every daylight hour during shark season, an observer stands at the lighthouse scanning the islands for signs of shark activity. SUSAN CASEY

An eighteen-foot shark investigates a six-foot surfboard. PETER PYLE

The fate of
a surfboard at
the Farallones.
PETER PYLE

Scot Anderson (in orange) observes a feeding. Also in the boat are director Paul Atkins and cinematographer Peter Scoones of the BBC film crew that visited the Farallones in 1993 to film *The Great White Shark*. PETER PYLE

Whiteslash, an eighteen-foot female Peter described as "gentle and maternal," cruises the whaler. PETER PYLE

Great Murre Cave (right) and Little Murre Cave, cleaved into the rock below Shubrick Point. SUSAN CASEY

Juvenile northern elephant seal, the favored food of great white sharks, lounging on the marine terrace.
SUSAN CASEY

California sea lions basking on the old stone steps at North Landing.
SUSAN CASEY

Twenty-five thousand western gulls make Southeast Farallon Island their home. SUSAN CASEY

Riding the Billy Pugh at East Landing, with *Kingfish* and the Dinner Plate in background.
SUSAN CASEY

A cassin's auklet chick.
SUSAN CASEY

The sixty-foot steel cutter *Just Imagine*, with skipper Tom Camp. SUSAN CASEY

An unquiet cove: *Just Imagine* (with Tubby tied off to starboard) at its moorage in Fisherman's Bay, 150 yards west of Tower Point and 200 yards east of Sugarloaf. SUSAN CASEY

Marine scientist and shark-tagging expert Kevin Weng from the Block Lab at Hopkins Marine Station, Monterey.
SUSAN CASEY

Part of the *Just Imagine* diet: a cabezon, a fish with a face that could scare small children.
SUSAN CASEY

"Just get there as fast as you can": Peter Pyle rowing Tubby across Fisherman's Bay. SUSAN CASEY

Scot Anderson on the marine terrace, with Saddle Rock in the background.
SUSAN CASEY

The outer edge of the fearsome Maintop Bay, a spooky, boat-eating stretch of water that makes everyone uneasy. Not surprisingly, the sharks seem to love it. SUSAN CASEY

Unfavorable boat-launching conditions at East Landing. PETER PYLE

The Perfect Wave, a pristine right break that rolls along Shark Alley. PETER PYLE

penings all summer. On August 24, Deborah Franzman, a fifty-year-old teacher who counted swimming with seals among her hobbies, was fatally attacked by a sixteen-foot great white at Avila Beach, two hundred miles north of Los Angeles. It had been nine years since a white shark killed someone in California, and the shark message boards and chat rooms buzzed. Some thought Franzman had been courting danger. *"Swimming with seals?* Why didn't she just put a dinner bell around her neck!" wrote one member before being chastised for insensitivity by fellow shark enthusiasts.

Meanwhile, a stone's throw down the coast, three great white sharks had congregated near the San Onofre nuclear plant and were photographed from news helicopters and by pilots from nearby Camp Pendleton every day for a month. After numerous sightings and subsequent beach closures, the sharks became such local fixtures that they were given the names Sparky, Fluffy, and Archie. As word of the trio's persistent presence spread, sightseers thronged the windswept beach. "We could have went to any beach in San Clemente, but I thought it would be fun to maybe see someone get bit or chased by a shark," one visitor explained to the local press. Others had asked the park rangers, "What time do the sharks appear?" When a fourth shark had shown up, it seemed prudent to cancel the annual Labor Day surfing competition. No one could figure out why Fluffy, Sparky, and Archie were loitering around this particular spot, until city officials admitted that they had buried a forty-foot fin whale at this beach two years ago.

Closer to home, in August, Peter had been startled to receive email queries from a group of open-water swimmers planning a relay from Southeast Farallon to the Golden Gate Bridge on September 20. As a precaution, they said, they would be wearing an electronic repellent device called the "Shark Shield," and what were his thoughts about this? "I discourage this idea," Peter hastily emailed in response. "In September the sharks are just back from the mid-Pacific and they're hungry. I don't think the electronic wrist watches would be effective given the white shark's hunting strategy of rushing up from the depths." Recounting the story to me, Peter scoffed. "So the shark's thinking, 'Hmmm, I don't like this noise,' but at that point it's hauling ass upward at forty miles per hour. What's it gonna do? Make a U-turn?"

The race, which would have taken place yesterday, had been canceled when the escort boat's insurance company balked. In fact, no coverage could be had for any boat participating in this competition, nor for any part of the swim, period. The notion that this event had almost taken place disturbed me so much that I'd phoned one of the organizers, a seventy-year-old man named Joe Oakes who also ran a swimming race called "Escape from Alcatraz." Despite Peter's warnings, he remained undeterred. I'd mentioned that I was a swimmer myself and that while I certainly understood the allure of open water, given what I'd seen out there I really couldn't imagine diving in at East Landing and stroking away, particularly in the fall. Oakes laughed. "There are always sharks," he said in a dismissive voice. He had complete faith in the repellent device, likening its effect to a brisk whack on the animal's snout. "They don't like that one bit. Hey, do you want to be on the relay? Get us a boat, and you've got yourself a team."

AN HOUR LATER, PETER, KEVIN, AND I BOARDED *JUST IMAGINE*, TYING the whaler alongside. I realized immediately that it was even harder to climb between pitching boats of wildly varying sizes when they were tied together. Fingers mashed between the railings would fare about as well as a caterpillar clapped between two blocks of cement. Poor timing on the swells could easily result in hang time from *Just Imagine*'s railing or, worse, falling between the boats as they smacked against each other.

The sailboat was roomy but hard-used, with fore and aft bunks, a pocket kitchen, a semicircular dining banquette, and, surprisingly, a bathroom with a full-size shower. Overall, it looked nothing like the pictures of yachts you see in travel magazines, the ones where assorted Italian magnates and an accompanying herd of fashion models are lounging around on deck drinking Cristal and wearing Pucci sarongs. *Just Imagine* was to glamour yachts what cargo planes were to Lear jets, what Clydesdales were to Arabians. Its decor listed heavily toward seventies-era rec room—acres of shellacked knotty pine, dusty bottles of no-name brandy, a stained-glass porthole, and, in the center of the floor, a groovy bas-relief carving of a woman wearing nothing but long hair.

Unfortunately, Tom explained, on the trip down from Seattle they had encountered some bad weather and they had jibed and, well, part of the starboard side had been ripped off. We looked: yellow twine and duct tape crisscrossed an area once occupied by a railing. "Best not to walk on that side," he said. Also, Tom mentioned offhandedly, the refrigerator had gone down, and the plumbing did not quite seem to be working either. I stared at him. "What do you *mean* the plumbing doesn't work?" I felt panic. "Well, just now I tried to flush the toilet, but there was this backwash . . ." He opened a cabinet and pumped a long lever hopefully. "See, there's no vacuum—hey! What do you know! It's working!" Something gurgled ominously in the head, followed by a vicious blurping noise. "So there is plumbing?" I confirmed. "I guess there is! That's cool!" he said, with surprise in his voice. I glanced at Peter and Kevin. I supposed I could drink warm beer and I'd have to donate most of my groceries to the island crew, but plumbing seemed non-negotiable.

I stood off to the side while everyone else attempted to create a mooring setup that would stay secured for the duration. The process was anything but simple: Should the bow face north or south? How far should the sailboat be from the buoy in the middle of the bay? What about the anchor? How many ropes? It went on. Peter and Kevin climbed into the whaler, untied it, and idled beside us so they could ferry the ropes to the buoy, while Tom and Bob argued about where *Just Imagine* should lie. The spot they chose was quite far offshore, straddling the mouth of the bay. It was obvious that whatever shelter the cove offered would be next to useless in this spot, especially in the event of northwest winds (which happened to be the prevailing winds). This anchorage also aligned *Just Imagine* with a gap between Sugarloaf and Arch Rock, so that westerly gusts would come barreling through at a ninety-degree angle to the boat, broadsiding it. Peter noticed this immediately and asked if the yacht shouldn't be moved in slightly, but Tom wanted to hook the anchor on a reef edge that traversed the area. He crouched at the bow holding the windlass, a device that lowers and raises the anchor. Slowly, the chain paid out. Tom spoke to *Just Imagine* as he was doing this, and after several minutes of encouragement, he suddenly yelled, "Oh no, oh no, OH NO, *GODDAMMIT!*"

"What's wrong?!" I asked, alarmed.

"Oh, I thought for a second there I lost the anchor," he said, looking relieved. "But I caught it just in time. That wouldn't have been pretty."

Given that *Just Imagine* was now more than two hundred yards from the buoy, Peter and Kevin had to tie four ropes together to reach it. This, of course, made for three weak links, and as a precaution they looped another set of ropes along with the first. When they reboarded, I could tell they were startled by the way that the yacht was now secured on both ends—ropes off the stern, anchor chain off the bow. Tying a boat up this way, stretched like a hammock, is not usually recommended as it prevents the boat from tracking with the wind, and sure enough, even though the gusts had died down and right now there was really nothing but a breeze, *Just Imagine* began to buck from side to side. Peter and Kevin stood at the stern with their arms crossed, looking perturbed. They were convinced that if the wind picked up there might be real trouble, but Tom and Bob, who had strong opinions about the matter, were adamant.

We climbed down the wooden ladder into the cabin to get a lesson in how things worked. As we moved through the interior, Tom spent a long time rhapsodizing on the craftsmanship of the woodwork, fondling objects he found squirreled away inside cubbyholes, and giving us a thorough inventory of the moldering food that was left over from the Seattle trip. The contents of the broken fridge had been spoiling for more than a week. I couldn't wait to throw the rotten lunchmeat over the side, see what came along to check it out.

He glossed quickly over the instrument panels, which looked like something you might encounter at NASA mission control. Colored switches, lights, gauges, keys, and dials lined the wall nearest the hatch. There was talk of which knobs to turn and which buttons never to touch, which dials should be monitored and which warning lights could be ignored. He explained the workings of the arcane 12-volt electrical system in about twenty words, mentioning offhandedly that if an earsplitting buzzer went off, as it was sometimes apt to do, we should shut down everything immediately, call him, and maybe go ashore. Peter took notes. I was suddenly very tired and distracted, catching only odd snatches of instruction.

Moving to the fore, Tom opened a wood-paneled drawer of documents and maps, explaining that this was where he kept *Just Imagine*'s important papers. Joking, I noted that these, then, were the things we'd need when we took the yacht to South America. Tom wheeled around to look at me, his face hard, the laid-back demeanor nowhere in evidence. *"I'd have the police after you so fast,"* he said, in the low, measured voice of someone completely unamused. There was a moment of awkward silence, and then, noticing the tension, we all laughed uneasily. Clearly, he did not think my joke was that funny. Surely though, he couldn't think I was serious. In that split second, I'd seen something akin to panic in Tom's eyes. Here he was, explaining the ins and outs of his precious boat to a group of strangers: how to run the engine, what to do and not do with the propane valve, how to unscrew the special handmade rack that held the dried fruit. And then he would be sailing in the opposite direction, leaving us in charge, having moored his baby in one of the most notoriously dangerous marine spots on Earth.

. . .

PETER AND KEVIN SHUTTLED TOM, BOB, AND BRIAN TO THE *FLYING Fish*, which still had fishing lines trailing behind it. I stood on *Just Imagine*'s deck and looked around. Fisherman's Bay was a classic U-shaped cove, ringed on all sides by vertical rock. The bay was tricky. It looked like a lee, but it was actually quite exposed, and in the past boats had ventured in seeking shelter and never made it back out. At the southern tip of the *U*, in a thimble of a gulley, was the North Landing. The gulley's mouth was barely fifteen feet wide, and from there it narrowed almost to a point. Drop offs required the boat driver to dash in between swells, maneuver next to the one flat rock in the gulley, hoping that the passengers had enough dexterity to leap quickly, and then dart back out before the next set of waves came surging in. At one time there had been a crane here too, but the entire derrick was ripped from its concrete platform by a storm in 1905 and had never been replaced. That was the thing about North Landing: At first glance it looked benign, much more manageable than East Landing. It wasn't.

Just Imagine's anchorage centered it between Sugarloaf, the massive rock 200 yards to the west, and Tower Point, 150 yards to the east. Adjacent to Tower Point was the even more massive Shubrick Point. This northeastern stretch of the island was all Sisterhood. I would literally be sleeping above them. Earlier, as we boarded the sailboat, Peter had volunteered that he'd seen Copepod Mama—eighteen feet if she was an inch—feeding right where we were anchored. And Scot had once watched the same shark drag a carcass into the shallows, directly in front of the Fisherman's Bay buoy. Seals had been hit close to shore in here, and the sweep of water at the bay's mouth was noteworthy for the number of jumbo-sized elephant seals that had floated there, headless—alpha kills that only a Sister could've made. Then, there was Ron's experience in this neighborhood. He'd had his closest call ever right off *Just Imagine*'s newly positioned bow.

On Christmas Eve day 1998, he was diving here when, a little ways in the distance, he saw a giant Sister who "made Stumpy look like a baby." The shark was oddly unscarred, pristine even. For her to have grown so large without collecting any of the wounds that tattooed the other animals was just plain weird, and the first indication that this wasn't an average shark. As she approached, Ron made a move that in retrospect was not the smartest, swimming at her, fast, from behind. It was one of his typical offensive tactics—he thought he'd make her go away. Instead the shark pulled an immediate donut and charged at him. She was the "fattest, maddest" shark he'd ever seen. Luckily, there were some rocks close by. Which Ron hid under for quite some time.

Remembering the awe with which he and Scot had discussed the shark, whom they'd dubbed Mrs. Clean, I longed to see one of the ultra behemoths. "The ones that manage to get that big, they're *different*," Ron had said in a hushed, humble voice, and Scot had nodded soberly. That mystical aura was something that I hoped to witness for myself, maybe even while standing right here, on this deck. Given the sailboat's location, it didn't seem unreasonable.

Peter drove the whaler back to *Just Imagine;* Kevin rowed out in Tubby, an eight-foot-long white rowboat that would ferry people from the island to our floating shark research base. He crossed the four hundred yards from North Landing to the sailboat with a few strong strokes. Tubby was the third member of the Shark Project flotilla, and despite her size she was important. Since Tubby was plastic, and not a very robust plastic at that, she could be hauled up on the rocks by a single person and didn't require the full production of being lifted on and off the island by crane. Given this season's boat-launching restrictions, that was a key point. When we weren't chasing sharks in it, the whaler would remain tied alongside *Just Imagine*.

Peter and Scot had chosen Tubby carefully, paging through marine catalogs looking for the squarest-shaped rowboat they could possibly find. "Eight feet is definitely in their range," Scot had admitted, but after years of decoy research he believed that a square object would not be attacked. He wasn't prepared to say that it wouldn't be investigated though, and that was enough to make the prospect of rowing around here feel somewhat less than carefree.

The whaler was tied along the port side of *Just Imagine*, while Tubby floated off the starboard. It was an awkward arrangement, and trying to keep this unlikely family of boats from slamming against each other required a series of bumpers that hung like junkyard art over the sailboat's side. The scariest move of all was the leap from *Just Imagine* into Tubby, which had the stability of a disposable pie plate and no railings to grab in order to cushion the impact. I dreaded the idea of doing this and hoped I wouldn't have to. After all, Tubby's job was to shuttle people to the island, and I wasn't going there.

By now it was past four o'clock. The sun blazed in the late afternoon sky; the water was deep sapphire with a light diamond chop; it was high tide. There was no point in unpacking the groceries since they couldn't be refrigerated anyway, so the three of us decided to take a lap in the whaler.

At Indian Head, we set out the surfboard. Less than ten seconds had passed when Peter and Kevin saw it at the same time: a boil next to the board, then a dorsal fin slicing around it in a polite arc. The shark made a quick investigatory pass beneath the whaler and then swam off. I didn't even see its body. "It was small," Kevin said, dismissing it as a tagging candidate. Older, larger sharks took priority—with Sisters at the top of his list. "Yeah, just a little tiny twelve-foot white shark," Peter said, laughing. "Well, at least we know they're here. That's a relief."

The sky took on that rich end-of-day glow. Fog began to move in even as the sun was shining, and its tendrils slowly wrapped around the islands, twisting like liquid. Light played between the wisps, which moved and settled according to density, like a layered cocktail, before shifting and reweaving again. Then, through the veiled sunlight, we saw a shimmery white rainbow straight from heaven's prop room. I'd never seen anything like it; Peter identified the otherworldly vision as a trick of the light called the Specter of the Brocken. It rose like an ethereal mirage over Maintop Bay, in stark contrast to the dark cleft of rocks and the black water below. He steered the whaler beneath its arch, and we drifted through it, while above us birds turned to metal in the silvering light. According to legend, Franciscan monks believed that anyone fortunate enough to see the Specter of the Brocken should go right out and throw themselves off a cliff, because its beauty was so rare and singular that life could only go downhill from there. Looking at Kevin and Peter and the mist sweeping in and the birds glittering above us and a pair of humpback whales gamboling on the horizon and knowing there were white sharks cruising below, I could almost believe it myself.

CHAPTER 7

Zodiac attacked today sometime during the afternoon. The starboard pontoon suffered two bites on the stern portion, which tore out the wall, deflated boat and submerged outboard. Zodiac was seen sinking at 1600.

—FARALLON ISLAND LOGBOOK, NOVEMBER 4, 1985

SEPTEMBER 22–24, 2003

The Hunchback was a humongous Sister with a Quasimodo hump whom Peter had encountered one wavy afternoon in Mirounga Bay. He'd been alone in the whaler, filming an attack that had drawn a gaggle of Rat Packers. At least three sharks were on the scene, buzzing him and taking their turns at the kill, but then suddenly they were gone. A vast shadow loomed beneath the boat, darkening the water as though the sun had been shunted behind a fat cloud. Peter gazed down, puzzled. Was there a whale below him? Occasionally, humpbacks and blues surfaced underneath fishing vessels, a situation that no one enjoyed, and he was considering whether to throw the boat into gear when the shark's head glided into view, heading in the direction of the carcass. Her scale made the seal look like a bath toy. She had a distinctively notched dorsal fin that appeared dainty compared to her outsized body, and she was at least three feet longer than the whaler, somewhere in the neighborhood of twenty-one feet. Peter had felt uncharacteristically rattled by the sight of her, though he forced himself to stay put and continue to film, realizing that there weren't many opportunities to document a creature so extraordinary. As it turned out, "she was quite docile."

A great white so big that she blocked out the light: I couldn't get that notion out of my mind, and I had dreamed about her last night. As the sailboat heeled in Fisherman's Bay, I was transported to the deck of a rust-colored freighter, plowing through turbulent, icy water somewhere off the coast of Alaska. Whitecaps salted the surface, and every few yards a white shark would thrust its head up. Sharks everywhere, the ocean was thick with them. When the Hunchback glided by, all the sounds were instantly muted: the wind stopped; the seabird cries and the churning water hushed to silence. Peter and Scot were on the freighter as well, but I was the only one wearing a survival drysuit, as though I was expecting to go overboard at some point. This dream water was even spookier than the water at the Farallones. Along with the sharks, it teemed with the unexpected, and typically unseen, denizens of the deep sea. Beside the freighter I could make out the slime eel, a primitive creature with five hearts and no eyes that bores its way inside fish, devouring them from within, and a pack of hatchetfish with icepick teeth. There was an albino sturgeon with ruby eyes, and a bioluminescent viperfish, glowing like fire. Enormous jellies floated among them, trailing poison tentacles. And as we looked down from the freighter's deck, the Hunchback ghosted by, orbiting like a stray moon.

When I woke up, I had to think hard for a second or two about where I was. Not that I normally slept on an eighteen-inch-wide lime green foam pad. *Just Imagine* had a fairly impressive captain's bunk up front, featuring a double bed with an actual mattress, but the air under the bow was stale and the skylight above was jammed shut in a snarl of nuts and bolts, and Tom had warned that it tended to slam down on the fingers of anyone trying to wrestle it open. Instead, I'd chosen the bunk nearest the hatch, where ocean breezes could blow in all night. It was just a shelf, really, that I was sleeping on, and it shared the aft compartment with the naked lady carving. The berth had a complicated lattice of blue Cordura straps on the side to hold me in, if it came to that. It probably would. I'd already realized that this setup wasn't conducive for being gently rocked to sleep—more like briskly shaken. And last night the water had been calm.

Fisherman's Bay sparkled in the sunlight and its surface was still, with no wind to speak of. Animal noises echoed off the rocks. There were elephant seals and California sea lions and harbor seals and Steller's sea lions playing in the shallows and clearing their throats, accompanied by a chorus of bird cries. Cormorants and murres shared Sugarloaf with squadrons of brown pelicans, who patrolled the bay on a mission for fish. The pelicans cracked me up. With their ungainly bodies and their long, prehistoric beaks, they seemed sent from *Flintstones* central casting. On land, they looked as though they'd fly with all the grace of a curling stone. But at liftoff, their enormous wingspans lofted them effortlessly, and when they detected a potential meal they folded their wings and transformed themselves into torpedoes, piercing the water and then swooping back up into the sky.

I spent an hour checking out the scene through my binoculars. Sea lions seemed to make up the bulk of the population in the bay. They swanned around North Landing, occasionally hauling themselves up onto the old stone staircase, a relic from the egging days, that led straight into the sea. The sea lions were remarkably agile. They could spider their way up a vertical incline with surprising speed and then flip back down with the poise of platform divers. They traveled in packs, porpoising and performing evasive maneuvers throughout the waters closest to the island, an area referred to around here as "the danger zone." Elephant seals were more skilled at lolling in the gulches than any kind of acrobatics, and they approached the island alone, which was why they got picked off by the sharks so often. They reminded me of oversized garden slugs, except with cute button eyes. The sleek and spotted harbor seals looked a bit like inflatable pool toys, and there were more of them in Fisherman's Bay than I'd seen elsewhere on the island. Steller's sea lions, of which there were only a handful here, were meaty-looking big boys that you wouldn't want to mess with, though the sharks occasionally did. A Steller's bull was holding court near the Tit; his size, I thought, would daunt even a Sister.

I went back into the cabin to make coffee, but after failing to light the burner three times I gave up, remembering Tom's cautionary note regarding excess use of propane within a closed space. My stuff was strewn all over the boat; I decided to try to organize it. I'd given much thought to gear and clothing. In the past, whenever I'd visited the Farallones I'd forgotten at least one critical item, usually something obvious like a sleeping bag or a waterproof jacket or long underwear or polarized sunglasses. This time, I'd spent hours at my computer surfing REI.com, trying to anticipate every eventuality of shark season. Would I need repellent of any kind? Nah. A camping stove? I hoped not, as I had always found them scary and apt to maim; an explosion waiting to be let out of its can. Antimicrobial socks? Fingerless gloves? Gore-Tex dental floss?

One of the least useful things I'd brought was an ultradeluxe Therm-a-Rest. As any camper knows, your average Therm-a-Rest is an inflatable nylon pad that acts as a slight buffer between you and the hard, wet ground. In generic form these pads are simple, and they're cheap, running anywhere from $30 to $40. However, as might be expected, the enterprising folks at Therm-a-Rest had invented some pricier models because . . . why not? The $199 DreamTime model caught my eye. It was identical to all other Therm-a-Rests except that it was so thick it practically qualified as a mattress, and it promised "decadent comfort." So what if the Dream-Time was so bulky it needed to be checked as oversized baggage? Wouldn't it be ideal, I'd thought, for those nights when I opted to sleep under the stars on *Just Imagine*'s deck? But that was before I realized that Guiles hadn't been kidding about the kelp flies.

They were at their peak now, a carpeting plague, crawling up pant legs and down shirt fronts, overwhelming a person's every moment outside. And these flies were not the cleanest insects—

their preferred habitat is the inside of a seal's anus. The anus flies spent their time in one of three ways: tormenting us, tormenting the poor seals who had to house them in such an inhospitable place, and copulating with abandon in giant fly gang-bangs. This morning I'd counted a vertical stack of thirteen flies. Swarms of anus flies would put a definite damper on sleeping topside. With difficulty, I crammed the DreamTime into a closet.

Likewise, I was having second thoughts about another purchase.

After my strange experience with the chest-constricting presence in the house, it had occurred to me that a Ouija board might get some serious action at the Farallones. At worst, it would give me something to do one night. I set out to buy one. Sadly, the contemporary model is nothing but a plastic shell of the original, and it didn't seem right to bring a piece-of-crap Ouija board to a place with such a proud history of ghosts. Surely the spirits would relate better to something more authentic? I googled "antique Ouija boards" and was springboarded to various witchcraft sites festooned with graphics of demons and pentagrams and runes dripping with blood. One of them played eerie, tinkly piano music that was frankly upsetting. I went ahead anyway and shelled out $160 for a handcrafted wooden board.

When the board arrived, I was startled to see that it was the size and heft of a sidewalk slab. It bore a sign that warned: "IF AT ANY TIME during usage you suddenly feel cold or threatened, it is a good idea to stop immediately. These are signs of an evil spirit! Over all, this game is NOT completely safe. DON'T be crazy and use it at a graveyard!"

Now that I had dragged the thing all the way out here, I really didn't want it. I shoved it into my duffel bag.

My radio bleeped with a special tone that meant Peter was calling. Everyone on the island carried Motorola walkie-talkies at all times; practically the first thing that Peter had done when I arrived was to set one up for me. The devices served as both a communications and a safety system. (In an emergency, yelling for help would be futile in the rushing wind.) He and Kevin had finished programming the tags and were on their way out to the yacht. I'd seen the tags last night. They looked like little karaoke microphones, but sleeker. At one end was a metal barb that hooked the tag to the shark, ideally right below the dorsal fin. At the other end hung a black bulb-shaped float. The effect was not unlike a chandelier earring, with the tag subtly swaying alongside the animal as it swam. Kevin had lashed the tags to long harpoons using thick elastic bands.

By midafternoon's high tide we were out on the water, with Brown on Sharkwatch. Earlier, while we were standing on *Just Imagine*'s deck, transferring gear into the whaler, Ron had swung by. He planned to make his first dive of the season later this week and had come by today to check the conditions. He idled beside us in *GW* and raised a dubious eyebrow at our mooring. "What kind of anchor's he got out there?" Ron asked. I was the only one who had seen it up close; I had no idea what kind of anchor it was, but I described its cross-hatched shape. "Sounds like a Danforth," he said, with distaste. "All wrong for out here." He told us that the island was an anchor cemetery. "I see them all the time on the bottom. They get bent up like pretzels."

We returned to Indian Head, where we'd had such instant success yesterday. The water was wildly alive, red with krill and teeming with fish and birds. Krill are tiny crustaceans, and they're pink, like a Lilliputian shrimp cocktail. "These are big ones," Kevin said, looking over the side. "They're lunkers." And where there's krill, there are whales. To the west, humpbacks rose and spouted.

Peter reached into the boat's glove compartment and pulled out a transistor radio, which he strapped to the railing. The San Francisco Giants were playing the Houston Astros in the National League playoffs, an event that ranked right above surfing in the leisure hierarchy of his mind. And he wasn't the only baseball fanatic on the island; all of the bird biologists were rabid fans. Yesterday he and Brown, an avid Red Sox fan, had spent a long time on the radio debating the merits of Barry Bonds versus Pedro Martinez with the same eye for detail they brought to the identification of a vagrant oriole or pipit. Perhaps it simply came down to a love of watching small objects whizzing through the sky.

Peter fiddled with the dial until the sounds of a sports announcer and a roaring crowd boomed out. He picked up a fishing pole and began to untangle the line that was attached to the surfboard. "Listening to baseball and watching for sharks. What could be finer?"

While waiting for news of attacks, we drifted in the sun with the decoy set out. The board received some halfhearted attention, a few drive-bys, but no one was getting serious enough to bite it or even bump it. The most extreme move was a mild tail flick. Just the fact that they *were* out there, unseen perhaps, yet always a possibility, thrilled me. But the sharks' new take-it-or-leave-it attitude troubled Peter. It supported Scot's theory that the cage divers' constant use of the decoys was desensitizing them, and that for future research purposes, decoys might not work at all. The sharks' lack of interest was all the more unusual since it was early in the season, and few of them had managed to kill a seal yet. High tide came and went without an attack.

As the hours ticked by, more than a dozen fishing boats began to mass off East Landing, resembling a small, itinerant town. This was the Monterey squid fleet. We'd seen them yesterday too. They worked through the nights, shining powerful lights that lured squid to the boats, which they then scooped up in purse seine nets. Unfortunately, the lights also attracted the nocturnal seabirds, which flew toward them, only to be picked off by the gulls.

Commercial squid fishing was legal within the marine sanctuary, oddly enough, but traumatizing the seabird population at the wildlife refuge was not. The two jurisdictions overlapped here. Peter had already received an email from the Fish and Wildlife Service asking him to keep an eye on the squid fleet.

Peter piloted the whaler through the gang of boats. Most of them were about sixty feet long, *Just Imagine*'s length, but stockier. Some had already caught squid and were in the process of brailing in their nets. In these waters the species was *Loligo opalescens*, or California market squid, an invertebrate shaped like a toy rocket, about eight inches long and milky in color, with dime-sized eyes that could see twice as well as a human's. Contrary to most people's expectations, Kevin told me, squid were wily and clever, some of the more intelligent creatures in the ocean. And among the most athletic—they traveled through the water by jet propulsion, leaving fish in their wake. For mating, these animals favored orgies. It was thought that they communicated with each other using their own language of color, pattern, and luminescence; instantly, they could turn themselves spotted or striped or dark as ink or a shimmery pearl color to lure other creatures toward them, or to fake out predators. Scientists had determined that squid made rapid and complex decisions, reacting to situations as they arose. For instance, when they realized they were trapped, they would panic and swim against the net.

We wove in and out of the herd, looking to trade a six-pack of Negro Modelo for some fresh squid. As we approached the first boat, we saw that there was a sea lion twisted in its net, a victim of bycatch. The animal was struggling frantically as it was hoisted out of the water. A crew of fishermen dressed in fluorescent coveralls lined the railing, looking uncomfortable. Their only options were to cut their nets so the sea lion could escape, or shoot it, and they sure as hell weren't going to cut their nets. Our presence made them visibly edgy—if you're about to kill a marine mammal, execution-style, in a wildlife refuge, you don't exactly want spectators. They angled the nets away from us so we couldn't see what they were doing. Rather than gawk, we drove away.

A dingy black boat that was occupying Stumpy's territory agreed to give us some squid, although the captain seemed surprised by the request. They were a dry boat, he said, and didn't care for any beer. Kevin leaned over to pass a bucket across, and as he did, he found himself looking straight into the eyes of a mako shark head, freshly severed. We took our bucket of squid and got out of there, scooted back to *Just Imagine* as the sun set.

In the sailboat's galley, Peter pan-fried the loligo with a little garlic. Today's catch didn't taste like the light, springy calamari you get in good seafood restaurants. Our squid, when cooked, turned an unappetizing mauve color, swimming in a viscous pool of its own grease. It was repulsive, like eating a strip of rubber doormat. "Maybe we didn't prepare it right," Peter said. I felt a racking stomachache come on, and washed the dishes doubled over in pain.

Suddenly, I smelled something truly fetid coming from the bathroom. I opened the door. Gallons of murky red liquid sloshed around in the shower, burbling up through the drain. It had the combined stench of sewage and gasoline, but it looked like watered-down blood, with chunks of something floating on its surface. "I think the red stuff might be diesel fuel," Peter said, grimacing. "I don't know about the other bits." Ridding ourselves of the alien fluid required opening the "sea chest," a closet that contained the sewage pipes. Setting aside the question of why diesel fuel was spewing into the shower, Peter twisted a couple of wrenches and pumped various handles, as Tom had instructed. The red glop slowly headed back down the drain, to hell or wherever. I didn't care, so long as it was gone.

THE NEXT DAY, WHILE I WAS SITTING ON *JUST IMAGINE*'S STERN DECK picking mashed anus flies out of my hair, Peter announced that he wanted me to learn to drive the shark boat. I stopped picking flies and stared at him. He went on to explain that during the week between Kevin's departure and Scot's arrival, there would be times when I would have to handle the whaler alone, maybe even in stormy conditions. I might have to dock it alongside *Just Imagine* after, say, dropping him off at North Landing. I might have to maneuver the boat during a shark attack so he could put in a tag or capture a video ID. I might have to rescue somebody who got into trouble with Tubby. Maybe, when no one else was around, I might have to deal with some unforeseen marine emergency.

Until this moment, it was true, I had ducked every technical item on the checklist out of certainty that, whatever it was, I was the least qualified person to do it. But Peter was basically telling me that I couldn't afford to think that way anymore. On occasion it would just be the two of us working our shark flotilla, and I needed to be skilled and reliable and on top of all things nautical.

This plan made sense, of course, but it terrified me. Although I did know how to drive a boat. Sort of. Since I was a kid my family had kept a summer cottage in Canadian lake country, and before a road was put in recently, the only way to get there was by water. My father always had an inboard-outboard cruiser of some type; these days it was a twenty-foot Sea Ray. Over the years I'd been taught basic boating skills and been something less than a natural: I could never remember, for instance, which side of the channel the red buoys should be on. And I failed to master steering a boat in reverse, even after a decade of trying. In my checkered boating history there were mangled propellers and sheared cotter pins and dead engines and less-than-gentle encounters with docks and, one time, there was even an explosion.

I tried to imagine docking the whaler against *Just Imagine* by myself—getting it into the right position, gauging the wind and the waves, throwing on a brief burst of reverse and then neutral, and then cutting the engine, all as precisely timed as a tango. After which: leaping six feet over the railing onto *Just Imagine*'s deck with fore and aft ropes in hand, tying a smart bowline followed by a half hitch on both ends of the whaler at just the right tension. (I'd seen Peter and Kevin do this many times.) But the only image that came to mind was one of being sandwiched between the two pitching boats with no way out from above and the Sisterhood below. I remembered Tony Badger sternly telling me, "If you fall over the side, even in good conditions, your chances of getting out are zero.

ZERO." He'd held up his thumb and index finger to form a circle, in case I didn't get it. "I know it sounds crazy, but people die right next to boats all the time," he'd said.

As Peter outlined the course of my boating instruction—"You can start right now!"—I watched Kevin rowing across Fisherman's Bay. When he arrived, he casually jumped out of the teetering row-boat, vaulted across *Just Imagine*'s wounded starboard, and secured Tubby with an effortless and elaborate pair of knots. He had the boat thing down cold. But it wasn't only boats; every time a tool was needed for anything—cutting a piece of rope, gaffing a fish, un-bending a hook, performing open-heart surgery—Kevin simply whipped it out of one of his pockets, and solved the problem on the spot. Basically, he was wearing a Home Depot in his pants.

The chance to be with people who possessed these elegant sur-vival skills, I realized, was a big part of what had drawn me here. This was an oasis of competence in a bumbling world, clean and straight where things were usually compromised and bent. Scot, Peter, Ron, and now Kevin—I'd watched them, and the way they op-erated was different. Necessity dictated it: Fumble around here and the place would spit you out like a watermelon seed squeezed between slippery fingers. The Farallones specialized in the harsh ejection of anyone lacking the perfect balance of the two essential ingredients—humility and skill. I hoped there was still time to get the mix right.

I had a chance to observe extreme competence at close range later that afternoon when I met up with Ron in Mirounga Bay. Since our first meeting two years ago, we'd spoken at length sev-eral times, and I'd come away from every conversation even more intrigued by him; he was unlike anyone I'd ever met. Ron main-tained a clearheadedness that few manage to pull off. No adding or subtracting of emotions that didn't need to be there, no fretting or exaggeration, no what-ifs. And this equilibrium was even more im-pressive when I learned that he had experienced more than his share of close calls—on the water, with the sharks, and in life.

"I pushed all the boundaries," he'd admitted. In his younger days in Southern California, he had experimented with drugs, getting in deep and tangling with the law. Twelve-step programs had helped him steer out of the skid, and diving became his salvation.

And now things were in order, and stayed that way. Only one problem remained, and it didn't have a tidy solution. At some point during his drug-using days, he'd contracted hepatitis C. Though at present there's no cure for the illness, in characteristic Ron fashion he faced it head on, and did everything he could to keep its debilitating effects at bay. He'd become an unlikely convert to holistic living, pursuing alternative treatments that ranged from homeopathics to biofeedback to ingesting bovine liver cells obtained from France. There was very little processed food, pesticides, *crap* in Ron's diet. Even his dog, Alice, a chocolate lab, ate organically; her special dog food, a blend of eggshells, vitamins, and raw free-range hamburger, was handmade by two women in Petaluma and occupied the bulk of space in his freezer.

Healthwise, things were going as well as could be expected, with some days better than others, but at times he felt the symptoms creeping up on him. Under the circumstances his diving days did not stretch out in front of him indefinitely, but he was sanguine: "I just kinda do the best I can to keep going. That's all I do."

When he'd passed by earlier in the week, I'd asked if I could spend a few hours on the *GW* with him while he dived. "Anytime," he replied. Urchin picking was 100 percent weather dependent though, and he made the trip only when the market justified it. Lately, the price of urchins had been falling, and he'd reduced his Farallon schedule. But today he was anchored in the middle of Shark Alley with his neon-orange dive buoy set out, and when Peter drove me over, I climbed aboard easily. Ron had customized his boat so its stern sat lower to the water, making it a snap to get in and out of, a valid concern when you worked by yourself in the middle of the ocean. He stood on deck rinsing pieces of his wetsuit in a plastic tub. Peter mentioned that there hadn't been much in the way of attacks, and speculated that the sea lion bycatch from the squid boats amounted to a free meal for the sharks. "So they're wrapping sea lions," Ron said dryly. "Well, that's just such a surprise."

I sat on *GW*'s aluminum deck while Ron suited up. This was a minimalist's dive boat, no junk lying around, no snarled ropes, nothing clattering or rolling underfoot. He pulled on sets of elbow and knee pads, sturdy neoprene boots, long, industrial-strength gloves, and a hood that left only the center of his face showing. It was so tight that his cheeks bulged. "Beats wearing a coat and tie," he said, smiling. But then his eyes turned serious. "Let's see if it gets busy today."

"On the water?" I asked, thinking he meant the squid fleet.

"No, below. Sometimes when the sharks aren't on the surface, they've got a lot going on down there."

I lost sight of Ron immediately as he dropped over the side; the instant he entered the water he ducked underneath his boat. He did this whenever he was ascending or descending so as not to present a tempting silhouette on the surface. This was a signature innovation, and a smart one. He'd described the early cowboy days when there were numerous urchin divers out here, and back then no one, not even Ron, had quite enough respect for the sharks. "We'd swim across the surface all the time. Our attitude was 'Bring it on.' *Right.*" The result of such behavior was obvious: Ron was alone here now, and he had developed his own rules, tailor-made to keep him alive. "I thought maybe if I do things differently, I can narrow the odds of something happening," he said.

The air compressor chugged, and the yellow air hose that was attached to it snaked sixty feet down into the darkness. Ron dove with a hookah rig rather than scuba tanks, with the hose functioning as an umbilical cord that tethered him to the boat. I watched it, remembering the story he had told me about the time a shark had gotten tangled in the line. He'd been on the bottom prying up urchins and felt himself swaying, as if from the current. Suddenly, he was jerked about three feet upward. Lifting his head, he saw a shark directly above him, the air hose caught between its dorsal and tail fins. The shark had struggled to get free, flinging Ron around like a trick yo-yo. Finally, after what must have seemed like a very long time, the animal cleared itself and swam away.

I leaned over *GW*'s edge until my nose was almost touching the water, but the surface was flat and inscrutable, concealing the parallel universe below as effectively as one-way glass. All appeared tranquil for the moment. The radio hissed white noise, and the depth finder blipped across a colorful screen. Earlier, Ron had explained that smaller fish didn't show up on this sonar, but the sharks were large enough to register as angry-looking red slashes. I watched the screen for a while and didn't see any. The hose hung off the stern, making no sudden jerking motions, tracking slowly in different directions as he moved across the bottom.

If you spend time around great white sharks, however, you quickly learn that calm can change to out-of-control on a dime. In fact, Scot had experienced his closest call with a shark in conditions exactly like these. He'd described the incident during my first visit, and I'd been struck by how, even seven years later, he was humbled by it.

The water had been dark, "glassy calm and dead silent." He decided to tow the surfboard around, but on this day—nothing. No sharks, not even any boils. After an hour he reeled the board back in. Scot was bent over the edge, leaning to pick it up, when the shark hit, blasting at a steep fifty-degree angle from beneath the boat. There was a heart-stopping crack and the board flew into the air as three thousand pounds of shark breached, six inches from Scot's hand. It was the sound that rattled him as much as anything, like a gun going off in his ear. For several moments, he stood frozen. It took him some time to regain his composure.

After this, a new protocol for retrieving the boards was adopted: no body parts hanging over the water. Recalling the incident, I backed away from the side.

An hour later there was a rush of bubbles and, quite suddenly,

Ron was back on the deck. He pulled off his mask and unbuckled his thirty-five-pound weight belt. "Ahhh, there's so much krill down there," he said, shaking off the water. "All these things swimming around in front of your face." He made swatting gestures.

"See any sharks?" I had to ask.

"Nah, couldn't see anything. With all the krill, it's like looking around in a dark closet. But that doesn't mean they aren't there." He began to winch up his urchin bags, three enormous nylon-mesh sacks that each held seven hundred pounds of catch.

Peter and Kevin came back over, tied off the whaler, and boarded the *GW*. Kevin asked how the urchins were looking. Fantastic, apparently. The roe was fat and the color was a bright orangey-yellow. Ron offered to let us taste one. Now seemed like a good time to knock back an urchin; these were of such exquisite quality that sushi chefs in Tokyo would be fighting over them tomorrow morning when the fish market opened.

As with oysters, urchin desirability is a combination of size, taste, and aesthetics. Ron explained that the Japanese, who bought most of the California stock, liked theirs just so: symmetrically circular and less than four inches in diameter, the smallest legal size. He was highly selective about what he picked, and given that he was the only one diving out here, his Farallon-caught urchins were unique—the equivalent of truffles. Even so, there was stiff competition. "China and Russia started selling urchins to Japan," he said. "Boy, it's hard to compete with those guys. Even though their product is of a lesser quality."

He placed one on deck. The urchin was the lush red color of a heart, and it waved its dozens of legs like an insect that had been flipped onto its back. The legs, or maybe they were arms, were shaped like spiny skewers. Using a tool that resembled a can opener, Ron cracked it in half. You'd think that would mean it was dead, but the spines kept waving without missing a beat. Inside the shell was a drippy brown goo and some grainy yellow blobs the consistency of custard. These were the gonads, more palatably known as "roe." Both males and females have them; urchins are hermaphrodites. Ron held out a piece on his knife. The gonads tasted fresh and salty, like the ocean.

I was surprised to learn that urchins marched around on the seafloor. I'd assumed they were rooted, in barnacle fashion. In fact, there's a far livelier scene going on down there than you might realize. Even the sea anemones, which look like colorful flowers or wavy coral, have intelligence; Ron said they often reached out and stung him on the part of his face that wasn't covered by his mask, somehow discerning that skin was vulnerable, while rubber was not. You don't necessarily think of the scenery as possessing free will, carnivorous intent, and a plan, but Ron once saw a sea anemone ingest an entire live murre, a bird the size of a small mallard duck. This is not something that happens accidentally.

The radio bleeped. "Peter, you copy?" It was Nat.

"Roger, go ahead."

"You've got an attack off Indian Head. A floater."

We clambered into the whaler, leaving Ron to unsuit and unwind and prepare for the two-hour drive back to Bodega Bay and a profitable appointment with his urchin processor.

THE YEARLING ELEPHANT SEAL BOBBED, HEADLESS, AT THE FAR WEST end of the island, almost exactly on the spot where we'd set out the surfboard our first night. A fiery cloud of blood billowed around the body. A few seconds passed, and the shark was on it; a dorsal fin sliced by our stern. Its head rose from the water and, rather serenely, began to tear pieces of meat from the seal. Peter filmed with the underwater camera, occasionally reaching around to steer the idling whaler; Kevin stood poised with a tag, and I was busy shooting topside video, my latest responsibility. I fumbled with the lens cap and the on/off switch and finally got the camera trained on the kill. The scene was decidedly unfrenzied, and no other sharks showed up, which was unusual on Rat Pack turf.

"As far as attacks go, it doesn't get any mellower than this," Peter said, sounding almost bored. We were right beside the shark, within petting distance, although that's a bad idea. I could see three white scratches on its head, and a black puncture the size of a silver dollar, and the line where its white underbelly met its black top coat, and I could see the seal's blood as it ran between the shark's teeth. I could see straight into its eyes, although I can't tell you exactly what I found there. Absolute focus, maybe. The shark wasn't remotely distracted by us until after its meal, when it began to circle the whaler, giving the propeller an investigatory bite. Kevin reached over with the harpoon and tagged it easily. As the tag went in, it made a sort of crunching noise, but the shark barely reacted. This was a fifteen-footer, most likely a male, and he was new. Peter didn't know him.

Observing the shark's size, gender, distinguishing marks, and individual behaviors as it swam around the boat was a challenge in the lightless water, but it was important to make sure the animal that was about to be tagged was not *already* wearing a satellite tag, unless you enjoyed watching thirty-five hundred dollars go swimming down the drain. A couple of times in the past, this had almost happened. There were other research programs tagging white sharks in other locations, like Guadalupe Island or Southern California or Año Nuevo Island near the southern tip of the Red Triangle, and it was possible for one of those taggees to show up here. Some sharks had old transmitters from previous tracking studies still affixed to them, along with other assorted paraphernalia. One shark, a smallish and inexperienced Rat Packer who constantly sidled up to the boat, was laden with so much electronic gear that he came to be known as Radio Shack.

The lone shark vanished thirty minutes later, no one else made a run at the leftovers, and we powered up the whaler to head back to the mother ship. I was driving. And I was starting to get the feel of it, although sometimes when I thought I had shifted into neutral, I was really in reverse. It was the end of a one-attack day, and the sunset was coming on like a determined postcard. I began to relax, but then Peter nudged me conspiratorially. "What do you say we shoot the Gap?"

The Gap was a tiny surge channel between Sugarloaf and Arch Rock passable only when high tide and meek water conditions coincided. Almost never, in other words. Darting through there in the whaler was a high-adrenaline move made purely for sport. Even at its most benign the Gap was white water, and it was a tight fit around the boat. A rogue swell could knock you against the granite on either side.

"Sure," I said, trying to keep my voice nonchalant. Wimping out was not an option—the two of them had just tagged a great white shark, for crissakes, and Ron had spent most of the day underwater at Shark Alley. I could hold the boat straight for ten seconds.

I was clutching the wheel as I steered into the boiling passage, trying not to be distracted by the one-hundred-foot walls on either side. I felt the sea rumble beneath my feet and lift us on a roller-coaster crest, and then a wave grabbed the whaler and swept us into Fisherman's Bay as if we were surfing. Pelicans wheeled overhead, while sea lions splashed and barked in the gulches. *Just Imagine* lay in front of us, bathed in golden and violet light. My hands unclenched. I looked at Kevin, who was wearing his trillion-dollar smile, and I broke out in one too. We twirled in a little eddy. Peter shook my hand. "Congratulations! You are the fifth person ever to shoot the Gap."

The evening was so lovely that Peter and Kevin decided to stay on the yacht. After less than a week, I was already down to dry goods, pretzels, and the like, whatever didn't need refrigeration to stay edible. But Peter brought some fillets from an albacore he'd caught, and Kevin cooked them, making a ginger marinade from scratch and sharpening all the kitchen knives by hand. Peter and I sat at the table, drank Sangiovese, and offered moral support.

After watching Ron dive today on what would be the ideal tow-in spot to surf the perfect wave, Peter resumed his talk about getting out there sooner rather than later. This afternoon he'd mentioned it to Ron, who had nodded his approval and said, "I've thought about that." Until that point I hadn't realized that Ron surfed too, but of course it made perfect sense.

Kevin didn't say much, but he looked intrigued. He was also a surfer, and he knew exactly which wave Peter was talking about. They were both wearing Maui's fishhooks around their necks, a Hawaiian symbol that signifies taking the shark as one's *amakua*, or spirit animal. Peter leaned back in the banquette with his glass of wine. "I've been thinking about it for so long," he said. "I don't want someone else to come out here and do it. But I don't want to rush it, either. If you put out the wrong vibe, then something bad could happen. I want to be in the right space. It's gotta be done right."

After dinner we climbed onto the deck and looked out at the squid fleet, which was hovering three hundred yards away. It was disconcerting to see the barren inkiness of the surrounding skies lit up like a switchboard. Suspended from above, the boats' squid-luring lights shone a cold artificial blaze. Tiny black dots wove in and out of the glare; Peter could tell which specks were gulls and which were cassin's auklets. A big night of hunting lay ahead; no doubt the curious, ravenous sea lions would be out nosing around, infuriating the fishermen. They often dove right into the nets as the catch was being hauled up, hurriedly eating their fill before attempting last-second Houdini escapes. Sometimes they didn't make it and got ensnared, like the animal we'd seen last night. When this happened, the sea lions were goners. Yesterday morning one of the interns had discovered one washed ashore: The animal's head had been shot to pieces. Watching the fleet, I wondered what else besides squid was coming up in those nets. We'd already seen one dead shark lying on deck—how many more might there be? Flies crawled on us, even in the dark, and we turned to go back into the cabin. As we did, we heard the crack of three gunshots across the water.

* * *

IT WAS BROWN'S THIRTY-FIRST BIRTHDAY. AFTER A FEW ROUNDS OF back-and-forth with his better judgment, Peter decided that I could attend the celebration dinner. One little party—and I'd be off the island in a matter of hours. What harm could it do? I figured he'd been feeling sorry for me the past few days, subsisting on Power-bars at sea while everyone else ate home-cooked organic meals on-shore. I hadn't seen Brown or Nat yet, though I'd heard their voices on the radio. They hadn't made it out to the boat. Not that I blamed them. *Just Imagine* was starting to smell, and it was taking me down with it. The marine toilet was a nasty piece of business; it constantly exploded on my shoes, and when I attempted to pump the graywater, reaching into the sea chest, it exploded on my shirt. Meanwhile, the red sludge had put in several more appearances. I was beginning to get it: *Just Imagine* was not happy to be here. Like a furniture-gnawing pet left with a sitter while its owner was on vacation, the yacht was expressing its displeasure in passive-aggressive ways.

Peter rowed Tubby across Fisherman's Bay toward the island while I crouched unsteadily in front, resisting the urge to look over the side for signs of the Sisterhood—telltale shadows, say, or boils the size of trucks. The one time I did not wish to see a twenty-foot-long apparition was while sitting in Tubby. I stared at the rocks, thinking of the stories I'd read about great white shark teeth found embedded in the hulls of small boats. There wasn't much conver-sation. Peter was bent forward in concentration, hauling on the oars. Flies clustered on his legs.

As we neared the island, I was reminded again that by allowing me to step ashore, he was putting a lot on the line. Technically, as long as I stayed on *Just Imagine* I wasn't here illegally, though Peter still wasn't anxious to call attention to my presence. After all, both the U.S. Fish and Wildlife officers and the PRBO directors knew me. I'd met them all; they'd given me one of their coveted over-night permits only last month, and by now I was supposed to be back home, hunched over my computer churning out stories about the Brandt's cormorant population. For me to be anywhere near this island during shark season had been expressly forbidden. Forget about becoming part of the *crew*.

In Peter's mind, however, the fact that I'd received a prior permit meant that no one would object to a bit of an addendum. I wasn't so sure, and I was nervous. Things were wound far more tightly now than they had been on my first visit. I didn't want to cause trouble. But I suppose I didn't want that badly enough to stay on the sailboat.

As we neared the narrow gulley that marked North Landing, I prepared to jump onto the rocks with a rope. Even though the water wasn't overly choppy and the swells weren't out of hand, it was still critical to time the waves correctly. Jump too early, and you'd end up in the drink. Jump too late, and you'd end up in the drink as Tubby and Peter flipped over onto the rocks. Lacking experience with precision movements on algae-coated slickrock, I skidded and impaled my leg on a pointy outcropping. But I made it, and while I tied off a line, Peter wrassled Tubby onto the shore.

A steep cliff rose from the foot of the landing. This was the backside of Lighthouse Hill. No convenient switchback path here, though. A full, vertigo-inducing neck tilt was required to scan the expanse of crags between North Landing and the Light. The only route was straight up; the only takers would be mountain goats with suction-cup feet or eggers who'd drawn the short straw. Gulls glared sullenly from ledges.

We walked to the house down a thread of a path, beaten into the stone. I felt grateful to be on land, and the smell of guano and warm earth and heavy moisture seemed almost soothing. Now that breeding season was over, there were fewer seabirds here, but that's like saying there are fewer cars on the San Diego freeway when it's not rush hour. Without chicks the gulls were noticeably mellower, less likely to draw blood, and the hard hats had been put away until next spring. Still, I worked my peripheral vision to check for any suspicious movements aimed at my head. Two hundred yards away, a posse of birds jetted past the cliff. Peter, who had been expounding on the strengths and weaknesses of the Giants' infield, stopped midsentence and said, "Puffin with a bonehead sculpin in its mouth." He pointed to a blurry Coke can–sized object as it hurtled in front of the rocks. I could barely make out the puffin, never mind identify the species of baitfish it was carrying. Sightings were rare to begin with. The entire island population numbered only 120 tufted puffins, down from 2,000 in the early nineties.

As weatherworn as it was, the house glowed in the incandescent light of dusk. Kevin sat in the workroom, surrounded by tags, typing on a computer. His desk faced a window with a panoramic view of Mirounga Bay and beyond, to an infinity of ocean where gray, blue, and humpback whales were feeding, throwing off impressive geysers. In the kitchen, Mark, a tall, affable intern from Louisiana, was cooking dinner. A vat of spaghetti sauce simmered on the stove.

Brown and Nat were out somewhere, and Peter took their absence as an opportunity to hunt for a birthday present. Pickings were slim, to say the least. Maybe for Brown's birthday he'd get a three-minute shower, which he could take navy-style, shutting off the water while he was lathering, or an elephant seal skull that someone came across, or an extra beer. But Peter had a private stash of memorabilia he'd amassed over the decades, and it was in this tangle of stuff that he hoped to find a worthy and meaningful gift. We walked next door to the coast guard house, where he pulled out a crate filled with photographs and feathers and assorted other flotsam, the kind of memento stockpile that you find in attics. He began to rifle through it. "A lure? Nah, he doesn't like fishing." Peter was especially fond of Brown and had acted as a kind of mentor to him. They were a generation apart, but the things they shared—sharks, baseball, surfing, birds, and, of course, this place—vastly outweighed their differences. The main points of contention were technological: Peter's insistence on using DOS-era computer programs to store data, for instance, and his reluctance to adopt digital video for filming the sharks. As a result, Brown often found himself bent over software manuals from the seventies and eighties, trying to unlearn every bit of user interface progress from the past ten years, or patching together shark images from diverse sources on the Farallones' ancient computer equipment. He kept a healthy sense of humor about it, but you could tell he'd rather not have to.

Peter thumbed quickly through a thick batch of pictures. "Lots and lots of shark attack stuff," he said dismissively. His wedding photos were mixed in there too, along with endless bird images and shots of various seals and sea lions missing gaping hunks of flesh and looking stunned. "Oh, here's a Steller's sea lion with a big bite out of its chest." I couldn't put the pictures down, but in his opinion, none of them was special enough to mark the occasion. "I used to have more things I found in the tide pools," he said. "If you want, we can go to one of my secret spots to look for elephant seal teeth." I looked at Peter, bent over underneath his omnipresent Giants cap hunting through his box of nature souvenirs, like a kid showing another kid something cool in his treehouse. These islands, I realized, were his sacred hideout—both spiritually and literally. One time, I'd asked him if there was anything about the Farallones that he *didn't* like. I imagined he'd take the opening to complain about the weather, or the lack of hot water, or some other gripe. Instead he'd frowned, and gaped at me like I was sort of slow. "No," he answered without hesitation. "Why would there be?"

It dawned on me that Peter took any criticism of this place almost as a personal insult. One time I'd overheard him telling Brown that he loved the island, which he often referred to as "the rock," more than life itself. And he'd declared it like a sworn truth, and not with any kind of exaggerated drama. Ten years ago during seabird breeding season, the marine operator had hailed the Farallones with an urgent message for Peter; he was patched through to his mother, Leilani, in Honolulu. His younger brother, Lew, who had been struggling with leukemia, had "moved on," she said. The news wasn't entirely unexpected, but that didn't make it any less wrenching. When Peter and Lew had spoken the week before, his parting words had been "Hang in there." Suddenly, that sentiment seemed flip, inadequate. Peter climbed to the murre blind and sat there for the rest of the day. When the coast guard offered to helicopter him off the island, he declined; it would be several days before he could face the mainland.

After another fifteen minutes of rummaging, he settled on a framed photograph of Bitehead majestically cruising in profile. We wrapped the present in an old newspaper and headed down to dinner.

Nat was in the kitchen, making the last adjustments to Brown's birthday cake. So were the other two interns, Kristie and Elias. Fine-boned and alert, Kristie spoke in a singsong voice that reminded me of a bird itself. Elias was smallish and rugged-looking, with a full beard. He seemed laid-back, except on the subject of birds. Earlier, I'd overheard him ask, in a tight, urgent voice: "Excuse me, Peter? Can I bother you about the molting strategies of pigeon guillemots?"

Brown sat at the head of the table, sunburned, wearing a UPS T-shirt that said, "What Can Brown Do For You?" His ponytail was gone now, but he still didn't look anywhere near thirty-one. Kristie and Kevin were setting out the silverware, and Peter was opening the wine, and the rest of us were just about to sit down when Nat said, "Oh, I'd better let the bats out."

During the day, hoary bats slept in the three trees near the houses and could be plucked out like fruit. Hoary bats are almost as tough to study as great white sharks; they're equally elusive, even though they range widely throughout the boreal forests of North America. But unlike many bat species, which will cluster by the millions in a single cave, hoary bats are happy-go-lucky hoboes, traveling solo, stopping to rest wherever and whenever the urge hits, and not even bothering to nest. To find them at all required a full-out scavenger hunt, except at these islands, where bats that flew off course in their migrations stopped by regularly, just like the land birds. This made chiropterists—bat scientists—crazy to come here, to spend time with hoary bats as they could nowhere else. Since that wasn't possible, Nat and Brown had begun to monitor the bats, taking snips of their fur, watching their behaviors, counting and weighing them. The information would then be dispersed to the bat community.

I followed Nat as she walked to the coast guard house, entering through the back door into the kitchen. Two wooden crates, each the size of a suitcase, sat on the floor. She grabbed them and carried them outside. When opened, the boxes were divided into eight small compartments, like private berths in a railcar. Each contained a hoary bat. The bats were a mottled sienna color, with veined, complicated-looking wings that gave the appearance of gothic hang gliders. They had giant ears. As Nat gently lifted them one-by-one out of the cage, they unfurled themselves to fly off, making pissed-off clicking and hissing noises.

I reached out a finger to stroke one of the cute little angry bats. Its head snapped forward to bite me; it was in no mood for placatory gestures. Nat, wearing leather work gloves, liberated them all, although she almost missed one that was wedged deeply inside its compartment, curled behind a branch. The bat showed us its mouthful of pinlike teeth, rasped and clicked a blue streak, and then whirled off into the night.

Back at the birthday dinner, celebratory shots of Jack Daniel's were being tossed back as aperitifs. "I think this is a big year for bats," Peter said. "We're already at seventy." As it happened, Peter was the first person ever to observe hoary bat sex. "It looked like one bat, just one fat bat," he said. "But then I realized, 'Hey, they're doing it!' " He'd taken photographs and sent them to bat experts, who had become very excited. All these years, all the technology in the world, and no one had managed to get an eyeful of this event before. Nor had many people been privy to humpback whale sex, until one day in 1986 when three of them swam up to

Saddle Rock and mated on the spot, while Peter watched through a scope. Thus, he became one of the first to know that humpback whales have sex in threesomes, with the third whale acting as a sort of assistant.

Just another item to add to Peter's astonishing list of sightings, along with the unheard-of great white shark behaviors and the countless rarer-than-rare birds and the time sixty-one blue whales cruised past the island and the morning in 1996 when he came upon the first northern fur seal pup to be born at the Farallones, after the species had been virtually wiped out 160 years earlier.

But perhaps the most bizarre thing he had ever witnessed here, in recent history anyway, involved a shark named Jerry Garcia.

Jerry had gotten his name on a cold and blustery fall day in 1995, when Peter had watched as an expensive-looking powerboat arrived at the Farallones, hung offshore for about fifteen minutes, turned, and left. It was odd for a boat to make the pilgrimage in weather so rough. "The wind was blowing thirty knots," Peter recalled. But he suspected he knew what the boat was up to. Jerry Garcia (the leader of the Grateful Dead, not the shark) had died the previous August, and Peter had it on good source that sometime during the week friends and relatives would be coming out to scatter his ashes in the vicinity. He looked on with Ed Ueber, the manager of the Gulf of the Farallones National Marine Sanctuary, who was visiting the island, as the boat tossed in the waves and Garcia was flung to the elements. "They really should have a chumming permit," Ueber noted. "But . . . I didn't see anything."

The next day Peter encountered a new shark, a twelve-foot male with a crooked, partially lopped-off tail, and in homage to the previous day's events, he christened the shark Jerry Garcia. From then on, he and Scot spotted Jerry regularly in Maintop Bay, where he was observed hanging out with other Rat Pack sharks. (There was some consideration given to changing the Rat Pack's name to the Deadheads, but it never quite took.)

Then, on October 4, 1997, two marauding orcas attacked a white shark in Maintop, flipping him onto his back and, working in efficient tandem, holding him there until he drowned. The smaller of the two orcas swam around for a while with the shark sticking out of her mouth, toothpick-style, and then proceeded to eat him in front of a boatload of wide-eyed tourists on *Superfish*. When the showdown commenced, Mick had radioed Peter and told him he'd better get out there, and fast.

Peter and two interns arrived in time to observe the two orcas pinning the shark down by his nose. It was Jerry Garcia. The kill was masterful. "Orcas clearly know what the hell they are doing," Peter said.

No one had ever seen the ocean's two top predators battle it out in gladiatorial style. News outlets around the globe ran Peter's underwater video of the aftermath, during which the orca cruised by the camera with a scrap of Jerry Garcia's liver hanging from her mouth. Scot and Peter's favorite clip came from the *CBS Evening News*, which featured the story under the portentous headline: "Battle of the Century off the California Coast." Dan Rather introduced the segment, informing viewers that the video they were about to see was the first filming ever of the "two sea titans facing off." But, Rather added, "when push came to shove, it was no contest. It was brains and blubber over the lean, mean teeth machine."

From a research perspective the most fascinating part was this: immediately after Jerry Garcia was killed, *all* of the Farallon sharks vanished. Just lit out of the place, every last one of them. Scot and Peter waited six weeks for the sharks to return, but no one showed. "It was like the cops had arrived and shut the party down," Peter said. Ron concurred; no sharks. But as far as making a scientific pronouncement that the sharks had fled, hunch and a single event weren't proof enough.

And then it happened again, on November 19, 2000. And again, Peter was there. The island was ultrasharky at the time; the previous day six sharks had visited the decoy board in succession, and there had also been an attack involving multiple diners. But when a pod of orcas hit a shark just north of Shubrick, scattering pieces of tissue in a giant slick, the other sharks bolted. This time, however, several of them were wearing satellite tags, and when the data came back they showed that within hours Tipfin, for one, had plunged over the edge of the continental shelf and hightailed it back to Hawaii. Attacks ceased instantly, and the ghost-town ambience underwater was once again confirmed by Ron. "It's eerie when there are no sharks here," Peter recalled.

Another incident meant more mysteries: How did the sharks collectively know to scram? Why didn't the orcas move into the prime hunting grounds here, since they obviously could? In the course of my research I'd come across a reference to a band of orcas slashing its way through Fisherman's Bay in 1937, snatching seals off rocks and terrifying a boatload of people who were being unloaded at North Landing. This didn't happen anymore; orcas were rarely seen within a mile of the islands. But why? The food was here. What sort of subaquatic zoning rules allowed for the sharks to have the drive-thru more or less to themselves?

It was almost midnight when the journal entry was completed, the birthday cake was reduced to crumbs, and the dishes had been washed. Peter had planned to spend these next few hours spying on the squid boats from the lighthouse, documenting the seabird havoc, so rather than row me back to *Just Imagine*, he suggested that I stay on the island. This was a swell idea, I thought; the idea of rowing Tubby in the dark was not very appealing. Especially as during dinner, Peter had admitted that there was a part of Fisherman's Bay that he dreaded passing over, noting that it was "definitely shark territory." Brown had nodded in agreement. "You know as well as I do that they could just *annihilate* Tubby. Just get there. Go straight to the sailboat as fast as you can."

The main house was full, so I carried an armful of blankets over to the coast guard house. I wore my headlamp as I walked up the stairs, which creaked ominously the way stairs always do in horror movies. Its beam illuminated stains on the ceilings. I threw my blankets down in the only bedroom that had a mattress, a terrifying old thing lying on a cracked linoleum floor.

Black handprints smeared the wall at knee level. The air was heavy and dark and still, although the room was painted a soft peachy color.

Back home, if someone tossed me a pile of flea-bitten blankets and directed me to a filthy mattress in a haunted, rodent-infested house with no power or water, I would be less than enthusiastic about bunking down. But here I was, and, actually, I was content. Lying in the dark, listening to high-pitched mice sounds, I wondered why.

Being on this island, I decided, bestowed the luxury of forgetting. Forget the news, the chaos, the jihad, all the crazy zealotry and eviscerating hate. Forget the relationship travails of Britney Spears and forget transfats and absolutely forget about fourth-quarter results. This didn't make the world seem smaller. Instead, it was liberating, like slipping off a lead backpack. And the sense of freedom was so enormous that it made everything else—lack of first-run movies, or never having clean pants—seem trivial. This place was harsh, but when you were here, your world was manageable. There were never more than seven other people to contend with, and every boundary was sharply defined: from where the land ended and the ocean began, to how much food was left in the pantry. You couldn't control it, perhaps, but you could defend it.

In spite of the geographic isolation, no one was ever truly alone on this island. It was a fact that spun me 180 degrees away from my New York life, where I often felt cut off both from the natural world and from any close-knit group of people, and where I spent my time stamping out rather predictable days. Here, nothing went as planned because there were no plans. You just never knew what was on the agenda. Great white sharks would swim up to you and hoary bats zipped into the trees and Steller's sea lions formed harems and blue whales practically brushed the shore and mountain bluebirds and yellow-breasted chats and dusky warblers fluttered down like wayward confetti. The common denominator was this: Only wild things came here.

CHAPTER 8

Both bites were very close together, suggesting that the shark bit twice in rapid succession, rather than attacking, releasing, and attacking again. The oblique angle of the bites suggests that the shark came from below, hitting the boat with a lot of force at a 45-degree angle.

—FARALLON ISLAND LOGBOOK, NOVEMBER 5, 1985

SEPTEMBER 25–29, 2003

The weather was changing. Drifting in zinc-dark water off Indian Head, the sky pressing down on us like damp laundry, Peter and I sat in the whaler and fished. Since the Giants weren't playing today, the transistor radio stayed in the glove box, and out here, away from the bird gallery on the island, there was silence. I cast a line from the bow, and on the glassy surface I could see exactly where it hit. It was one of those times when you could practically feel the barometer falling and the ocean taking a step back, winding up for something nasty. The light was steely and the air had turned so cold that we both wore parkas. Peter dialed the radio to the marine weather forecast. An official-sounding, computer-generated voice came on: "Point Arena to Point Pinos, winds northwest ten to twenty knots, seas three to five feet at eleven seconds . . . ," it droned, sounding totally self-assured, the way only software can. All day and all night the omniscient Weather Voice churned out readings from data-collecting buoys along the coast. These automated buoys were anchored at sea, and they collected minute-by-minute measurements of wind speed and direction, pressure, wave height, and period (the number of seconds that pass between two waves). A shorter period meant rough water, with the peaks tumbling fast and relentless. When the period was equal to—or less than—the height of the wave, there was trouble. Ten-foot waves coming every ten seconds was an equation that sailors dreaded, the oceanic equivalent of a bucking bronco. Ten-foot waves coming every eight seconds was worse. And, of course, conditions could get much meaner than that, and did.

The Voice was hypnotic, looping on and on with a metronomic cadence. In the past, live people had provided the marine weather, but when thick accents and even some broken English started creeping into the reports, making it possible to mistake, say, "winds *fifty* miles an hour" for "winds *fifteen* miles an hour," the robot voice was instituted. At the Farallones, close attention was paid to the readings from the Point Arena buoy, only one hundred miles north of here. This spot usually received the same weather that was headed toward the islands, but about five hours earlier. As we listened, it became clear that Point Arena was getting punished, and that later tonight so would we.

In the gloomy light I could still see clear to Middle Farallon, poking out of the water with all the insouciance of a predate zit. One time, during shark season in 1988, several admittedly hungover biologists had peered out from Southeast Farallon and been startled to note that there were actually *two* Middle Farallones. When advised of this, Peter ran to the lighthouse to check it out: sure enough, a second twenty-foot mound lay next to the original. Further examination revealed the new lump to be the carcass of a blue whale, and everyone wanted to take a closer look, so an expedition was hastily arranged. The Dinner Plate couldn't be launched due to a boom malfunction at East Landing, so Peter had pushed off from North Landing in a Zodiac, along with another biologist who'd decided to bring his six-month-old baby along for the ride. As they neared the whale, they began to see the fins, two-and three-foot-high black dorsals, slicing like knives. There were at least four great white sharks on the case, ripping immense horseshoe-shaped chunks of meat from the whale, and suddenly, being three miles away from the island in a ten-foot rubber dinghy with a six-month-old baby on your lap seemed like an ill-advised equation.

There was a heavy tug on my line, and I began to reel it in. Catching something never took more than a few minutes here. Our quarry was rockfish, wacky-looking bottom dwellers, ancient and armored, with long spines and quills webbed into an elaborate weaponry of fins. Because they came in endless combinations of vivid colors—tangerine with mustard speckles or olive green dappled with neon lime, or vermilion and scarlet swirled together in an iridescent sheen—they seemed like Dr. Seuss characters. They had cartoon names, too, like the treefish and the gopher and the quillback, the chilipepper, the cowcod, and the dwarf. There was even a fish down there called the sarcastic fringehead.

My catch was a ling cod, a spotted, flatheaded fish with a face that would scare small children. I hauled it up on deck, backing away as it jerked and shimmied, heaving its gills and slapping its tail. Peter reached down with a tape measure. It was twenty-three inches long, one inch undersized. Picking up the ling cod, something that I was deeply reluctant to do myself, Peter gently pried the hook from its wraparound lips. Then he slipped it back into the water. "Sorry for the inconvenience, Bud," he said, as the fish shot back to its home in the netherworld.

We were going to have to keep fishing. Grocery-wise, I was down to a hunk of Ghirardelli chocolate, two boxes of crackers, four fast-blackening bananas, and a case of wine. Rockfish were a major addition to the menu. The other day Peter had brought out some eggs from the island, and we'd scrambled them with the meat of an olive rockfish that was accidentally killed when its air bladder burst through its mouth. Many of the rockfish lived a good ways down, fifty feet and deeper, and when they were yanked to the surface, the rapid pressure change sometimes caused this to happen. When it had been lifted into the boat, the fish looked like it was blowing a giant, tissue-colored bubble. It was gross, and both Brown and I had turned away, pretending to be very interested in something on the horizon while Kevin and Peter tried to figure out the most humane way to put the tiny olive out of its misery. They debated piercing its swim bladder, a supposedly painless option, but even though Kevin actually *had* a needle, neither of them knew precisely how to do it. So they'd opted for the gaff, and behind me I'd heard the fish's head make a squelching noise, like a ripe cantaloupe hitting the pavement.

I had no choice but to embrace my new rockfish diet. This morning, Kevin had departed on *Superfish,* and arriving shortly thereafter was a U.S. Fish and Wildlife employee, who would remain on the island for the next eleven days, along with a team of coast guard contractors. They were here to execute the elaborate maintenance project and debris removal that had prompted Peter to base this year's Shark Project from a floating platform in the first place.

Marching orders from the mainland were to stay out of the way while all this work was going on. Both landings would be shut down and, except for Tubby, no boats could be launched. In general, this restriction didn't make much difference; it had been anticipated, Sharkwatch could continue, and we were already working from the water. However, federal officials on shore meant no more casual visits for me—for food, for a change of scene, for anyone's birthday. Not even for emergencies.

"Okay, sharkies. It's twelve minutes to high tide," Peter said, looking at his watch and then up at the sky, where he picked a flesh-footed shearwater, "a pretty rare bird," out of a pack of sooty shearwaters zinging by under the low ceiling. He had just cast his line, and I was trying to spot the flesh-footed oddball through my binoculars when suddenly Peter saw a dorsal fin. It was an almost imperceptible blip, just a few inches of dagger above the surface, and if there had been any chop at all, it might have been invisible. He whirled around. The fin popped up again, only ten feet away now and circling tighter. "Mako!" he said. This was a different brand of shark, a five-foot missile with a shorter, slightly rounded dorsal fin. The mako pirouetted around the whaler as though it were cutting through glass. As the shark flashed by we could see its aluminum-blue back, so metallic that it seemed like it ought to have rivets. "He's looking for a ling cod," Peter explained. Makos were notorious for dogging the catch as it was brought to the boat, neatly severing the flesh so that fishermen felt a quick release of pressure on their lines and then found themselves reeling in a disembodied head.

Makos and great whites are cousins, two of the lamnid sharks, with salmon sharks and porbeagles rounding out the family. The lamnids are warm-blooded, unusual for a fish, but great if you happen to be a predator. Tunas are also warm-blooded, and it's no accident that they, along with the lamnid sharks, are among the ocean's sports stars—their muscles are always warmed up. So are their eyes, brains, and nervous systems. Makos, for instance, can swim sixty miles per hour and leap twenty feet into the air. Salmon sharks carve away as much as 25 percent of the annual salmon run in Alaska, and white sharks . . . well, we know what they can do. Warm-bloodedness also revs up digestion and, in particular, fat metabolism—a handy feature for an animal that habitually polishes off two-ton elephant seals. An efficient heating system known as the *rete mirabile* (Latin for "wonderful net") keeps the bodies of lamnid sharks up to twenty degrees warmer than the water they're swimming in, allowing them to hunt and travel in colder regions where they otherwise couldn't survive. Cooling anything slows it down, so when the water is chillier, cold-blooded fish are at a disadvantage for dodging a souped-up mako with dinner in mind.

Another characteristic these sharks share is a striking economy of movement. Powered by thick, scythe-shaped tails, their swimming motions appear effortless, almost as though a current was sweeping them along. And then there are the teeth. The lamnids all have serious arsenals in their mouths, arrayed in multiple rows. No spindly needles or snaggly hooks here. Adult white sharks have broad, flat, triangular teeth with distinct serrations, designed to tear twenty-pound gulps of flesh from large mammals. Makos and salmon sharks, with their daggerlike, nonserrated teeth, are better equipped for dining on fish. Because the teeth are embedded in cartilage rather than bone, they fall out with regularity. That's what the extra rows are for. When a shark loses a tooth, the one behind it simply rotates forward like a bag of chips in a vending machine. An average shark loses thousands of teeth in its lifetime.

One thing's for sure: the sharks in these waters were earning a living. There was no lounging on the bottom (nurse sharks, wobbegongs) or garbage eating (bull sharks, tigers). Peter gave me his rundown on the locals: "Blues are graceful, the perfect shark. Makos are compact and edgy. Whites are just . . . cool."

Even to me, it was obvious that makos did not have the charisma of great whites, nor their haunting presence, although the fish was beautiful in its machine grace. Peter pulled in his line, not wanting to subject a hapless rockfish to the double indignity of being first hooked and then eaten alive. We watched the mako trying to look inconspicuous for a while, and then, eventually, it faded into the twilight depths.

We both cast. Almost instantly, Peter pulled in a monstrosity. It was a cabezon, the toad of the sea. The fish was mottled brown and beige, with vicious-looking quills and a great beast of a head atop a long, snaky body. It looked at us with baleful eyes and unmistakable hatred. This one was almost three feet long, the heftiest we'd seen, although the cabezons and lings used to regularly grow five feet long. It was the same sad refrain here, as elsewhere: Those larger fish were gone now.

Rockfish were especially vulnerable to overfishing because they tend to stay near one spot for their entire lives—and their lives could last more than one hundred years. When the long-liners and the bottom trawlers raked the area, the curmudgeonly rockfish stood no chance. Both fishing methods were still legal within the marine sanctuary.

I heard the thunk of the gaff. Earlier, I'd halfheartedly expressed the desire to kill and clean my own catch, but after an attempt or two that resulted in fish being flung across the whaler, Peter had quietly taken over this chore and between the two of us there was no more talk of me gaining backwoods know-how.

He knelt on the deck and cleaned the fish in several swift, almost savage motions. It had little teeth. Peter's hands and forearms were smeared with dark blood, which he wiped on his pants. The process was fast and surgical—he wanted every last scrap of meat. This, to him, was the only justification for killing: because you needed to eat.

This attitude put him at odds with some of his fellow biologists. To many specialists, the name of the game was "collecting," taking a handful of whatever you found, or one of anything that seemed rare or unusual. In the past, being an ornithologist had basically meant being a good shot, striding through the marsh or the tundra or the jungle with a pair of binoculars in one hand and a 12-gauge shotgun in the other. A scientific journal called the *Oologist* summed up the philosophy in 1892: "The murre, common as it is, is a beautiful bird, and a nicely mounted specimen vies well with most seabirds in one's collection."

As a rule, Peter was opposed to "collecting" and had butted heads with other biologists at the Farallones who'd wanted to bag some of the off-course migrants. However, he once worked on a Pacific seabird survey where it had been unavoidable, where the taking of a few individuals would truly help the entire species, and when that was the case, his rule was this: waste *nothing*. Every last snip of information needed to be gleaned. "We looked at every feather," he recalled. "Took their stomachs out. Analyzed the contents. We learned everything we possibly could out of every death, and that was really important to me."

Peter simply hated waste of any kind. He was the island's leftover king, and when it was his turn to cook dinner he'd make a kitchen-sink hash of whatever was languishing in the refrigerators. Sometimes meals would make three or four appearances at the table before people finally balked on the grounds of potential food poisoning. Only then would Peter throw the food out—which meant feeding it to the gulls. Scot had the same inclination, but on the mainland he took it even farther, pulling his truck over to the side of the road to scrape up roadkill deer. "If it's warm, I'll take it home," he'd said to me, describing how he would skin and dress the squashed and dented critters, making jerky out of them, or vacuum-packing the meat. One time, he had actually discovered a dead great white shark washed ashore at nearby Limantour Beach and, research permit in hand, had performed an impromptu dissection. Afterward, he'd brought chunks of its meat to a barbecue. I was beginning to understand that people who lived this close to nature couldn't afford to be sentimental about it. When you got right down to it, animals were food. In the aftermath of one particularly bloody shark attack, Peter had grabbed an abandoned morsel of elephant seal, taken it back to the house, and grilled it up with a few onions. "It was steaklike," he recalled. "Very rich and oily with a bit of a liver aftertaste. Not bad, but you'd get tired of it quick."

He put the rockfish meat into a cooler built into the whaler's side, flipped the carcass over the side, and wiped his hands on his pants again. "You know, I was always a little uneasy about eating the bottom fish around here. But I think it's okay. No way am I eating the mussels though, man." I understood his concern. We were fishing in the middle of America's first and largest undersea nuclear waste dump.

ONE OCTOBER EVENING IN 1980, PETER AND TWO OTHER BIOLOGISTS were cooking up some freshly caught rockfish and watching the news. Walter Cronkite came on. "Plutonium has entered the food chain," he announced, with even more gravitas than usual. As he said it, the camera cut to an aerial shot of Southeast Farallon Island, panning right in on the roof of the house they were sitting in. The story had just broken, Cronkite reported, that a UC Santa Cruz biologist had discovered elevated levels of radiation in fish swimming among some of the 47,500 barrels of nuclear waste that the navy had dumped in a 540-square-mile area around the Farallones between 1946 and 1970. One fish registered ninety times the normal levels of plutonium, and another had five thousand times the "allowable" amount of radioactivity in its liver.

Dinner preparations came to a halt. Peter took the rockfish outside and fed it to a gull named Pukey.

The radioactive debris came from Hunters Point Naval Shipyard, near San Francisco, home of the Naval Radiological Defense Laboratory, and Los Alamos, birthplace of the atomic bomb. Hunters Point, in particular, had been so sloppy with its toxic byproducts that, since 1989 when it was declared a Superfund site, $338 million has been spent trying to clean it up. And the work continues.

Although no records of the clandestine dumping were kept, the navy has claimed that the drums contain "low level" radioactive waste, things like the carcasses of test animals, paint scraps, old clothing, tainted lab equipment, gloves, and uniforms. Later, however, it was let slip that approximately six thousand barrels contained "special waste," a euphemism for very bad news. Plutonium and uranium were most likely present in this high-potency batch, as was cesium, which is less toxic than the other two but still not something you'd want to sprinkle on your breakfast cereal. Even the "low level" stuff was known to contain phenols, cyanides, mercury, beryllium, tritium, strontium, thorium, and radioactive lead.

Back in the early, heady A-bomb building days, no one really understood what kind of poisons they were dealing with—it didn't help that even lethal doses of radiation were quiet and invisible and undetected by human senses. Attitudes were heartbreakingly nonchalant. Also, much of the work at places like Los Alamos and Hunters Point was conducted beneath such a cloak of secrecy that most of the staff were unaware of what was underfoot. A woman named Janie Gale, who worked in the Hunters Point nuclear lab's library in 1948, outlined her degree of awareness in a newspaper interview: "They'd say 'Oh, we had a spill today.' I didn't know what a spill was. I had no idea there was anything toxic at the shipyard. I never heard the word 'decontamination.' It was a shipyard and they repaired the ships, I thought."

They were repairing the ships, all right. In the late forties, at least sixty warships that had been used for atomic target practice in the South Pacific were towed back to Hunters Point for decontamination. After they were sandblasted and scoured with chlorinated lime, flushed with detergent, and doused with solvents, a dozen were still so hot they were deemed beyond hope, and plans were made to secretly sink them far out at sea. Present on this roster of lost causes was the USS *Independence*, a ten-thousand-ton aircraft carrier, one of the navy's largest. In 1955 it was quietly scuttled in the Gulf of the Farallones.

Originally, the navy maintained that it was buried in a classified "safe" place four hundred miles offshore. But people claimed to have seen the ship going down right outside of San Francisco Bay, and sure enough, a precisely warship-sized and -shaped object was identified by sonar only twenty miles from the Golden Gate Bridge. To make matters worse, before it was sunk it had been loaded up with *extra* nuclear waste, crammed from stem to stern with "mixed fission" products. Though no one can tell you exactly what "mixed fission" means, it's likely to have included the most noxious remnants of the ship-cleaning operation. And some of the boats, including the *Independence*, had been so close to the mushroom clouds that their steel hulls had burst into flame.

There has never been a thorough study of the effects this nightmarish payload might have on the neighboring marine life, which includes at least five commercial fisheries. The most commonly cited reason was lack of cash. Poking around among the barrels was a multimillion-dollar proposition and the money never seemed to be available. Nor were the expensive submersibles required to do the job. Locating the barrels posed another problem. They'd been dumped in water three hundred to six thousand feet deep along the edge of the continental shelf, an area threaded with submarine canyons and gullies, sheer drop-offs, and crennelated rock. Recently, new sonar technologies helped pinpoint the nooks and crannies where the barrels lay, and in 1991 the Environmental Protection Agency and the National Oceanic and Atmospheric Administration spent a million dollars to hire a deepwater submersible named *Sea Cliff*. Three people could make the dive. Ed Ueber, head of the marine sanctuary and himself a former navy man, was one of them.

When I'd first heard about the nuclear waste, I'd been stunned. Surely, I thought, even back in the clueless forties and fifties they'd known that there were better spots for atomic dumping than one of the world's most fertile patches of ocean, a place that the government *itself*—going back to 1909 when Theodore Roosevelt had first declared the area a refuge—had designated worthy of extraspecial protection.

The mystery of what was percolating its twenty-four-thousand-year half-life on the ocean floor at the Farallones grabbed me, and I'd sought out Ed Ueber to ask him what he'd seen down there. We met for beers at San Francisco's Cliff House, sitting by the window on a day so clear you could make out Great Arch rock. Ueber, in his sixties, looked dapper in shirtsleeves and suspenders, and he gave off the warm vibe of your favorite college professor. He was completely, charmingly frank. In part, this might have had something to do with timing: he'd just stepped down from his post. Yet a survey of every interview he'd given on the issue proved him to be a straight-talking antibureaucrat by nature. He explained that despite pressure from environmental groups clamoring for an investigation, the government had shown a lack of enthusiasm for examining the barrels or the hot warship in any great detail. It was much easier to ignore them. (Anyway, it wasn't like the fish were *glowing*.) Given how difficult it was to study the dump, there wasn't enough data to prove that the marine life was dangerous to eat, or that the decaying barrels were anything to get alarmed about—and many parties preferred it that way. "We don't know the basis of the situation, so we can't say there's a problem," he said.

"That's like saying we don't have mad cow disease because we haven't tested for it."

The *Sea Cliff*'s dive concentrated on a nine-hundred-square-meter area that was estimated to be the resting place for 3,600 of the barrels. As expected, the underwater terrain was rugged, and as Ueber and the others dropped down 2,900 feet, the sinister-looking barrels loomed into view, fringed with barnacles, sponges, sea cucumbers, and anemones, and colonized by rockfish, bursting with all the reclaimed glory of an artificial reef. The report later stated that the drums ranged from intact to "completely deteriorated," imploded by the pressure of the depths. A photograph on the adjacent page showed a sablefish, a commercial species, nestled up against one of the barrels. When the picture became public, suddenly the Japanese market no longer wanted these fish. Damage to the sablefish industry was estimated at ten million dollars.

So it was not the biggest surprise to discover that since then, no large-scale studies had been undertaken. It didn't help that the *Sea Cliff* had come up from one barrel site hot with radiation and had to go through decontamination itself. While there are no patently disastrous results in what's been measured so far, only 15 percent of the dumping region has been examined. In some of the bottom-dwelling creatures that were sampled, background radiation levels were hundreds of times higher than normal. Furthermore, Ueber told me, the EPA had averaged those samples, combining readings from animals that lived closer to the barrels with those that didn't, diluting much of the data.

Maybe dropping atomic waste at sea will prove to have no obvious or devastating effects; maybe the ocean manages to just gulp it all down like a sour-tasting pill. More likely, though, the underwater radiation has been trickling up through the food chain. "No one knows what's in those barrels," Ueber had reminded me. "*No one.*" The U.S. Geological Survey report on what is now known as the Farallon Islands Radioactive Waste Dump spells it out chillingly:

"The potential hazard the containers pose to the environment is unknown."

AS THE WEATHER TURNED, THE PERFECT WAVE BEGAN TO CURL ACROSS Shark Alley in a way that caught Peter's eye. "I've seen my wave," he told me. "I've seen it five or six times." I'd heard him discussing plans over the radio with Brown, who, unlike Scot, was also itching to tow into Mirounga Bay. We were experiencing the season's sweetest surf, and all over Northern California the big-name, big-wave surfers were out trolling around, looking for epic and undiscovered breaks. Mavericks, the surf mecca just south of here, near Half Moon Bay, was "kind of like old school now," Peter had concluded. "It's done. It's crowded. Let's make sure we get our rides in before those guys get here."

There had been a Farallon reconnaissance mission by a group of surfers in November 2000, during a week when Peter was off the island. It so happened that the perfect wave was showing off when they arrived, and as they were watching it, growing excited, Groth had approached and warned them against trying anything, mentioning that he'd seen sharks on that spot only an hour before. As a test, a surfboard was placed in the water. Almost instantly the board was hammered—and not gently. The surfers had left abruptly, the story had made the rounds, and, according to Peter, "Nobody from the outside has thought about it since."

But the first-ride honors wouldn't go unclaimed forever. As a sport, surfing was ever more competitive, the pressure to one-up the last guy was excruciating, and, furthermore, there were always the insiders to worry about. "Don't scoop me on it man," I'd heard Peter say to Brown, with a bit of an edge to his voice. After all, Brown and Nat were now spending more time out here during the fall than anyone. And they were both expert surfers.

"No man, you're the first guy."

But for the time being, Peter had his hands full on shore. An attempt to plug in a power washer had blown out the island's electricity. And earlier, some bricks that were piled upstairs in the coast guard house had fallen through the floor to the kitchen below. Peter radioed in a cranky mood, grumbling about the sudden spate of emergency repairs. To be fair, lately things had been running more smoothly than usual, thanks to recent upgrades to the power system and the house, and a strict maintenance regime. Even in its finest shape, however, the island produced a laundry list of fix-it headaches: faulty valves, panels blown off by storms, sudden disasters involving plumbing, leaks, clogged filters, flashing warning lights on balky generators, contaminated fuel, corroded paint, busted pumps, snapped cables, endlessly malfunctioning batteries. There was propane to hook up and solar panels to be scraped of gull droppings and ozonator filters to be cleaned and a gravity tank, whatever that was, to be pumped. The houses got coated with a green algae that had to be blasted off with a high-pressure hose. After a day or two, the algae returned.

The breakdowns weren't happening only on land. As the weather turned testier so did *Just Imagine,* and we were on each other's nerves in a big way, locked in a battle of wills: I wanted to be here, and the yacht didn't.

The list of busted and haywire systems grew daily. For about a week now, for instance, the battery voltage—the power source for running everything from the lights to the radio to the water heater—had been falling steadily for no apparent reason. Peter and I had spent time with various manuals trying to fix it, but we had failed. Whenever the voltage dipped below a certain level, a jarring alarm buzzer would erupt, usually in the middle of the night, at which point I had to start the engine immediately and run it until the battery had recharged. This always made me nervous, as if by powering up I might cause the boat to lunge forward, rip from its moorings, and plow into Tower Point, or thunder into the open water. So I tried to conserve power. I kept the internal lights off and wore my headlamp at all times. The only light that resolutely stayed on at night was the mast light, which would—in theory—

prevent any vessel (squid fishing or otherwise) that had the notion to anchor in Fisherman's Bay from ramming into the bulky, parked object blocking its entrance.

Meanwhile, the plumbing was still dishing up surprises. The red ooze had crept up through the kitchen sink while I was washing dishes, and the toilet malfunctioned at a clip that manners prevent me from describing in full detail. In an attempt to fix it, we had gone so far as to pry up one of the panels in the floor to get a better look at the septic system. Down in the gaping hole lay a snarl of rubber pipes in a nasty broth of greasy gray water—I supposed this was the bilge. I'd heard the word used in reference to marine waste products, and this qualified, to say the least. There was a dull film on the water's surface, and it smelled like it had been sloshing around down there since approximately the era when the naked lady had been carved. Thankfully, Peter seemed to know his way around a septic system. I stood back as he reached purposefully into the maw. "Hmm. I think this is the blackwater line that isn't pumping . . . ," he said, fingering an ominous-looking pipe. BBLLAMM! A valve exploded, sending a hose clamp shooting straight up into the air like a champagne cork and then clinking down into the murk. A violent hissing noise issued from the hose. "Oops," he said. "Hope that wasn't something we needed." I looked in the bathroom and noticed that the toilet had flushed. But the victory was short-lived. Within the hour the head had vacuum-sealed itself shut, and when the seat cover was forced open, it spat up blackwater with *Exorcist*-like vigor.

Last night's fifteen-knot winds had the boat pitching and surging like an amusement park ride, and a cacophony of groaning and grinding noises filled the cabin, making sleep impossible. They reverberated up from the anchor as its chain rubbed back and forth across a rock edge. The image of a prisoner trying to saw off a pair of handcuffs came to mind.

Admittedly, the whole floating shark research platform concept was being tested at the moment. But it was also true that things kept happening to remind me of why I still wanted to be here. On the island, two extraordinary bird sightings had set things abuzz: a

Baird's sparrow and a red-tailed tropicbird. Both were off-course migrants that were exotic to begin with; in fact, Peter had laid eyes on a Baird's sparrow only once before—and throughout all of California the bird had been glimpsed on only four occasions. (Three of the four sightings had taken place at the Farallones.) Kristie had spotted the bird near a patch of scrub vegetation known as "Twitville," and Peter had positively identified it, not a simple thing to do. (If you leaf through a bird guide, within the span of twenty pages of sparrows you'll notice that only minuscule markings set them apart, and sparrows are canapé-sized to begin with.) The red-tailed tropicbird made its home in the far northwestern reaches of Hawaii. It was a showy white bird with a single red tail feather that trailed behind it like the train on a Valentino gown. This specimen had no business being here, but here it was, swooping around for the better part of an hour. Peter had described the sightings to me over the radio as "fucking radical."

And earlier this afternoon there had been an impressive attack off Indian Head involving at least five sharks. The seal was a full-sized adult with a seemingly endless supply of blood, and the water off the west point of the island had been whipped into a scarlet froth as the waves tumbled against each other from all directions. The sharks had been thrashing near the whaler, and then one of them had breached, but sort of in reverse, leading with its tail. Peter suspected that they had gotten too close to one another while feeding and "freaked," I believe was his biological term. It had been far too crazy to put in a tag, although Peter had recognized one of the sharks: "That's Tipfin, man!" Back from Hawaii for another season.

After more than an hour of feeding and investigating things on the surface—the whaler, its motor, a surfboard—the last shark had slipped away. At least five individuals had been caught on video, most likely a gang of Rat Packers. If a Sister had been part of the group, the others would have scattered rather than lingering so confidently. "Well that was gnarly," Peter had said happily and then turned up the Giants' game on the transistor.

Now he'd gone back to the island for the night. I'd watched him sprint to shore in Tubby, haul the rowboat onto the rocks at North Landing, and then set off down the path at a jog, ready to return to the warmth of the house. The sky was gloomy and cold, with stormy plumes reaching down to the north. I stood at the bow and watched as the squid fleet fired up their stadium lighting and positioned themselves for the night. Heavy chop slapped *Just Imagine,* and in turn the sailboat backhanded the whaler, tied alongside.

I clicked on my headlamp and went down into the cabin. "Tonight won't be that bad," I told myself, as I settled into the banquette with a dinner of crackers and cabernet sauvignon. "A little windy, maybe."

My assessment changed within the hour. According to the Weather Voice, the wind was gusting ten to twenty knots, with six-foot waves arriving every ten seconds. Which, if you went by marine charts, was a "fresh breeze." To me, this seemed akin to describing a raging, blackout drunk as "slightly tipsy." There was nothing *breezelike* about these conditions. The whaler hammered at the side of *Just Imagine* with direct, cracking hits. The noise grew louder and eventually became so disturbing that I crawled on deck to shift the bumpers and retie the lines. Outside the wind whooshed by, the yacht was slippery from fog, and both boats swung from side to side as I tried to undo bowlines and cleat hitches without losing any digits. Sea lion barks and elephant seal snorts echoed off the rocks, and above me the lighthouse cast its beam into the night, as though searching for something, rather than pointing it out.

Falling off a sailboat in the night would be a bad way to go. Especially one that was tossing in the middle of the Pacific. What could possibly be lonelier than being swallowed by the abyss, stripped of anything that might maintain your illusion of control, and of all the comforting reminders of land? Imagine the terror of meeting a great white in the total blackness. First, it would circle. Next, the bump. On the first pass the shark would hold back, completing its due diligence, brushing by—perhaps you would feel its distinctive skin, covered in sharp-edged denticles, which are literally tiny teeth. (A shark's skin alone can draw blood.) By the time the shark returned

for a second bump, however, it would be officially hunting you. . . .
I shook my head, dismissing the image. Clinging to the cable railing,
I made it back into the cabin and was promptly knocked to the floor
when *Just Imagine* hit a high roller. Back home, some sailor friends
had recommended that I crawl through the sailboat during bad
weather to avoid getting batted around like this. At the time, I'd
thought that was funny: *Crawling. As if.* But I wasn't laughing right
now. I got down on my hands and knees.

The plastic dishes that had been in the sink picked themselves
up and crashed to the floor. (Few things on the boat were glass, for
obvious reasons.) Now, every thirty seconds or so, *Just Imagine* was
rearing up and then slamming down, sending anything that wasn't
strapped down careening through the cabin. I thought about radioing Peter, but there was nothing he could do. Plus, my radio had
gone skidding across the floor, and I had no idea where it was.

At the moment it was hard not to think back on all that had
gone down in Fisherman's Bay: the drownings and the shootings
and the egg mishaps and all the capsized and wrecked boats and
the Sisters making stealthy loops on the bottom like phantom jets.
The bow seemed more stable somehow, so I made my way up
there, crawling into the captain's bunk and padding myself on all
sides with mounds of blankets. Unfortunately, being up front
meant I was that much closer to the keening anchor chain, and by
now the wind had begun to actually howl. A dozen eggs that had
been sitting in the galley smashed against the opposite wall. Books
flipped off shelves; batteries bowled from port to starboard and
back again.

I was torn. On one hand, it seemed like a fine time to mix alcohol
and sleeping pills to escape the anxiety; this was the exact type of
event that sedatives were invented for. Alternately, it would be wise
to stay clearheaded in case emergency action was required. Such as
swimming. I'd stood on deck yesterday and calculated the distance
from *Just Imagine* to the rocks: 150 yards to Tower Point and about
200 to Sugarloaf. "It would take less than two minutes to swim to

the island," I had informed Peter, with false cockiness. "Yeah, well, that'd be the longest two minutes of your life," he replied.

After one particularly extreme round of waves, I voted for the drugs. But still I remained awake—this was like trying to sleep on a trampoline while people were jumping on it. Unidentified stuff continued to catapult around. At two o'clock, and after a few pulls on the ancient bottle of house brandy, I fell into a kind of half sleep. The noises became different: they took on the high-pitched, eerie tones of crying children and voices whispering. Light, feathery, and aquatic, they rose up from the water like an exhalation.

IN THE MORNING THE WIND WAS STILL BLOWING TWENTY KNOTS, AND the sky was angry and dismal, but—I was still here! It was daylight! The whaler was not on the bottom of the ocean! (Although it was noticeably banged up.) I went topside and scanned the bay, feeling thankful. Suddenly, in the midst of my private celebration, I noticed a large puddle of blood on the deck. And then, right above it, a long smear on the cabin door as though a bloody hand had raked down the side. And in front of the smear, near the bow, there was *more* blood—a small lake. In fact, there was blood *everywhere;* it was bright red and so recently spilled that it was still dripping. In a panic, I radioed Peter. He sounded cheerful and well rested and he immediately launched into a monologue about last night's dinner, going on about the chocolate banana chiffon cake they'd had for dessert—a vegan recipe, apparently; he'd bring a piece out for me . . .

Two people cannot speak simultaneously on a radio. You have to wait for one person to finish first, say "over," and release the transmit button. When I got my turn to talk I was a mess, screaming about whispering voices and pools of blood. Relax, Peter told me, a bird must have hit the boat. And probably, judging by the volume, a sizable bird like a cormorant. In a completely calm voice he advised me to look for a feather so that he could identify it, explaining that if a large bird went down and bled that much, there would definitely be feathers left behind. Right, okay. A bird. I'll come up with a feather. For half an hour, I hunted all over the deck and couldn't find a single one.

C H A P T E R   9

If Robinson Crusoe had been cast ashore on this island, I wonder how he would have lived?

—CHARLES WARREN STODDARD,
WITH THE EGG PICKERS OF THE FARALLONES, 1881

SEPTEMBER 30–OCTOBER 6, 2003

"Well. I don't *think* an elephant seal could've gotten up here." Peter had spent the last ten minutes searching the deck for evidence of kamikaze feathers and found none.

"Not unless they're able to levitate about six feet into the air and clear these railings."

There was an edge to my voice. On the heels of our radio conversation Peter had Tubbied out to examine the blood and, I hoped, figure out who it belonged to. He was taken aback, I could see, by the volume of liquid, and the way it ranged from stern to bow, as though a sprawling avian death match had unfolded across *Just Imagine's* entire upper deck. He'd pointed to a green smear near a dollop of blood and said, "This looks like eelgrass. Whatever this was, it was eating eelgrass."

"That's *guacamole*. From when I threw the rotten burritos overboard."

"Oh."

We decided to move on; it was clear that for now the source

would have to remain a mystery. I was rattled. First, the voices; now *this*. Of all the blood I'd seen at the Farallones, this batch was the most disconcerting. Maybe that damned Ouija board was to blame. As usual, my views on the supernatural were conflicted. I couldn't admit to a belief that blood-spraying ghosts had been attracted to the sailboat, but still, I would've welcomed a chance to get rid of the board. My nerves were ragged, and I was anxious to get off the murderous yacht, so the two of us set out in the whaler under dishwater skies and relentless chop. Earlier this morning Peter had been tinkering around onshore at East Landing and seen a large shark, potentially a Sister, breach right off Shubrick, clearing the water entirely and landing with an explosive splash. We headed there now.

Great white sharks were known to breach when hunting, and their aerobatics had even inspired a video series known as *Air Jaws*. The footage had been shot in part at South Africa's False Bay, where torpedoing up through a school of porpoising Cape fur seals is standard procedure. At the Farallones, breaching was less common, perhaps because the doddering elephant seals didn't require the effort. When Peter witnessed his first airborne shark, in 1982, he'd assumed that the animal was a whale. Over time, however, it became clear that the sharks were doing their share of the leaping. Scot interpreted the breaching as failed seal decapitations, but Peter had other theories. Sloppy hunting, in his opinion, didn't account for the instances when a shark would breach three or four times in succession. Repeat breaching almost seemed like an attempt at showing off, and he wondered whether it constituted a kind of social signaling or pre-mating display. "Their whole mating system is completely unknown," he said. "How do they meet? And how do they decide? The males have to do *something* to get the females." There was another, less romantic, possibility: perhaps the sharks were trying to rid themselves of parasites, as whales did.

I was driving. I'd tried to beg off; the water was, in Peter's appraisal, "snotty," and I just didn't feel like it. I didn't want to have to think, or worry, or demonstrate any kind of skill. I wanted to sit in the whaler's scooped-out bow staring passively at the surface and wait for some amazing creature to poke its head up. That was all. Peter wasn't having it. He gave me a withering look that said: *wrong attitude*. Then, trying to be encouraging, he added, "We're so overdue for an attack on this side." And he was right—the Sisters were being elusive. While the newer sharks, the smaller sharks, and the less clued in sharks had been keeping us busy at Indian Head and in Mirounga Bay, we had yet to encounter a shark on the island's east side.

The whaler bucked through hatchet-edged waves coming at fast intervals from unexpected directions. It was the kind of water in which a fledgling shark boat driver could bury the bow or bite the tip of her tongue off, should she become careless. Two hundred yards due east of the island, I felt the motor cough and miss a beat. I gunned it, and the engine, pushing back, completely cut out. Sputtered. Quit.

Peter reached over and tried to restart it several times, with no success. "Don't flood it," I warned. He graciously ignored me and turned to the back of the boat, removing the engine cover and checking the fuel lines. The wind was blowing at least ten knots from the northwest, and we teetered in the chop, ripping east, drifting quickly offshore. Rather than mess with the engine long enough to float out of radio range, Peter Maydayed the island for a tow, and within minutes Elias was motoring toward us in the Dinner Plate, dressed in foul-weather gear and looking valiant, like a toy boat captain on a mission in some children's adventure storybook. It was a relief to see him; the water had turned a foreboding obsidian, and looking back toward *Just Imagine*, I saw that Fisherman's Bay was draped in a dark fog, punctuated by whitecaps.

Almost exactly above the spot where Peter had seen the shark breach this morning, we threw Elias a tow rope and then scrambled into the Dinner Plate. It was more substantial than Tubby, I reckoned, looking nervously over the side, but not by much. The shark boat was clearly down for the count, so they dropped me at *Just Imagine* and headed back to East Landing, where the crippled whaler would be winched onto the island for repairs.

I stood on deck looking out at the unfriendly landscape as Elias and Peter faded into the gloom. The clouds had knitted themselves into a steel muffler, and for now it was a monochrome world. Standing downwind, near several puddles of dried blood, I caught an unmistakable whiff of sewage. The stench could be traced to a silver fitting that looked decorative but obviously was not; a brackish stream oozed steadily from it with a sibilant hiss. While I puzzled over this—why was shit coming out of the roof of the cabin?—a sporty catamaran emerged out of nowhere and made a tight U-turn next to the yacht. Far too tight, in fact. He was traveling fast in close quarters, gambling with his turning radius, and he practically took out Tubby. Not only that; one poorly timed wave and he would've swiped *Just Imagine*'s starboard a lot harder than Tom and his crew had managed to do when they'd jibed. The boat's name, *Big Fat Fun*, flashed into view as it swept by, and the fear in the skipper's eyes was plainly visible. He was alone, dressed in a balaclava and slicker, driving with his motor on and his sails down, and laboring to get out of here as quickly as possible. Breaking the crux rule of boating etiquette, he didn't bother to wave.

Peter radioed to confirm that, sharks or no sharks, we were done for the day. He would be staying on the island to work on the whaler, which appeared to have a busted fuel filter. There were other chores to be dealt with as well, something about a ruined pipe, and also there was a Giants game on. I fully understood my abandonment. Why would you spend time on *Just Imagine* unless you were forced to? But it was only two o'clock. A long afternoon, evening, and night stretched in front of me.

I went below, figuring that I'd lie in my sleeping bag for a while, reading a book I'd brought about the role of predators in nature, and then maybe do some chin-ups. Wooden handholds sprouted from the yacht's ceiling in various spots and they were ideal for this exercise, although I believe these grips were intended for more prosaic uses, such as staying upright while the boat was barrel rolling. Anyway, they were my favorite feature, perhaps because the handles seemed excessively sturdy and unlikely to break. I was up to seventeen chin-ups now, a lifetime best.

The sailboat pitched irritably, making reading impossible. I crawled into my bunk and tightened the straps. Somehow, this wasn't how I'd envisioned shark season: sitting alone and foodless in foul conditions on a sailboat that seemed bent on retaliation for having to be part of it. And *where* were the Sisters?

By now, I'd imagined, I would have known them by sight. After all, we were neighbors. I pictured the Big Girls asleep in deep and twisted subaquatic caves, gliding out when the time was right, like Ferraris that were only rarely driven. Though technically it was still early in the season, Peter had phoned Scot to discuss the lack of female sharks. Scot continued to wonder about the role of the squid boats; the lights and the underwater noises of the nets being hauled in and out, and the heavy engines roaring, he felt, would certainly affect the animals' hunting patterns. "They're smart. They'll go elsewhere." But, he added: "It's not over till it's over." During October the average number of shark attacks was one per day, though there were sometimes as many as five. Right now we were *seeing* sharks daily, but mainly when they were bumping the decoys. There had been fewer than usual live attacks, with seals and blood and much exposure of teeth. Peter recounted this conversation to me, noting that "when Scot gets here, the mojo will change. You'll see, things can turn quickly."

I fell into a half nap and awoke with a jolt just before sunset. Though the anchor chain was still wailing and grinding, and the sailboat was surging and straining against its ropes, things seemed oddly quiet—the absence of the whaler, I realized, meant there was nothing for *Just Imagine* to pummel. Feeling disoriented, I poked my head up through the hatch. Instantly I could see that the water had become stormier, and the sky was in on it too. Through the

Gap, surf swept across the raking two-tiered reefs of Maintop Bay with a force I hadn't seen before. The wind was building.

Alarmed, I flipped on the Weather Voice, just in time to hear the report from the Point Arena buoy: "SMALL CRAFT WARNING. Winds twenty to thirty knots; seas ten feet at eleven seconds." The Voice delivered this information with mechanical unconcern. But as the sailboat resumed its night noises in the quickly falling light, I felt less nonchalant. Compared with these new, scarier numbers, last night *was*, in fact, a "fresh breeze." I hailed Peter, who was in the middle of cooking dinner. He tried to calm me down, adopting the faux-soothing voice that air traffic controllers use in movies when all the pilots are dead and they're trying to walk someone who's never flown a plane through landing a 747. "It looks *bad* out here," I said, struggling to tamp down the panic in my voice. "Even the squid boats are gone!"

There was a long silence. "Over? Peter? You copy?"

"This is what I was worried about," Peter answered wearily.

These were not the most comforting words I'd ever heard.

"This sailboat can't roll over, can it?"

"No, no, no. There's no way. It has a big old keel."

I was momentarily reassured until he continued: "The problem would be if the rope or the anchor chain broke, and the boat swung toward Tower Point . . ."

"What do you mean if the rope or the anchor chain broke?"

"I think I'd better come out."

It was past nine o'clock when Peter rowed across Fisherman's Bay in the ten-foot swells, something that was surely advised against in Tubby's owner's manual. The hatch opened, and a gush of wind and ocean noise whirled into the cabin, followed by Peter's boots coming down the ladder. I sat at the table in my headlamp. I was embarrassingly relieved to see him, especially since he'd brought me some food. "What's that noise?" he asked, his brow scrunched in concern.

"Which *one*?" The sailboat was performing a symphony of ominous noises, Satan's orchestra tuning up underwater. As the gusts broadsided it from the west, *Just Imagine* listed so heavily to the east, toward Tower Point, that the starboard portholes were almost submerged.

"That grinding noise. It sounds like something's scraping on rock. I haven't heard that one before. I'm going up to see what's the deal with that anchor chain."

Peter crawled back up the ladder and out into the wind. Ten minutes passed. I began to worry that I'd have to go up on deck and he'd be gone, an unexplained puddle of blood in his place. But a few moments later he emerged down the hatch. "Man, it is *howling* out there," he said, shaking his head. He held a shredded, utterly destroyed length of rope—the remains of a line that Tom had looped around the anchor chain for support. With this additional line secured off the bow, the sailboat had less play. With its destruction, the newly loosened anchor chain enabled *Just Imagine* to sway with a lively whipsawing motion.

"I am not unworried," Peter said, examining the rope.

The gravelly rasping of the chain across the edge of the reef had intensified. It was impossible to ignore the change in tone. "Okay," he said, turning to me and speaking slowly. "If *Just Imagine* were to swing all the way over and smash against the rocks, Tubby would be our bailout. We'd jump in Tubby and get outta here." I was in agreement: a ride in the rowboat was a better option than a midnight swim.

An ominous rumbling noise erupted topside, followed by a loud staccato of objects skittering across the deck.

"What the hell was *that*?"

"The gas cans, and probably a spare radio or something. We better save it before it goes overboard." Peter went back up the ladder, returning a moment later with a video-camera case and a tin can.

"I think the bucket went for a sail," he said.

This was a loss. The plumbing situation was dire. I needed that bucket.

Suddenly, there were several more thunks and a rambunctious

surge from the bow, followed by a loud moaning. "What was *that* noise!" It was his turn to sound surprised.

"I don't know. But it's not the first time I've heard it."

"Well, I'd like it to stop right now. Because that's a new noise since I've been on. Now it sounds like the . . ."

"It's not a new noise. That noise is very familiar to me."

Peter sat at the table, looking uneasy. "I'm wondering if another rope broke," he said. I handed him an oversized plastic mug of red wine and took a long drink from my own. Now we were surging back and forth more erratically. "We'll know if something major happens," he said. "If it does, our whole motion is going to shift. And it hasn't. I don't think."

An ugly noise clanged up through the bottom of the boat. It was a full-on collision sound, the type of thing you'd expect to hear if you hit a solid object, a rock maybe, or the wrecked remains of the boat that was stupid enough to anchor here before you. But it was only the force of the waves churning across the bay. A radio and some batteries went crashing to the floor, whacking the naked lady in the head.

"Sailboats are made to withstand this kind of weather," Peter said. He didn't seem entirely persuaded, though. "In the open ocean they go through far worse than this." What he didn't say—he didn't have to—was that when the boat was actually sailing, it was free to track with the wind.

I asked if he and Scot had ever been out on shark attacks in truly dicey weather. It was hard to imagine tooling around in the whaler next to a few feeding sharks in conditions like these.

"Oh yeah, lots," he said. "Most of the times they're not really worth it. The slick goes away fast, the boat's just pitching, and you're trying to film. There was one really crazy one, though."

A furious storm had come up a few years ago, he said, out of nowhere. It was late September, prime shark season, and he'd been on the water when he spotted two large fins about a mile north of Sugarloaf, just sitting there quietly, like periscopes. At that point the weather was completely benign, and there were no gulls swarming, no blood slick. Curious, he radioed Scot, who was at the lighthouse, and then he drove toward the fins. Suddenly, the sharks began to thrash, kicking up enormous crests of water. Scot saw it too and sprinted down to launch the Dinner Plate.

As Peter motored toward the attack, he realized that it was farther offshore than he'd estimated, more like two miles. At the site, an elephant seal carcass bobbed, so slashed up that its edges fluttered like ribbons, and it was surrounded by three large sharks. They were circling but, strangely, not eating. It had all seemed very ominous, portentous even, like Macbeth's witches around the cauldron, and at that moment he'd turned and noticed that the entire western horizon had blackened behind a wall of clouds. Scot arrived as the winds began to build, took one look at the scene, and recommended a hasty retreat. Neither the Dinner Plate nor the whaler was the right place to be during an ocean squall.

Peter, suspecting they were poised to witness something interesting, was reluctant to leave, but when the winds hit twenty-five knots, he too had turned toward shore. By the time he reached the island the storm had ratcheted into a gale, rain and hail thundered down, and using the boom was out of the question. Scot and the Dinner Plate were trapped in Fisherman's Bay; the huge swells had made it impossible to round Shubrick Point. Peter ferried him to North Landing and then tied off to the buoy, prepared to ride out the storm with the two boats all night, if necessary. But the storm left as abruptly as it had come, and within an hour he was back onshore, wrapped in blankets.

Unfortunately, tonight's weather wasn't going anywhere. But it didn't seem to be getting any worse, so I lashed myself into my bunk, leaving Peter to the creepy captain's cabin, and both of us to worry about *Just Imagine* beelining toward the rocks during the night. As I tightened the straps around my sleeping bag, I realized that I had to give the Farallones this: Even as the place was trying to kill me, I had never felt more alive.

. . .

IN THE MORNING, PETER WAS GONE. A NOTE ON THE LADDER EX-
plained that the boat noises had kept him up and he'd rowed back
to the island at 4 a.m. I radioed. "I can't *believe* you took Tubby out
in that!"

"It was a bit heavy," he admitted.

Today was another Small Craft Warning day, filled with the
promise of more discomfort. But the whaler was fixed, and despite
the offputting conditions, we decided to go out. Casting the surfboard at Indian Head, we drifted down Shark Alley. Peter seemed
uncharacteristically quiet. I asked him what was on his mind.

"I'm worried that having the sailboat out here has become a bad
idea," he said, looking somewhat pained. He was thinking about
the nights I'd spent on *Just Imagine* being flung around at the
mercy of the weather. He was thinking about the groceries that
had gone rotten and the toilet that wouldn't flush and the anony-
mous blood splattered all over the deck.

I told him that as far as I was concerned, everything was going
fine. And mostly, I meant it. Yet I also knew that if the weather
continued to deteriorate, the responsible thing to do was get *Just
Imagine* out of here. But that would require Tom, who was traveling this week, to come and pick it up, and anyway, Scot was arriving soon. Surely between him and Peter, they'd be able to fix the
mooring.

I was well aware that if the sailboat had to go, so did I. I wasn't
ready for this to happen. I hadn't seen a Sister. I hadn't spent time
with Scot. If I retreated now, all the drama of shark season would
continue without me, and I would be sidelined once again on the
mainland.

"This is a character-building experience," I reassured him, trying to sound upbeat. But he wasn't looking at me. In the nanosecond before I said it, a small boil had risen near the surfboard, and
he noticed it just as the shark surfaced. It was a midsize Rat Packer.

He made a fast figure-eight around the board, bumped us, rolled onto his side looking skyward with one black and ancient eye, flicked his tail, and disappeared. The shark's head was raked with long white scrapes. "That was Plimpton," Peter said.

The encounter broke the tension and seemed to end the discussion of an exit strategy for the borrowed yacht. And although the night that followed was gruesome, again, and the noises hammered at my nerves and I spent the night staring out at Tower Point, waiting to see it suddenly loom large in the porthole, when Peter radioed to see how I was doing, I told him that things in Fisherman's Bay were much, much better; really quite good.

It wasn't even a total lie. Over the next two days there were no fresh breakdowns aboard *Just Imagine*, though the weather remained a concern. The island buzzed with chain saws and jackhammers as coast guard contractors assembled the piles of debris to be carted off by the helicopters next week. From *Just Imagine*'s deck I watched them standing on the rocks at North Landing, fishing. The Farallones had never been a popular assignment for coast guard types. Several seasons ago, in fact, a crew had protested "inhumane working conditions," citing the kelp flies. And that particular group had flown in a satellite dish for their weeklong assignment. The guys on the island now, Peter told me, had airlifted in their own food. Their menu veered dramatically from the organic and healthful food the biologists ate and toward Dinty Moore beef stew and nacho-flavored Doritos. Whole palettes of packaged goods had been unloaded as the contractors settled into the coast guard house.

I had some new company in Fisherman's Bay. Less than twenty yards off the bow, resident for several days now, swam a baby gray whale who seemed to materialize every time I stood on deck. Its prehistoric-looking, knuckled back arched above the surface; her elegant barnacled tail waved playfully. Occasionally, we made eye contact. As far as whales go, this one was truly pocket-size, and Peter had wondered aloud if a shark might not take it out.

No one had ever witnessed a shark attack a whale before, but blubber was the ultimate shark delicacy, and there was no more certain place to find great white sharks than at a newly bloated whale carcass floating somewhere in the Red Triangle. Scot had a network of fishing buddies who would give him a heads-up whenever one surfaced. Unless the carcass was beyond rancid, the sharks would be there, shearing off long strips of fat.

Right now, the Farallones were exceptionally well populated with whales. In the shark boat we'd been almost uncomfortably close to humpbacks that would suddenly surface, often in pairs. The humpbacks were sleek and elegant, acrobats with long tapered fins. Feeding out a little farther were the stately blue whales, the largest animals on Earth. The blues were imposing and humbling as they burst from the water or rolled by, their long backs streaming on forever. At one time two hundred thousand of these boxcar-size mammals had ranged the world's oceans; now there were fewer than ten thousand.

Back in the whaling days, gray whales were known as "devilfish," and they were notorious for killing fishermen and charging boats. But, it was discovered later, this had more to do with the harpoons stuck in their backs than innate aggressive behavior, and after the practice was stopped, people learned that grays are downright friendly. In Baja's San Ignacio lagoon, for instance, they congregate en masse, nuzzling tourist boats and allowing themselves to be stroked, reveling when their bellies are scratched. My whale, as I had come to think of her, was clearly interested in the sailboat. Maybe it had to do with the smell. One little known fact: The water that spouts out of a whale's blowhole in such a picturesque way reeks like the most toxic fart imaginable. And that pretty much described the yacht's odor, especially downwind of the hissing silver fixture.

MAINTOP BAY WAS THE MOST PERILOUS SPOT ON THE ISLAND. IT HAD the most exposure, the biggest surf, an array of treacherous hidden rocks, and fierce currents to suck you toward them. Cast into shadow by Southeast Farallon itself, Maintop was always blacker than the seas around it. For boats it was never the best place to be, as the prevailing northwest winds and the western winter swells walloped it straight on. If you got into trouble in there, you were out of luck. The shoreline was sheer and there was nowhere to ditch in an emergency, something that many people had discovered too late: Maintop had been the site of numerous drownings. Shards of wrecked ships still poked out at low tide. Peter and Scot were always wary as they drove through it, and even warier during attacks. Not surprisingly, the sharks seemed to enjoy the area.

One morning in 1991, Scot had just summited at the lighthouse for his first watch, and he was warming up, doodling, drinking his coffee, when he happened to look up and notice a guy bobbing in the center of Maintop, a bright orange life preserver wedged between his legs. The man was surrounded by a few floating coolers, but there was no boat to be seen. Scot did a double take. He had no idea how the guy could have gotten there, short of dropping out of the sky; no one had noticed any fishing vessels approaching the island.

He radioed to Peter that "there was someone in Maintop Bay," and Peter, of course, assumed he was referring to a shark. Upon learning that it was, improbably, a person, he rushed out in the whaler—floating in Maintop was not a highly survivable proposition in November—and somehow managed on his own to roll the two-hundred-pound man into the boat. A coast guard helicopter beetled out and airlifted the man, whose name was Bill Kaboose, to the hospital. During the entire rescue, Kaboose remained in shock and never uttered a word. And afterward, they never heard from him either, not so much as a thank-you note. They did find the remains of his boat though, and the fishing equipment that had been on it was handily deployed to cast surfboards out to sharks. In recognition of what a trick it must have been to haul Kaboose from the bay, the marine sanctuary granted Peter the O'Neil Award for Seamanship. It was an unlikely story with a crowd-pleasing ending:

"I do like to think that the Shark Project saved one life," Scot said.

This afternoon Peter and I were floating hopefully off Shubrick, getting heaved around so badly by swells that we'd been about to give up, when Kristie radioed down from the light with news of an attack. "It's over in Maintop." Peter glanced at me, started the engine, and said, simply, "Hang on." And then he hit the throttle so hard that the whaler literally took air, bouncing off the troughs.

First, the mass of gulls came into view as we rounded Sugarloaf, and then, there it was: the body in a crimson slick, the brightest color for miles. Everything else was muted in the fog and asphalt light. Peter pulled the whaler close to the beheaded seal and cut into neutral, grabbing for his pole camera. I fumbled with the topside camera, having difficulty and filming the inside of my jacket for a time—one hand was locked in a death grip around the rail and the other was shaking to the point of uselessness. I didn't like Maintop Bay. It churned like a malevolent washing machine, and the rocks were close by.

Instantly, the shark appeared alongside us. It was the largest I'd seen, at least sixteen feet with the girth of a trailer home. Every detail of the scene put my nerves on edge: the menacing water, the heft of the shark, the alarm-bell-red blood, an extra-aggressive band of gulls screaming overhead. For the first time I could see how easy it would be to end up in the water during an attack. Peter alternately filmed and lunged toward the console to reverse the whaler from its path toward the rocks. The shark tore a slab of seal and went down, giving us a moment to get it together, but then it surfaced in the next second and seemed almost angry at the boat, whipping the side with its tail, and soaking us. The seal had been ripped in three, and the pieces began to drift apart.

"Watch for other sharks," Peter said, standing on the gunwale, staring down. I leaned over the edge trying to make out shapes or shadows or boils in the lightless water. "There!" he yelled, pointing toward me. A hulking body swept by, and I focused the camera. The shark charged to the surface, jaws slashing at a piece of the carcass, coming in for its close-up. It was the sharpest, closest look

I'd had at a great white shark's face and its alien head and the white underbelly of its throat, which was bulging, and at that moment it was as though time stopped. By now I'd seen more than a dozen white sharks, but I still felt the same raw amazement every time one loomed beneath us. It never diminished, not even slightly. Rather, it grew. This was a standard sentiment. Scot had spoken to the Animal Planet crew about his own sense of awe: "I've probably seen more white sharks attacking more things than almost anyone on the planet, so I have a respect for what they can do. And it's something I'll never shake." His response to me was simpler: "I feel sorry for anybody who hasn't seen one."

We stayed in Maintop for an hour, filming and struggling to stay off the rocks. The slick dissipated, and as the seal was whittled down to kabob-sized remnants, Peter turned up the Giants game, which had started during the attack. It was a make-or-break play-off game, and if they lost, they would be eliminated in their World Series run. He seemed more keyed up about baseball than any of the other action. "I've seen that shark before," he said, throwing the whaler into gear. "I recognize the spot on his right side. It's a large male." This was disappointing news. The shark was massive enough, I'd thought, to have been a Sister. Not by a long shot, Peter told me, laughing. "When you see a big female, you won't *believe* how badass they are."

I wanted to know how he managed to see anything when the water was this dark—and no, I didn't see the spot on its right side. Both he and Scot had the startling ability to track the sharks as they moved around the boat, even to the point of knowing where the animals would surface after they dove. On a clear-water day, they could pinpoint the creatures, even when they were twenty feet underwater. Whereas most of the time, to me, it was like staring into black paint.

"You learn to read the shadows." He paused. "That, and being at about five hundred of these attacks."

He drove into Fisherman's Bay. "No shooting the Gap today," I noted. The surge channel was engulfed in foam.

"Not unless you want another character-building experience."

The sky was closing in. "We're done," Peter said absentmindedly, adding, "You can drop me at North Landing." He was focused on listening to the ninth inning, so he didn't catch the color draining from my face. This offhanded instruction, *drop me at North Landing,* had huge implications. It was not unlike someone casually saying, "Jump when the plane hits thirty-five thousand feet" or "Pass me that eyeball."

To complete this routine task, I would have to do advanced nautical things. I'd have to maneuver the whaler in North Landing's pinched entrance, between sets of breakers, steering close enough to the rocks for Peter to jump off, and then nimbly exiting before the next swell barreled in. This would require skillful reverse driving, with no accidental shifts into neutral. Then, as the light fell, I would have to return to *Just Imagine,* align the whaler in fifteen-knot winds, and tie it off. I had never docked alongside the sailboat without at least one person helping, reaching out and grabbing hold of a bumper or a line. And even with assistance, those attempts had not been pretty.

What choice did I have? I tightened my grip on the wheel and went for it. It took five passes before Peter was near enough to shore to leap off, and even then he had to scramble a bit, and water slopped over the top of his boots. There was a brief ricochet off the rocks and an uncomfortable whining noise when I hit reverse a little too hard. It could have been worse. I'm pleased to say, however, that the docking was perfect. Although somehow the whaler's railing got ripped off.

SCOT AND I SAT IN THE SUN ON *JUST IMAGINE,* UPWIND OF THE HISSING fixture, drinking a brand of beer called Red Seal. The beer's slogan was "Vita Brevis," and even though the seal on the label still possessed its head, there couldn't possibly have been a more appropriate beer for the Farallones if a microbrewery itself had sprung up at the base of Lighthouse Hill. Scot had arrived yesterday, looking handsome and feral and as though he'd never spent a day indoors in his life, and damned if the weather didn't change on a dime. Wind slackened, fog blew off, clouds bleached away their tarnish. An experienced fisherman and deckhand, Scot knew his way around boats. After examining the whaler's splintered edges, torn railing, and walloped side, he'd taken one look at *Just Imagine*'s mooring and shaken his head: No. Peter visibly relaxed. He'd expressed relief to me when Scot had arrived, that now there was "someone else to shoulder the responsibility of all this." "All this," I was acutely aware, meant me and the sailboat.

We had to move *Just Imagine* over to East Landing in any case; when the maintenance project kicked into high gear, and the Chinook helicopters roared in to pick up the debris, they would be flying low over Fisherman's Bay, and the vortex from their rotors would whip the surface into a gin fizz. The sailboat couldn't be there. The copters would be zooming into a tight pickup zone and then slinging several tons of old timbers overhead; no one was prepared to guarantee that this operation would go off without a hitch. I envisioned a one-hundred-foot log dropping from the sky and spearing *Just Imagine*'s deck.

Scot had spent yesterday afternoon cleaning and checking his gear, meticulously arranging all the equipment he'd need. In a place this chaotic, things could go sideways in an instant, and he'd witnessed enough trouble to know that thoughtful preparation was important. I admired this philosophy. Somehow, though, I hadn't managed to incorporate it into life on *Just Imagine*, a seat-of-the-pants existence surrounded by broken systems and random upsets.

Today the three of us had hit the water with Seal Baby, a decoy Scot had fashioned out of gray carpet. In the past, Seal Baby had been attacked virtually every time it was dropped into the water. When I admired its lifelike appearance, Scot flashed a smile. "It looks like a seal, baby!"

One great thing about the carpet seal: When it was mauled, as it was so often, Scot didn't have to see its terror, or its awareness of impending death. The fact that Seal Baby had no face, no eyes that could bulge to the size of cocktail coasters when scared, that was ideal, and part of the decoy's design. Despite his obvious lack of queasiness, Scot hated to witness suffering and had remained affected for years by the image of a sea lion he'd once seen trying to exit the water with half its body missing. Around here, you didn't have to look far to find a fate that painful. Ron had once watched, horrified, as a baby elephant seal that was being pursued by a shark tried with every ounce of its strength to scramble aboard the *GW*, the panic seared into its bewhiskered little face. Ten days ago, Kevin and I had rowed Tubby into a pocket cove so we could examine a shark-bitten sea lion that had managed to drag itself onto the rocks. The animal had three furrows raked across its torso, each at least two inches deep. The wounds were extreme, though the sea lion would likely survive them; these creatures managed to heal from the most vicious maimings, like torn and mangled lumps of Silly Putty that, when squeezed together, somehow became whole again. Not without visible agony, however, and we were struck by the emotion on the creature's face. Its eyes blinked slowly and sadly, and it gave off a deeply resigned air as flies burrowed into its wounds.

This morning under restless but sunny skies we'd cruised Mirounga Bay and Indian Head, and trolled around on the east side too, accompanied by about fifty humpbacks, fifteen blues, and my gray whale. Seal Baby stayed in the boat; deploying it was Scot's call, and he was preoccupied with another passion. "Look at all the crazy invertebrates!" he said, leaning over the side with a plastic measuring cup, reaching to scoop up one of the countless types of comb jellies that lived in these waters.

Along with the toadstool-shaped yellow and orange *Chrysaora* jellyfish that migrated past the islands, most of which were larger than a human head, there were platoons and battalions of smaller, weirder jellied critters. Their names were tongue-twisting mouthfuls—heteropods, ctenophores, siphonophores, scyphomedusae—and floating around next to the boat they looked like tiny science-fiction characters. Before I came to the Farallones I'd never heard of these animals, which isn't surprising—they are as evanescent as soap bubbles.

The jellies living nearest the surface had transparent bodies, but their edges twinkled and flashed, as though traced by fiber-optic cables, blinking and undulating like neon signs. They were delicate; if you weren't looking for them, you'd easily miss them hovering, but once you realized they were there, you could never stop seeing them. They came in a boggling array of shapes and sizes and colors—from the *praya* siphonophore, a filament made of hundreds of individuals (think of a chain of people holding hands) that could exceed 120 feet in length, to the gumball-size sea goose-berry. Some resembled elephants with glowing eyes, and some looked like rabbits whose floppy ears swept prey into their mouths. Some were wing-shaped; some looked like they were made of zippers; others brought to mind elaborate, psychedelic spaceships. Many of them stung, including the siphonophore known as the Portuguese man o' war, and all of them were car-nivorous predators who survived by eating plankton, fish larvae, and each other.

In their element they were hearty little cannibals, but their ge-latinous bodies collapsed when caught in a net. Scientists could only hope to bring them up in a pail or a glass container, carefully raising them to the surface suspended in water. Even that method didn't work much of the time, though; the jellies still deflated or shuddered into pieces, and besides, some species were completely transparent and eluded all capture. None of them preserved well; in many instances, the animal could be studied only in photo-graphs, or by someone floating next to it in the water. And that, too, was difficult—many of them lived at great depths.

Scot dipped the cup into the water and came up with a strand of minuscule red dots suspended in what looked like a clear piece of spaghetti. It was a siphonophore, one that had a light but wicked sting. "I want to feel it," Peter said, rolling up his sleeve to expose the soft skin inside his forearm.

"If you really want to feel it Pete, put it on your eye," Scot said.

He placed a glob of it on Peter's arm and then touched the filament to his own wrist. "Susan? Do you want to feel it?"

I put out my wrist. It stung, but not that much. Anyway, it hurt less than rope burn, which I'd already received this morning.

Peter held his arm up to Scot's and mine. "It's a bonding thing." Scot looked away uncomfortably. I was beginning to sense that he didn't think much of the yacht arrangement. Complex logistics—the kind of juggling act that Peter thrived on and the convoluted set of circumstances that brought me here—bugged him. He did not invite distraction: not from me, not from the motley fraternity of coast guard contractors who'd descended upon the island, not from the world's relentless fascination with the group of sharks he studied. I'd noticed that, while Peter often gave public talks about the sharks and referred to them with personal pronouns—"White-slash is one of our biggest females"—as though it was just one big happy family out here, Scot was guarded, keeping his shark experiences tight to his vest, reserving them for scientific papers and for special occasions. When he was at the Farallones, his attention was directed 100 percent toward the natural world. Though he was always friendly, I recognized that a journalist's presence was an extra concern that he could've done without.

The siphonophore glistened in the measuring cup as Scot held it up to the sun. Back on the island he had built several Plexiglas aquariums, which he'd arranged against a black background so that the jellies stood out. When the shark action was slow, he studied the ctenophores and the siphonophores and the salps ("a completely unappreciated life-form"), videotaping them and tinkering endlessly with the lighting. The resulting films were magnificent, as intricate and luminous as the creatures themselves.

"How about giving Seal Baby a bath?" Peter asked. We were not exactly beating off the sharks. Scot seemed reluctant to set out the carpet seal, though he didn't give a reason. "It definitely doesn't feel active," he said, sniffing the air, laser eyes scanning the water, taking it all in. "But I've seen years when it's started out slow, and then it *rocks*."

• • •

"SEAS TEN FEET AT TEN SECONDS," THE WEATHER VOICE HAD AN-
nounced yesterday morning. "Winds fifteen to twenty-five knots."
The promised weather from Point Arena showed up around din-
nertime, and all night the boats continued to try to destroy each
other, the whaler fighting back with the jagged edge of its railing.
As usual, I got slapped around too. We'd planned to move *Just
Imagine* in the next couple of days; it couldn't be soon enough. I
was hanging on by my fingertips, I felt, in Fisherman's Bay. In a
moment of paranoia last night, I had pulled out my notebook and
written in block letters: "THIS COVE WANTS ME GONE."

The Voice weighed in with another Small Craft Warning tonight,
with conditions predicted to deteriorate further tomorrow, and
then it laughed, a long, diabolical machine cackle. Okay, it may not
have laughed. But given my dread-filled and sleepless nights of
late, this was demoralizing news. And there was no end in sight.
The long-range forecast, which came from another channel, was
beyond grim.

Things were tense in general. Yesterday the *Patriot* had approached us, one of the skippers waving chummily as though
they'd hoped to pull alongside and shoot the breeze, and Scot's
face had turned to stone as he pointed the whaler in the opposite
direction and hit the throttle. I was somewhat surprised. Recently,
it had seemed that the relationship between the shark researchers
and the cage divers was thawing slightly. In fact, earlier in the
week the crew of the *Patriot* had actually hailed us to point out a
shark attack that was happening beside them. Peter and I had
zoomed over to Mirounga and seen three sharks jetting around, including an outsized Rat Packer named Cal Ripfin. Cal was easily
identified because the top of his dorsal fin was chewed off, the result of trying to snitch a carcass from one of the Sisters last season.

For years now, though, Scot had held out the hope that the same
frustrations that had shuttered the other cage-diving operations
would get to this one. That wasn't happening. On the contrary,

Groth was building his business, adding dive dates to the Farallon schedule.

And it was disconcerting on the island, everyone felt, having all these contractors running around with demolition tools, hosting spare rib barbecues, and chain-smoking. The biologists had nicknamed them: there was Fat Bob, Old Bob, Lumpy Bob, Noriega, and the Drunk Guy, among others. Each of the houses contained an entirely separate culture, and the two were coexisting uneasily. Everyone was snappish. I wasn't in the best mood, either. Conditions had not improved aboard the bad ship *Just Imagine*. The plumbing was spewing frightening substances, voltage buzzers continued to wail, and the repertoire of distressing noises had expanded dramatically. Sunshine had been scarce; I'd spent entire days in the chop and gloom, without so much as a peanut butter sandwich. In fact, my food supplies were now a fond memory. I hadn't even gotten a rockfish lately.

"I'm reaching my breaking point," I told Peter.

"I can see that."

It was time to trot out the question I'd been practicing for the last twenty-four hours: Could I sleep at the lighthouse for a night? Underlying my request was a distinct sense of panic. Call it claustrophobia or chalk it up to tattered nerves—if I could just have one solid night's sleep, one chance to pull myself together, then I could face the yacht again. I was banking, of course, on him being too kind to refuse the request. I was right; he agreed to look the other way while I snuck up there. It was decided that I would row ashore just before nightfall and then scale the backside of Lighthouse Hill with extreme stealth. The evening offered a ready-made diversion: the Oakland A's were playing the Boston Red Sox in a crux game, and everyone would be glued to the TV in the coast guard house, hunkered down with large bowls of chips.

At dusk, the water in Fisherman's Bay was a surly mess, and I stood on deck, watching Tubby tossing around. The jump from *Just Imagine* down into the rowboat was an unpleasant flier, but it had to be done. Crouching as low as possible, I dropped in, hoping that a wave wouldn't jostle the craft aside at the last second. This was my debut at Tubby's helm. As I reached for the oars, one of them flew from its oarlock and sailed off in the direction of Tower Point. Peter had warned me about this design flaw. One morning he'd lost both oars and been forced to lean over the side, paddling with his hands to fish them out. Retrieving the wayward oar, I rowed a jerky path to the landing. As I approached the barnacled rocks, I attempted to jump but ended up straddling instead, one foot on shore, one in the boat. At that moment a swell bowled in and knocked me down, but luckily it threw Tubby in my direction. Crawling, and dragging the rowboat, I made land.

I hadn't set foot on solid ground in thirteen days, and it showed. My balance was off, leaving me woozy and disoriented. I looked up. The evening sky was still mostly clear, but fog swirled at the lighthouse peak, and it was moving in fast. I began to climb.

The rocks were easy to grab on to but tended to crumble, and they were slippery, not to mention well stocked with angry, pecking gulls. Careful two-stepping was required to avoid crushing any seabird burrows. The top third of the climb, I noticed, was a chute. Though I'd done a little rock climbing, enough to have learned not to freak out when clinging to the side of a wall, this wasn't going so well. I kept swaying and losing my bearings. Below, the waves churned into North Landing. I imagined eggs tumbling, bodies flailing. The cumbersome arrangement of gear on my back—sleeping bag, DreamTime Therm-a-Rest, and knapsack—didn't help. My center of gravity felt as though it was somewhere near the back of my neck.

I'd just begun the steepest part when my left hand slipped from its hold, causing a heart-in-mouth backward swoon before I recovered my balance. Afterward, I realized that it had been an extremely close call, so frightening that I couldn't afford to think about it at the time. But I did shoot a look over my shoulder at the place I would have fallen, a funnel of splintered rocks that deadended in a seething spit of ocean.

At the top, the wind was furious. I radioed Peter to confirm that

I'd made it. Leaving out the details of my near miss, I assured him I was fine, no problems. Except, I mentioned casually, it was so windy up here I might get blown off the edge. "Oh, I know how that whole deal works," he said, with a hint of impatience. "I've probably spent a few years of my life up there."

Gulls swooped by, performing aerobatic moves in the thermals. To the east, the ocean shimmered cold and metallic, untethered to Earth. To the south, the Perfect Wave was breaking beautifully, then pounding down mercilessly on the shallow rocks. Yesterday, while we drifted along Shark Alley, I had overheard Peter and Scot discussing it. They had both turned toward shore and were watching it break.

"I think you're on your own for that one," Scot had declared. "I ain't going."

"You won't even drive me?"

"Ah, I'll drop you off, I guess. But that means I'll have to *pick you up.*" His voice had an ominous tone. They both knew what the inflection meant.

Peter was silent for a moment. "No," he said. "If it comes to that, just leave me out there."

I tossed my sleeping bag inside the door. Dust and grit coated everything. A loud humming filled the air; the industrial batteries that powered the lighthouse lined an entire wall. I was reminded of a low-budget horror movie—this was the soundtrack of insanity. Above the batteries, urgent-looking signs warned of mishaps involving explosions and battery acid.

The only place to sleep that wasn't out of the question in terms of active vermin and extreme creepiness was right in the doorway, wedged in beside the bank of acid-spewing batteries. The passageway was just wide enough for the deluxe Therm-a-Rest. The alternative, moving farther back into the structure, would mean sleeping in the old lighthouse tower itself, with its abandoned spiral staircase and its trapped, suffocating air. At least near the door, I could bolt if I had to. I stepped outside, into a small sheltered spot. Edging around the side, both hands clamped on the railing, I

looked down through backside fog that was pooling at North Landing. The curtain had fallen; *Just Imagine* was no longer visible. This
was dirtier weather, closing in. I wondered how much longer I
could stick it out.

I stood in the doorway, wrapped in my sleeping bag, as the light
drained away and the indigo-black night came up, and the harsh
beauty of the landscape was replaced by the terrible beauty of the
elements. The lights from the houses shone with warmth. A dozen
people sat down there, eating dinner and talking baseball; they had
no idea they were being watched. Later, Scot and Peter would be
drinking Jack Daniel's and poring over shark video. Up here: the
Farallon equivalent of the lunatic in the attic. All I needed was a
white dress.

A three-quarter moon rose, with Mars like a bodyguard beside
it, glowing red. Gull feathers tumbled by in the gale. The sea and
the sky had melted into each other, and now they were just nuanced tones of infinity, dual voids. Overhead, the lighthouse beacon rotated. It was hard not to imagine that I was standing at the
very end of the world; that there was nothing but water, and after
that, more water, and that all the land was gone.

CHAPTER 10

The forecasts went from small craft advisories to gale force
winds during that day. Hazardous seas. Wind. Cold. Rain.
—FARALLON PATROL LOG, "NIGHTMARE!"
—*THE CORMORANT*, SPRING 1983

OCTOBER 7–9, 2003

Peter knocked on the lighthouse door at 7:30 a.m. I was asleep, but
barely. The floor was bulletproof cement covered with planked
wood, hard enough to bounce pennies, and the DreamTime
Therm-a-Rest had failed to deliver on its promise of decadent com-
fort. The wind was not quiet up here, nor was the buzzing phalanx
of batteries. All night, mice had played tag on top of my sleeping
bag, and I could tell by the way my head was itching that I had
bird lice. Opening the door, I stepped into total, disorienting fog.
Everything outside a six-foot radius had dissolved into a ghostly
ether. Peter stood there holding a container of orange juice and a
banana. "You can go back to sleep if you want," he said, looking
somewhat alarmed by my appearance. I ran my hand through my
hair to make sure nothing was nesting in it. "Sharkwatch is canceled until the fog lifts."

There was an advantage to being socked in. As long as the view
from below was obscured, I could slink down the front-side trail
rather than having to descend the cliff out back. And I was not

anxious to repeat this route, especially after having had time to consider yesterday's slip. I squinted into the mist. It would be better to hightail it back to the boat now, under cover of fog.

Peter and I agreed that, in thirty minutes, I would steal down the path and meet him at North Landing. He'd then make a round-trip in Tubby, depositing me on *Just Imagine* and returning to the island. Later this morning, he and Scot would row back out. We had to move the sailboat today. If the fog lifted, the helicopters would be arriving, and by the time they got here Fisherman's Bay needed to be obstacle-free.

I made my way down the zigzag trail. Although I was scurrying through zero visibility in a half crouch, running low and, I imagined, with cat-burglar finesse, the going was easier this time. For one thing, I'd jettisoned the DreamTime, stashed it in the cobwebby recesses of the old tower. Approaching the midway notch in Lighthouse Hill, where I could drop over to a manageable part of the backside, I skidded on some rocks and stumbled, ripping the knee out of my pants.

Somehow, I thought, picking myself up and wiping away the dirt and blood, this lighthouse foray hadn't been the respite I'd hoped for. I was still dizzy with fatigue, and rubber-legged on land, and now I was going back to the spiteful yacht.

The fog persisted. At noon, Tubby poked a hole through the murk, and I tied her to the side as Scot and Peter climbed aboard the yacht. I was anxious to put Fisherman's Bay in the rearview mirror, but the logistics were daunting: disconnecting the linguine of ropes, pulling up the cantankerous anchor chain, and then actually having to drive the beast. While Scot searched for the windlass to bring up the anchor, Peter drove the whaler to the buoy and untied the ropes. Surprisingly, none of this took much time, and suddenly we were at sea, with Scot standing confidently at the wheel and the yacht acting momentarily subdued, as Tubby and the whaler surfed along behind us.

As our shark flotilla rounded Shubrick Point, a ship named *White Holly* came into view. The 133-foot vessel had been hired by the

Fish and Wildlife Service to lug away the debris; the helicopters would winch their loads down onto its deck. *White Holly* resembled a miniature container ship, squat and strong as a sumo wrestler. Its ropes were slung around the East Landing buoy. The best anchorage for *Just Imagine* was right beside it, on Hurst Shoal, a reef that lay halfway between the buoy and Saddle Rock, 150 yards from shore. I liked this: The houses were visible from here, and I was pleased by the idea of being next to the bigger boat (although in truth it was just another object that the yacht could potentially slam into). Somehow the presence of other people, especially those with nautical expertise, was reassuring.

Scot anchored the sailboat effortlessly, providing sharp contrast to the circus atmosphere that had surrounded our original mooring, although he was disconcerted to find that *Just Imagine*'s anchor chain was unmarked, forcing a blind guess as to how much of its length had been paid out; you could be right at the end of your tether and not know it. This was peculiar, and sort of unsafe, and likely the reason the anchor had almost slipped off as Tom had deployed it. But Scot knew the water here better than anyone, with the possible exception of Ron, and he'd carefully estimated the depth and monitored the chain as it slid to the ocean floor.

Securing a boat was never easy, Scot noted, adding that mariners often described anchoring as the "test of a relationship." Typically, the process was a contentious matter involving widely divergent opinions about where and how. No one was arguing about it right now, though. This was a far better arrangement. *Just Imagine* was no longer double-tied, leaving its back end free to move with the currents and the wind. And even though at first glance the new parking spot appeared more exposed, with the wind coming from the northwest, we were actually in a lee created by the island itself. Instantly I could feel the difference, and the sailboat behaved more like a sailboat and less like an angry, lassoed animal.

Avoiding the places on deck that smelled like dead cattle, the three of us sat waiting to see if the helicopters would show up. The marine layer of fog was melting away, though the lighthouse was still engulfed. Among the contractor crew, there was a high level of motivation to wrap up this project and get the hell out of here. The weather wasn't making the Farallones any new friends, and some of them had been bunking in the coast guard house for ten days, which was about nine days longer than they preferred.

"The problem in Fisherman's Bay was that the sailboat wasn't just pitching, it was *surging*," Scot said. "And you know that's gonna be—" He stopped midsentence. "What's that shark doing?" I turned. The animal was about thirty yards west of us, with both its dorsal and tail fins on the surface. Its entire back arched out of the water, as though it was trying to tug something up from below. "I don't see a seal," Peter said, focusing his binoculars. Scot dispatched Seal Baby; the shark skirmished with its mystery prey again and then dove, returning briefly to take a pass at the decoy before bolting nervously.

"Tubby will definitely get visited in this spot," Peter predicted.

"I think you're right," Scot said, noting that rowing back from here was out of the question. We were anchored in a high-traffic area, a sort of shark thoroughfare between the seals piled in the East Landing gulches and the seals perched on Saddle Rock. It was a stretch of ocean that had hosted some fairly dramatic events.

I thought of a story that Peter had told me earlier, an almost unbelievable tale of negligence involving a charter boat named the *New Holiday II*. One fall afternoon it had emerged out of nowhere, pulled up to East Landing, and disgorged twenty plump, seal-shaped tourists, who'd jumped into the water and begun to snorkel. Peter had been at the lighthouse that day and remembers gaping in disbelief through the scope, feeling faint, screaming into the radio: "*New Holiday II*!! *New Holiday II*!! Get out of the water!! REPEAT: GET. OUT. OF. THE. WATER!" He considered calling for a medevac helicopter, as one was sure to be needed. To this day he doesn't know if the captain heard his transmission, broadcasting blind across the emergency frequency, or—more likely—whether one of the tourists saw one of the sharks. But as Peter watched helplessly from the light, the snorkelers scrambled onto the boat in a panic and the *New Holiday II* shot off, never to be seen again. On this exact spot, Swissy, the rehabilitated sea lion, hadn't been quite so lucky, nor had many of Scot's surfboards.

As the afternoon wore on, the fog remained parked over the island, and it was shortly confirmed that the helicopter operation had been postponed until tomorrow. We cracked open a round of Red Seal ale, and I was about to launch into my usual list of questions, aimed mainly at trying to get Scot and Peter to reminisce about encounters with the Sisterhood, when we noticed that over on *White Holly,* a shark cage was being lowered into the water.

A bikini-clad woman and a guy holding a cumbersome camera were wedged inside it, looking decidedly unsteady. Neither person was wearing a wetsuit as they plunged into the fifty-five-degree water. We watched the cage being rocked on its side by the swells and careening against the ship's hull. "Well, they won't be in there very long," I observed.

"What the . . . ?" Peter radioed to ask what they were doing. A whiskey-voiced woman replied with the explanation that they were shooting "promotional" photographs. Sure enough, the cage was hauled back onto the boat in less than a minute, and its occupants staggered back onto *White Holly'*s deck, looking shaken.

Later, in the logbook, Peter noted that this event reminded him of "Miss Universe's visit in 1984." On that occasion, he had been assigned to accompany the reigning beauty queen on a tour of the island that was supposed to have been capped off by a brief dunking in a shark cage for the cameras. The weather, however, had been uncooperative, and Miss Universe had remained on land. Her loss: Peter had intended to drive the Dinner Plate across Hurst Shoal, where we were anchored right now, and she might have encountered an exceptionally friendly Sister named Whiteslash.

Eighteen-foot Whiteslash, described by Peter as "gentle and maternal," was an accommodating shark, eager to investigate the whaler, which she had learned to associate with food. The lesson—and it took only one—happened in 1996 as Scot and Peter floated next to a freshly killed seal, waiting for its claimant to return. Thirty minutes passed, and then Whiteslash arrived, all four thousand pounds of her, tucking into the food while the researchers filmed. When the feeding was winding down and the guys turned to leave, the shark dropped the last scraps of her meal and followed them. Peter and Scot were astonished; this was something new. They could only guess that she hadn't made the kill herself but had been lucky enough to stumble across it in the presence of the whaler. And from that point on, when the research boat passed through her territory, Whiteslash would often materialize, swimming up to the stern hopefully, in anticipation of another seal. Her clockwork appearances and laid-back personality made her the perfect ambassador for the Shark Project, and on various occasions Peter drove visiting dignitaries out to see her. Whiteslash, he recalled, was enormous, wide as a bus, and liked to hang off the back of the boat, "smiling."

NEXT MORNING THE SUN WAS UP, AS WAS THE WIND, AND THE national guard Chinooks swept in like the Valkyries. Peter and Scot were onshore, and I had positioned myself at *Just Imagine*'s stern to watch the whole spectacle. As planned, shark work had been temporarily suspended, and so, of course, in true defiant shark fashion there had already been an attack today, with a big splashy breach, less than fifty yards from *White Holly*'s bow. I'd just climbed on deck with my coffee when it happened, and had seen the white flash of the shark's belly as it leapt and then heard the whiskey-voiced woman barking across the public address system: "It's showtime! Everyone to your stations. Shark attack off starboard!" A crowd of people leaned over *White Holly*'s rail, shouting and pointing in the direction of the attack, while a blood slick crept toward the island and the thick mammalian oil smell leaked into the air, fanned by helicopter rotors. Despite the effort it had made to catch its meal, and all the spectators waiting to watch it dine, the shark never returned, and the neglected carcass floated out to sea.

The radio trilled. It was Peter, relaying a request from *White Holly's* photographer, who hoped to position himself on *Just Imagine* so he could snap yet more promotional pictures of his ship in action. "Sure, whatever," I said, and then watched as a Dinner Plate–size contraption shuttled in my direction. There were two men on board: a wiry guy who looked to be in his seventies and introduced himself as Crazy Louie, and Karl, a twenty-something redhead with a soul patch, overloaded with several bulky camera cases. They had both seen the shark breach and were anxious to get out of their small boat, and they flung themselves aboard *Just Imagine*, firing questions. "If there's one attack, does that mean there will be another?" Karl asked, his voice tight with adrenaline. "Now that I've seen one shark, I need to see more. Will you ask those biologists if they need a photographer?"

I had a few questions of my own. Last night, deep into the wee hours, I'd heard whoops and guffaws and the sounds of raucous festivities echoing across the water from *White Holly.* That, in combination with yesterday's photo shoot involving the bikini-clad woman, had piqued my curiosity. "What are you guys *doing* over there? And what's up with that shark cage?" I asked Crazy Louie.

"Oh, that. Photo shoot. Very poorly planned out. Very dangerous," he answered, waving his hand dismissively and then proceeding to recite a poem, something about biting a grizzly bear "in the balls." As he regaled me, the helicopters hovered, churning up a whirlpool of backwash, and then, out of nowhere it seemed, six fighter planes thundered by in formation, buzzed the island, and boomeranged back over the skyline as quickly as they'd come. Hundreds of sea lions, frightened by the noise, stampeded into the water. Startled, I hailed Peter. "What was *that?*"

"The Blue Angels," he said. "Practicing for Fleet Week. What a nightmare. They're not supposed to fly this close to the island. I'm going to write a citation."

"Ask him if I can come ashore to talk to them about sharks," Karl said, nudging me.

The Chinooks had been saddled with oil tanks and massive timbers, and they yawed over *White Holly*, trying to deposit them. Craning my neck to watch the loads swaying back and forth above, while the sailboat rocked in the waves, I began to feel queasy. I stopped looking into the sky and focused my eyes on *White Holly*. It seemed as though someone had badly miscalculated how large a vessel would be needed for this job; there didn't appear to be much room for all the junk. At one point, the shark cage was smacked by a dangling diesel tank and crumpled in the middle like a crushed soda can. Bundles of steel swung crazily in midair, occasionally bashing the ship itself and almost taking out several of the deckhands. Crazy Louie flinched. "He's a talented captain, but young," he mused. "We've had a coupla close calls. . . . Oh! Would you look at that! Damn near took the rear fantail shroud off!"

Peter radioed to tell me there was an attack in Maintop Bay. "Not that we can get to it," he added. As the helicopters struggled, fuel ran low from all the hovering, and they signaled that they were done for the day, and planned to head back to the mainland. On the island, the biologists watched the contractors run for the last chopper like it was the fall of Saigon.

As they lifted off and veered to the east, Crazy Louie turned to me. "Come over tonight," he said. "And if you want, you can bring those biologists. We're going to have a big party."

"Yeah," Karl said. "Could they tell us a bit more about the sharks maybe?"

"But we're out of booze," Crazy Louie added. "Can you bring us some booze?"

"We're out of food too," Karl reminded him.

"No, we're not out of food! We've got food!"

"Well I guess we've got, like, some eggs and stuff."

"Over on the *White Holly,* we like our parties."

I declined as politely as possible, citing logistical problems: launching boats, night, sharks. As they shoved off in their runabout, I rushed down into the cabin, crawling into the captain's bunk and curling up in the fetal position. The last thing I wanted to do was attend a party on a boat. I wasn't sure if it was the seething turbulence from the Chinooks, or the motion of the boat in its new position, or the idea of egg-based snacks over on *White Holly,* or the apple I'd just eaten, but I had become seasick, a condition I'd feared for weeks.

After handling the Small Craft Warning nights and the days spent rolling around off Maintop and Indian Head, I didn't think that anything could bring this on, never mind a conversation or a piece of fruit. In fact, I'd become downright cocky about my seaworthiness and had stopped taking my daily Dramamine. *Mistake.* This was a distressing turn of events; seasickness raised the misery index to impossible levels. Darwin himself despaired over this state, referring to it as "no trifling evil." I lay there for an hour, occasionally running up on deck to retch over the side. Even with this additional distraction, I couldn't help but notice the lineup of iron-colored clouds, poised on the skyline like invaders. The wind was lying low for the moment, but I could sense it changing moods, preparing to sweep the ocean into disorderly swells.

The realization hit hard: I couldn't take another night of this. I turned toward the stern and considered Tubby, flailing away at the end of its tether. *I would do it; I'd row ashore.* I radioed Peter, sounding plaintive. I might have even cried. I told him that I was at the end of my rope, that the noises had started up anew, that I'd just realized I was anchored on the exact spot where the passenger ship *Lucas* had gone down, killing twenty-three. *"Mayday,"* I said. Uncle. Please. The Fish and Wildlife crew had gone—could I possibly come onto the island for a night? Just one? I would row ashore myself, I told him. The radio was cutting in and out, but I could hear the alarm in his voice. "No! *Do not* row across East Landing. Stay out of Tubby!" He did the humanitarian thing, as I'd known he would, and came out to fetch me in the whaler.

My legs felt wobbly, as though they didn't quite belong to the rest of my body, as I walked from East Landing to the house. The ground spun underfoot. Scot stood on the front steps. I told him that I had been seasick and now I was landsick. "Just go with it," he said. "You're going to be spinning for at least twenty-four hours. I think it's a good feeling, myself." I didn't. Sitting down made it worse, though, so I decided to go for a walk. This turned out to be an unfortunate move. An hour later, still disoriented, I returned to an empty house. As I sat in the kitchen, wondering where everybody was, Peter and Scot came in, flushed and happy, and told me that I'd missed a great attack. Where had I been? While I was ambling around in search of equilibrium, there had been a glorious sunset hit in Mirounga Bay. One of the sharks in attendance was the infamous Gouge, killer of Swissy, the rehabilitated sea lion. They had recognized Gouge immediately, due to the three distinctive scars on his head. Last year the wounds were fleshy and raw, but they'd healed neatly and Gouge was back on the job. Scot had tagged him, and for an hour they drifted in Mirounga Bay as the light fell and various sharks swooped in to check them out. They sat down at the kitchen table and cracked open beers, comparing notes on who they'd seen.

Everyone was exhausted from the helicopter rodeo and relieved that the island was back to its sparsely populated state. The contractors had cleared out so quickly, however, that much of their gear had been left behind. Several lumpish bundles still sat on the helipad, and tomorrow, apparently, another chopper would return to collect this pallet of personal effects and residual trash.

I brightened slightly at dinner, perhaps due to the fact that it was my first hot meal in a depressingly long time. "I'm back from the edge," I thought, reaching for a third helping of enchiladas. "Things can only get better from here."

In the journal it was noted that today's new arrivals had included a burrowing owl and a white-throated sparrow, as well as a dozen humpbacks and thirty blue whales, but the real news was that it had been a three-attack day, the first of the season. October and November both provided their share of multiple feeding events, but so far this season the sharks had been hitting singles. Typically, the action came in waves; sometimes things would be eerily quiet, and at other times there was hardly a moment to spare between attacks. Under livelier conditions, it wasn't uncommon to encounter four or five individuals at a carcass, all of them amped up from the presence of blood and eager to sniff around at the whaler. In fact, the researchers would sometimes have to back away from the scene because things were getting, in Scot's words, "too hot."

"Well, we've got at least one hungry shark out there," Scot said. "Gouge was really interested in the boat."

According to Kristie and Elias, who'd seen it, the Maintop attack had involved an impressive amount of blood, which quickly dispersed in the fifteen-knot winds. I described the breach near *White Holly* and the ensuing shark fever on board, as well as the urgent requests for Peter and Scot to head out there—with a case of beer or two, preferably—and deliver a shark talk.

That night I had a luxurious and restful sleep, free of unexplained jolts and collision bangs. The sense of relief lasted until precisely eight o'clock the next morning when Peter stuck his head in the door to inform me that it was blowing thirty-five knots of wind with a monster swell. "I don't think we're going anywhere today," he said. At dawn, he and Scot had listened, speechless, as the Weather Voice reported waves at the Point Arena buoy measuring nineteen feet at eighteen seconds.

I couldn't believe what I was hearing. We'd suspected that more wind was heading our way, but where had *this* come from? This was rogue weather, mighty and freakish. And none of it had been predicted by the Weather Voice. I looked outside. Roiling white breakers filled the window.

As violent storms went, this one was improbably pretty. The water glittered in a spectrum of blue under cloudless turquoise skies, and everything that wasn't sparkling was frothing. Maintop wore a whitewater cape, and Fisherman's Bay was a chaos of foam and waves. In front of the houses, surf heaved against the marine terrace, sending up a gauzy veil of mist. If you managed to ignore the gale-force winds, the snarling whitecaps, the fact that the ocean was heaped twenty feet higher than usual, and the stomach-flipping vision of the borrowed yacht getting mauled out front—well, it would've been a lovely day.

Yet as terrifying as it was to watch *Just Imagine* getting buffaloed at East Landing, it was immediately obvious that the sailboat wouldn't have survived even an hour of this storm double-tied in Fisherman's Bay. The force of the swells was immense, and today the Gap looked like Niagara Falls. It was as though the ocean was vacuuming, sucking away anything grimy or stagnant or stuck. Even the seals were being rearranged. As the surf fire-hosed the rocks, the gulleys were blasted clean and every last inhabitant was swept out to sea, creating a windfall for the sharks. I pictured them trolling enthusiastically along the shoreline as seals and sea lions pinwheeled off the island. Earlier this morning, Kristie had seen a young harbor seal with its hind end bitten off attempting to drag itself back up onto the marine terrace.

Getting dressed doesn't take very long when you sleep in your clothes, so in no time I was clawing my way up to the lighthouse, where Scot stood on Sharkwatch. Stepping out of the door, I was walloped by wind like I'd never felt before, demon gusts that could rip you from earth and deposit you in Oz at their leisure. The only way to get through it was to literally double over, bending at a ninety-degree angle from the waist.

I was almost blown from the path several times and was reminded of the old lighthouse keepers' claims that, during storms, they'd crawled this route. After three weeks aboard *Just Imagine,* I'd had my fill of crawling, but the Farallones seemed to demand full-time submission. At the top, Scot sat in a metal folding chair against the wall, hands jammed into his pockets, hoodie wrapped tightly around his head. "It's really nasty out here, that's all I have to say," he said, as I crouched beside him. "It's humbling to think about what it'd be like on that sailboat right now."

From up here the visibility was so magnificent that you could practically see the curve of the earth. I took intermittent peeks through the scope at *Just Imagine* spiking in the tumult, half expecting to see it turn a cartwheel at any moment. Now, it was alone out there. *White Holly* had departed earlier, after radioing a warning to the island that "the weather's only going to get worse."

Every few minutes Peter radioed, sounding nervous. "I think the sailboat has drifted. It's definitely slipped."

Scot shook his head. "And what do you think you're gonna do about it, Pete?" he said, exasperated, with the transmit button released. "It's a *storm*. Hey, let's go down there and almost get killed!" He turned to me. "This is what I do. I let him think it out."

He clicked on the radio: "Okay, I'll go take a look." Scot rose from his post and walked to the railing, looking over at East Landing and the boat. Then he came back to the shelter of the wall. "It has definitely slipped."

"Do you think we should put a rope on it?"

"You're not getting anywhere near that buoy today. It'll take your hand off."

"I think I'd feel better if it was double-tied to the buoy," Peter persisted.

"The weather's pretty serious." Scot's voice was measured and calm, but it had an intractable edge. "I don't think we should do anything in haste." Using the landing today, we all knew, would be an invitation to disaster.

When Scot went down for lunch, I stayed at the light, taking a shift. Walking around the tower's exposed perimeters in this wind was not advised, but I snuck a look around the side and noticed that Middle Farallon was underwater, completely submerged by waves, just a white, surging hump. I'd heard rumors about this happening during noteworthy storms—also that surf sometimes broke *over the top* of forty-foot-high Saddle Rock—tales that had formerly seemed abstract and possibly even exaggerated. Apparently not.

As I was wrapping up my two hours, I noticed that a pint-size helicopter had touched down on the island; it was here, obviously, to retrieve the contractors' remaining gear. The craft looked about as sturdy as a packing crate, and watching it getting cuffed around by wind was only slightly less terrifying than training the scope on *Just Imagine.* Clearly, the air version of the Weather Voice had also blown the call—what were they doing here in a gale? Two men struggled onto the helipad and attached the netted bundles to a sling that hung from the struts. The helicopter whirled into the sky, hauling a load that appeared heavier than the machine itself. No more than ten seconds after liftoff, as it swung over Mirounga Bay, a gust hit, the chopper tipped dramatically onto its left side, the sling released, and every last bit of cargo went hurtling into the sea.

It all seemed to unwind in slow motion. And the helicopter hadn't paused for a second when this happened; it had made a beeline for the mainland and was already out of sight. Now the water was dotted with a bobbing herd of objects. I could make out a bright blue cooler, along with oil barrels, plastic kerosene containers, and some large white scraps of plastic. Kristie appeared at the top step to the lighthouse. She'd seen the helicopter's load crater into the ocean too. "Did they *mean* for that to happen?" she asked, looking stunned. I radioed down, in case everyone else missed it: "The helicopter just dropped everything. Everything! Right over Shark Alley."

At the house I found Peter standing in the living room, staring at the rafts of garbage tangled in the surf. The wind wailed like a siren. "Everything's just crazy right now," he said, almost in a whisper, as if to himself.

Trying to be reassuring, I said, "The sailboat looks like it's handling it."

He perked up and nodded. "That steel hull and all. And, you know, I think the swell might be coming down."

Personally, I'd been thinking it was getting bigger. But I didn't say so.

The front door burst open, and a rush of wind swept into the house. "It's fucking raging out there!" Scot said, fighting the door closed. The wind gauge, he told us, was reading forty-knot winds with gusts up to fifty.

"We're in a full-on gale," Peter said.

The Weather Voice prattled on in the background: "Point Arena buoy: seas nineteen feet at thirteen seconds." That stopped the conversation cold. *White Holly*'s prediction had been right—it was getting worse. Scot sank into the couch. "We've got the wind *and* the swells. This is about as bad as it ever gets out here."

"Let's go wrangle some plastic," Peter said, trying to shake off his mood. "I need to do something physical." The three of us headed across the wind-scoured marine terrace toward the water, where a vast yard sale of junk had begun to wash ashore. Peter kept trying out scenarios for making it to the sailboat.

"I think I could get a rope around that buoy," he said, as we walked.

Scot shook his head. "I don't think there's anything we can do, Pete," he said. "We can't take a boat out there."

The aptly named (for the moment, anyway) Sewer Gulch was sheltered from the pounding surf by a narrow channel, and many elephant seals had piled into it, coiled around one another and surrounded by hoses, cracked shards of Styrofoam, half-empty bottles of salad dressing, individually wrapped antacid tablets, single-serving envelopes of ketchup, mangled flip-flops, shredded tarps. The seals looked enormous and mightily pissed off. Without hesitating, Peter walked to the edge of the rocks and carefully lowered himself. At his approach the coven writhed and belched, rearranging their seal pile as if to better position its more aggressive members for a sortie.

After a moment they seemed to calm down, and Peter was able to roam among them, gathering the pulverized junk and passing it up. At around 5 p.m., Elias radioed down from Sharkwatch with disconcerting news: "Peter, just thought you might like to know: Little Tubby's flipped over. It's upside down." This was a blow, symbolic if nothing else, and Peter climbed out of the gulley and walked toward the landing to view Tubby's predicament for himself. Scot and I followed.

"I can't remember the last time something flipped out here," Scot said, looking across at the sailboat. Peter was silent, staring through his binoculars. There wasn't anything positive to say, really. *Just Imagine* was doing a frantic pogo, and Tubby was down for the count; I could see its flat white underside turtled in the surf. Ten seconds was about all we could stand to watch, and the three of us picked our way across the marine terrace, depositing the helicopter debris in piles near the house, before going inside.

Wind speed had risen to the point where the anemometer, a weather gauge positioned near East Landing, had broken into pieces, half of it sailing off into the sky. The Weather Voice delivered a continuous loop of information, though by now it had lost all credibility, and no one believed a word it said. And it had a lot to say, all of a sudden: "High surf advisory continues from Point Arena to Point Piedras Blancas. A series of strong systems have moved into the Pacific Northwest. In addition to the large swell, gale-force northwest winds are forecast over much of the coastal waters this evening, adding to the hazardous sea conditions. Mariners are urged to exercise *extreme caution*. Those in and near the surf zone should take necessary action to protect themselves and property from dangerous sea conditions."

We had been listening to the radio every single day and had never heard the Voice talk about anything but numbers. Certainly, it had never dispensed advice. The Voice had never before seemed agitated or perturbed, never so judiciously inclined. It was an alarming development.

"This is the Farallones," Peter said, lighting the stove. "You can never tell it what to do." He was making dinner, still wearing his jacket and his Giants cap, sweeping armfuls of half-eaten entrées out of the refrigerator and into a big pot. He sighed and leaned both elbows on the counter, looking out the kitchen window, which rattled and shook with every jolt of wind. Actually, the whole house seemed to be twisting.

As we sat down to eat, Peter pulled out the journals. "I'm not going to write that much about the helicopter incident," he said. "What's there to say? Buncha shit went in the drink." His eyes were red with exhaustion and stress. "It has been a trying day."

There had been two attacks today, both in Maintop, but the weather had sapped everyone's energy and details were few. Peter, who'd been on Sharkwatch duty for both, described them with haiku brevity: "Big sharks. Lotta thrashing. Everywhere. Red."

A fat and sinister moon hung over the ocean, making it somewhat easier to check on *Just Imagine*. Luckily I'd left the mast light on, and it was a simple thing to stick one's head out the front door every half hour, confirm that the light was jouncing around in the same place, and then duck into the house. Seemingly, the worst was over; it was a foregone conclusion that if the sailboat had survived this day, it would make it through the night. After dinner, everyone had turned in except for Kristie and me, and we sat in the living room, reading. I was buried in the journals again, deep into an account of a ship called *Grunt V* that had a near miss here in 1994. "Sea very lumpy," someone had written. "Rain squalls. At high water *Grunt V* hit submerged rocks. Damage to both props and rudders. Current and swells carried boat to northwest end of Fisherman's Bay—bounced and grounded broadside to breaking waves. 12 passengers stranded on Southeast Farallon. Called urgent Mayday." The account made for an uncomfortable reminder about the sailboat, and at ten o'clock I dashed out, glimpsed the mast light, watched it gyrating for a second, and dashed back in. "*Just Imagine* is still out there!" I wrote in my notebook. "THANK YOU THANK YOU THANK YOU."

At 10:45 the day's fatigue caught up with me, and I was about to turn in, but instead of heading straight up the stairs, I found myself opening the front door for one last yacht check. I fully expected to see the mast light; this final peek was just for good measure.

Stepping outside and down the front steps, I hunched to meet the wind's blast. The sky was overloaded with stars; they seemed crammed into every square inch of the night. Which is why it took me a moment to get my bearings—which glittering pinprick belonged to the mast light? Confused, I looked to where it had been only forty-five minutes earlier and couldn't spot it. I stared harder. It wasn't there. Surely this is a mistake, I told myself. My night vision, some sort of delusion. I tore barefoot down the cart path, into the teeth of the gale. There was no mast light. There was no sailboat. In shock, I sprinted back to the house and flew up the stairs. "The mast light is gone! The boat is gone!" I turned and ran back down to the landing with Peter and Scot on my heels. We looked out. Waves churned over the anchorage, but the entire area was barren, yachtless. "*Where the hell did it go?*" I yelled. And then we saw it: a barely visible twinkle of *Just Imagine*'s only light, galloping over the horizon.

CHAPTER 11

OCTOBER 10–11, 2003

The ocean is filled with unfinished stories: endings with unknown beginnings, blind guesses where there are usually facts. On a blustery and frigid December day in 1981, the nineteenth to be exact, a yellow surfboard washed ashore at Asilomar Beach, near Monterey. Two men, who happened by on their way to do some surfing of their own, stumbled across it. The board sent a ghastly message: A massive, ragged half circle had been ripped from its center. And its provenance was all too well known: It had belonged to a twenty-four-year-old surfer named Lewis Boren, who had last been seen taking advantage of a fifteen-foot storm swell, surfing by himself just north of Pebble Beach. Boren was nowhere in evidence now. He had disappeared as of yesterday, and suddenly it was clear why, and how.

Later, after the board was examined and found to be smeared with blood that wasn't Boren's (rather, it belonged to the shark); after the scientists who examined the gaping hole concluded that the great white responsible was one of the largest ever documented—twenty feet long, or more—a memorial bonfire was held on the beach. Boren's surfing compatriots fed their boards into the flames as an offering to the shark gods and stared at the black water, wondering how they would find the heart to get back out there. When the body, identifiable by, among other things, a seagull tattoo on the right shoulder, was discovered half a mile up the beach, most of the chest cavity had been torn away, suggesting that the shark had sheared through both Boren and his surfboard in one mighty bite as he was paddling to catch a wave.

"We want him dead or alive," a self-proclaimed shark hunter named David Fisse announced at a press conference, vowing that he would hunt the creature all the way to the Farallones, where the man-eaters were known to hide out. "That shark killed someone," he said indignantly. "That's murder to me." Fisse and two assistants, including a Modoc Indian whom Fisse claimed could "shoot eyes out at two hundred yards," arrived in Monterey with an eighteen-foot aluminum skiff full of knives, shotguns, rifles, pistols, and a "bang stick"—a three-foot pole topped with a .38-caliber charge. Using this weapon, he explained, he intended to swim beneath the shark's jaws and deliver a shot to the spinal cord. The hit would incapacitate the shark but stop short of killing it, at which point he would lasso its tail and tow it back to the marina, where it would be auctioned off to the highest bidder. Fisse acknowledged that there were some potential complications with his plan. "A shark is tremendously strong," he told reporters. "I might antagonize him—they can do a lot of damage." For protection while diving, he planned to wear a motorcycle helmet. The hunt hit a snag when Fisse, neglecting to don a wetsuit for his first foray into fifty-degree Monterey Bay, developed hypothermia, forcing a rescue by a charter fishing boat. "The feeling is he's a donkey or a knucklehead," the charter captain said afterward, adding that by the time he was yanked from the sea, Fisse had been "pretty far gone" and on the verge of drowning.

The professionals stepped up next, two men from Florida who claimed to have collectively captured some four thousand sharks for aquariums, including eight great whites. They, too, held a press conference. Their goal, they explained, was to help scientists discern why white shark attacks were on the upswing, and to that end they planned to catch the animals using longlines baited with bonito and Spanish mackerel. Sponsors had signed on to fund the mission, dubbed the Great White Expedition, which would be shoving off from Fisherman's Wharf that weekend. Their first destination? The Farallon Islands.

Despite the concerted efforts, the shark that had killed Lewis Boren evaded all attempts at capture, and she (for twenty feet was clearly Sister-sized) was never seen again. Maybe she *was* one of the female sharks who returned to the Farallones every other year, one of the semimythical twenty-footers who had amazed Peter and Scot and Ron over the seasons. Maybe it was even Stumpy, chasing down yet another surfboard. No one would ever know. She had vanished beneath the waves.

WHO DO YOU CALL WHEN YOU'VE LOST A YACHT? AND WE REALLY AND truly had. Lost a yacht. In less than an hour, *Just Imagine* disappeared from sight, even through the scope. As the boat approached the horizon it was riding sideways, broadside to the terrible swells, and the mast light lurched through the darkness, rising and falling and bucking and yawing in a procession of twenty-foot free falls. At the edge of visibility the sky imploded into the sea, leaving one vast black question mark out there, unknowable as outer space. Until the sailboat vanished, we could see that it was heading south, but there was the hope that it wasn't also heading east, toward land.

There had been a brief but tense standoff on the landing, all of us shouting as the wind swallowed our voices. Peter had wanted to launch the whaler immediately and go after the sailboat and then— well he wasn't exactly sure what then, but at least it would be something. Later, he described a faint path that he had seen on the ocean's surface, an improbable calm corridor between the swells that he believed he could have followed to the yacht. He admitted that once there, however, he probably would've taken a flying leap and tried to land on *Just Imagine,* something I'm certain that he would've done and that he might have even pulled off, against the odds. However, a miss of any kind in these conditions was likely to be permanent. The stakes were far too high to contemplate, and Scot had quietly but firmly emphasized that no one was going out in any boats. In fact, we shouldn't even have been standing at East Landing during a storm this ferocious. In the past, waves had swept people from the island.

Without Scot's assistance, the option of launching our own search-and-recovery mission was off the table. The attempt would have required all hands. Somebody would have had to drive the whaler through the twenty-foot swell; somebody else would have been needed to crane it back up in the forty-knot wind. Moonlight glanced off seething boils in the gulch beneath the boom, and surf exploded against the cliff, shattering like a crystal goblet hurled at a wall. If it wasn't suicide to drop a seventeen-foot boat in there tonight, it was something very near to it.

I saw the truth of this register in Peter's eyes, and he seemed to snap back from the extreme place that compelled him to act, despite the dangers. It was a mind-set formed by a quarter century of experience on this island, by rescuing people and boats and animals and pulling off landings that nobody else could've managed, by countless hours of face time with great white sharks, by successfully walking a razor-thin line between bowing to nature in its more furious moments and challenging it to an arm wrestle. He was hard-wired to fix any problems that arose out here, with giant swaths of duct tape if necessary, with jury-rigged parts and triple-tied ropes and no hope of an easy or convenient solution. Even so, when the moment passed and we backed away from the whaler, I felt a wave of relief roll over all of us, Peter included.

I held out the dim hope that the coast guard would fetch the sailboat, sort of like a Triple-A of the sea. Cash would be required, I assumed, perhaps large amounts of it, but surely we could get *Just Imagine* back with a few well-placed Maydays? I asked if this was the case; no one knew. Things had never happened this way before. Among all the wrecked and missing boats, the lost boats, the boats with engine trouble and wrong-place-wrong-time misfortune, there had never been a renegade yacht covered in dried blood and hissing shit out of its deck fixtures, lighting out for the far Pacific with no one on board, towing the valiant Tubby.

The nearest radio was located in the carpentry shop, about fifty yards from the landing. It was a long, low building with a faint hobbity tinge, filled with every possible tool and widget, a competent person's miniature heaven. Peter reached for a handheld receiver that was mounted on the wall. It was only then that I noticed his ensemble: He was wearing his heavy weather jacket, his omnipresent knee-high rubber boots, and his faded Hawaiian-print boxer shorts. I stood beside him in my bare feet as he hailed the coast guard on channel 16, the emergency marine frequency. We were expecting solace, I suppose, in the form of smart, can-do action from the nation's front guard of the seas, but the response was not reassuring.

The operator's voice was groggy and slurred, as though we'd just woken him up. He sounded approximately twelve years old. Peter launched into the awkward one-way conversation that radio communication requires, explaining that a sixty-foot sailboat had broken its mooring at Southeast Farallon Island and was now cantering, skipperless, across the ocean.

"How many people on the vessel?" the operator asked, after having already been told the boat was unmanned.

"No people on board," Peter said. "It is a derelict boat. Over."

"What is the Farallon Island? Is that the name of the vessel?"

"Uh, negative," Peter said. "We are *on* Southeast Farallon Island. The vessel's name is *Just Imagine.*"

Between yawns, the operator clarified the extent of our predicament. The coast guard, he said, would do nothing to help us unless there were people aboard the sailboat as it spun across the sea, propelled by riot wind into the shipping lane. Our only hope, he said, was to roust a private marine salvage company and persuade it to chase down *Just Imagine.* And just like that, we were shunted to the mercenary world of for-hire yacht retrieval.

Marine salvage laws have existed for about three thousand years, and they've changed surprisingly little since then, the idea being that the smorgasbord of troubles you can get into at sea hasn't changed much since then either. Snatching an imperiled vessel from a wreckage fate is dangerous business, the reasoning goes, and so the law provides for a "salvage reward" going to whomever makes the attempt. Fair enough, in theory. But the "salvage reward" itself is notorious, involving a usurious sliding scale of fees ranging from 1 percent of the boat's value—to 100 percent. The amount of payola has to do with a subjective interpretation of exactly how endangered the vessel was, what type of paperwork a rescuee has signed and under which conditions, and other subtle distinctions that are well known only to marine salvagers. Inevitably, the average recreational boater is shocked when the person he's hired to rescue his boat turns around and, rather than producing the maritime version of a towing bill, demands an ownership stake. And inevitably these disputes end up in court. But the laws are clear, if seemingly piratical: Whoever first set foot on *Just Imagine* would be able to lay some sort of claim to it. *Power and Motor Yacht* magazine summed up the salvage philosophy in a quick sentence: "Face it, the guy has you over a barrel."

Alternately, someone who didn't care to spend months in litigation, someone who might have just been minding his own business in the middle of the ocean and happened upon an empty sixty-foot steel-hulled yacht, could simply board, and take everything. Drifting boats had been found with their roofs sawn off, their furniture ripped out, the electrical equipment long gone—stripped to the hull. And these weren't always happenstance meetings: Certain people listened to emergency broadcasts like the one we'd just made, and then set out after the runaway boats. In our case, they would also be receiving an impressive selection of women's size-small Capilene long underwear, a handcrafted Ouija board, and several decent vintages of Italian wine. Then again, *Just Imagine's* topside smell would probably scare off any potential looters.

As the emergency marine operator was signing off, his hands

washed of us in less than five minutes, he actually said to Peter, "Have a good day!"

Scot stared at the radio in disbelief: "Did he really just say, *'Have a good day?'*"

"I can't quite believe it," I said. "But I think he did."

Peter turned off the radio and hung up. It would be better, he said, to interview marine salvagers over the radiophone in the house. Less static; less likelihood of eavesdropping across the airwaves. We stepped out of the building's shelter into the freight-train wind and fought our way up the cart path. On the front steps, Elias was crouched behind a scope, taking compass readings on the sailboat as it slipped away in the darkness. We moved into the living room, and Scot scanned the numbers.

"It's heading due south," he announced. "Downwind. And the wind's offshore."

"I think it'll be okay," Peter said. He paused. "For tonight."

Kristie made tea while the three of us huddled into the closet-sized room off the kitchen where the radiophone sat on a desk. Peter dialed. The process was excruciating: Over the start-stop radio connection we had to wake someone up, explain the whole deranged scenario, clarify where the Farallon Islands were, and repeat several times that there was no one aboard the outlaw yacht. The first salvager we called turned us down cold, citing weather, and expressed some doubt that anyone would venture out in this storm. Perhaps, he suggested, we should just sit tight and wait until someone reported a sighting to the coast guard. I tried to imagine us calling Tom the next morning and, when asked what we'd done in the face of the emergency, replying, "Oh, nothing." Somehow, it didn't seem like nothing was the thing to do here.

The salvager offered to call another outfit on our behalf, a guy with a bigger boat who might be less intimidated by the monster swells. If the more intrepid yacht wrangler, let's call him Black-beard, was willing to help us out, we'd hear from him directly. Before the salvager signed off, though, he asked what the sailboat was doing out here in the first place. "It was a research platform for work on great white sharks," Peter replied.

"Roger that," the salvager acknowledged, with a slightly more respectful tone in his voice.

Peter hung up. "I find that when you need something, it's a good thing to mention the sharks."

We moved into the kitchen to wait for Blackbeard's call. No one spoke. Minutes ticked by. Eventually, Peter stood up and started pacing. "This is unbelievable!" he said. "The way this storm just came up! It doesn't happen like this!"

Scot glanced up from his tea with tired eyes. "Nature threw us a hardball, Pete."

"At least *Just Imagine* wasn't still anchored in Fisherman's Bay," I offered. If it had been, right about now we'd be picking slivers out of the rocks.

Peter stopped circling the table and looked at me. "I didn't say anything about this, because I didn't want to scare you," he said. "Every day I checked those ropes and they were holding. Then, yesterday, when I went to untie them from the buoy, one of them had snapped, and the other was ninety percent gone. It would've broken any minute."

I'd been instants away from careening into Tower Point, in other words.

Now I understood why it had been so easy to remove the ropes—they'd already removed themselves. And before it slipped the leash, the yacht had been on the brink of removing me, too. I felt a dull shiver of fear at the thought of the ropes suddenly being chewed down to nothing, but I also realized that, instinctively, I'd known all along that the sailboat intended to break free.

The radiophone rang. Peter grabbed it; Blackbeard was calling. This could be the answer. Or the beginning of a cold, hard reality check that no one would be coming to capture *Just Imagine* anytime soon. Blackbeard's voice was deep and growly, and he had the cocky drawl of a man who knew he was the one people called when they needed bailing out of some major screwup.

"What's the wind?" he asked, in the same unconcerned tone that someone else might use to ask the time.

"I think about thirty-five knots," Peter said, uncomfortably.

"And the swell is nineteen feet . . ." Blackbeard was calculating. He didn't like the numbers.

"Yeah, it's not very pretty out there," Peter acknowledged. "That's why the boat got loose."

He didn't turn us down, though, and a lengthy conversation followed, most of it involving discussion of fees. At some point, I handed over my American Express number. Blackbeard wanted to rent a larger boat, and he also advised hiring an airplane with two people on board, the pilot and a marine mammal "spotter," someone trained to make out tiny objects on the ocean's surface.

I hadn't been thinking of *Just Imagine* as a gnatlike speck on the water. It was, after all, larger than many Manhattan apartments. But I was beginning to realize that the ocean's true scale exceeded one's ability to grasp. Trying to envision the span of the Pacific was like hearing that Saturn was 840 million miles from the sun—too gargantuan an image to stuff between your ears. It seemed impossible that a sixty-foot sailboat could simply escape notice in perfect visibility, in broad daylight, but in reality, enormous things got lost at sea all the time. Even container ships disappeared. Sometimes lost sailboats drifted for months and ended up halfway around the world. After a time, however, the battery died and the bilge began to take on water and it was all downhill from there—the boat would slowly sink. Given the already depleted state of *Just Imagine*'s power system, I wondered how long we had. Certainly, it didn't help that the yacht, with its dark blue hull and white deck, would be indistinguishable from the whitecapped seas.

It was three in the morning and nothing could be done before daybreak, so a plan was formed for Blackbeard to round up his crew and call us at dawn, confirming that the spotter plane was on its way out. We'd calculated that the boat was drifting at approximately five knots per hour, a decent clip and a fair indication that it wasn't dragging its anchor. By first light it could be thirty-five miles away, and the search area would become exponentially larger with every hour that passed, like a spilled glass of water expanding in all directions. It was a discouraging image. Initially I'd presumed that corralling the sailboat would be a routine matter and had even entertained the notion that I'd resume my tenancy in a matter of hours. Just a little additional inconvenience, a story that would be funny someday, though perhaps not to Tom. But now it was dawning on me that there was a chance we weren't going to get *Just Imagine* back.

"Maybe Tom will be happy," I wondered aloud. "Maybe he wants a new boat."

"Thing was a bit of a beater," Scot said.

THE SUN ROSE BLOODRED. "RED SKY IN THE MORNING . . . ," PETER said darkly, looking out the kitchen window. The wind still blew thirty knots, with savage gusts to thirty-five and forty, and the swell had barely subsided. But when the sunrise drained off its fire, the sky was crystalline again, as though the storm had swept away every last dust mote. Things weren't any worse, let's put it that way, and our sense of hopefulness had been revived by three hours of sleep.

A nautical map was splayed across the kitchen table, and Peter leaned over it, plotting a course with a red pen and a protractor. He was using last night's compass readings to estimate the sailboat's probable direction; an accurate guess would save hours of needle-in-a-haystack searching from the air. Getting this right involved a mix of art and science—a nuanced reading of the water and a careful assessment of the ever-shifting currents. Several powerful streams collided at the Farallones, and throughout the year they waxed and waned like the moon. There was the California Current, massive and cold, lumbering down from Alaska, and the warmer Davidson Current sweeping up from Baja, and the North Pacific Drift, flowing from the east. Beneath them all, a deep undercurrent swirled along the edge of the continental shelf. Above, shoving things along the surface, was the wind. All of it— longitude, latitude, tides, wind speed, time of year, ocean salinity, even the fact that the yacht's hull was made of steel rather than fiberglass—needed to be thrown into the navigational blender. The end result would be a "drift profile," a hypothetical dotted line on the map, projecting *Just Imagine*'s escape route.

As with anchoring, theories on the route differed. Peter believed that, right now, the Davidson Current might be stronger than people realized, in which case the boat could end up heading north. Blackbeard was convinced that it was headed offshore. Or toward shore, maybe. But not due south. Later this morning coast guard computers would spit out the official version, based on hard numbers, but after the Weather Voice's bruising failure, it was hard to get excited about another machine interpretation of the elements.

After we received confirmation that our spotter plane was up and running, the day seemed to pass in a weird lost instant. Scot climbed to the light, where he witnessed yet another Maintop shark attack that no one could attend. I dispelled my nervous energy by charging up and down the zigzag path a few times, stopping finally at the top. As he scanned the perimeter, I sat on the steps and stared numbly at the scenery. I don't think the islands had ever appeared more beautiful to me than they did just then— with the banshee wind and glinting water and the prismatic clarity, and more whales than I could count. They swam around us on all sides, unfazed by the turbulence; it just stirred up more things for them to eat. I scoped the entrance to Fisherman's Bay to see if my gray whale was still there, but I couldn't spot her.

Under the circumstances, I knew that I had to leave as quickly as possible. It was only a matter of time before the powers that be caught wind of what had happened, and an outsider's role in it. If there was a break in the weather, *Superfish* would venture out here tomorrow on its whale-watching tour, and I could hitchhike a ride. It was scheduled to be a landing day in any case. Peter was going back to Inverness for two weeks, Kristie and Elias were leaving, and Brown and Nat, who had rotated off when the contractors arrived, were returning with a fresh batch of interns. Scot planned to remain through the end of the month.

I looked at him, standing on the concrete apron of the lighthouse, hands jammed into his pockets, eyes riveted to every odd ripple and eddy and enthusiastic gull. The radio remained silent, which could mean only one thing: no sighting yet. After a while, Peter called. "What's going on up there?"

Scot's reply was terse: "Lotta whalage." No one was in the mood for conversation.

We needed to phone Tom, we knew that. But we were also harboring the quickly disintegrating hope that the sailboat would be located by the time we spoke to him, thus improving the tenor of the exchange. Morning had turned to afternoon, however, and it was time to make the call. While Scot remained at the light, I fought my way down in the gale. As I neared the back door of the house, I noticed that the barbecue had gone for a ride. Pieces of it were strewn up the side of the hill.

Peter sat by the radiophone, waiting for me. Neither of us was enthusiastic about this task. Taking a deep breath, he dialed. Tom answered the phone in his booming, friendly voice—always happy to hear from us. How were things? Had we seen many sharks? And how was that goddamned 12-volt battery? Goddamn system drove him nuts! He wished he knew more about these 12-volt systems— Peter interrupted the effusive greeting with the universal windup to very bad news: "You might want to sit down." He explained the situation in all its horrible detail and then added, "Look on the bright side, Tom. You might not have to fix the plumbing."

As it happened, Tom did not want a new boat. Not even somewhat. He wanted *that* boat, the old, stinking, bleeding, busted one. I envisioned him receiving the news, sitting in his law office wearing a tie with little sailboats printed all over it, looking like he'd been knifed in the stomach. Our call came—literally—from out of the blue. Today's weather in San Francisco was sunny and hot, a little blustery perhaps, but nothing noteworthy, and the swell was a concern only if you were a surfer. The conversation was brief; he was quite obviously knocked for a loop, and he wanted to call his insurance company, his wife, and Bob, his sailing partner. Tom said that he would be back in touch early this evening. By then, in all likelihood, the yacht would've been spotted.

"He took it about as well as he possibly could have," Peter told me. He looked drained but relieved. The only thing that we could do at this point was wait for Blackbeard's call. Which would come any moment now. Surely.

Two o'clock came and went, followed closely by three o'clock, and still there was radio silence. When Blackbeard finally hailed us, it was almost four, and daylight was ebbing. He didn't have good news.

Through a scrim of static he informed us of several false sightings, most of them involving large whitecaps. As for the real thing: no sign of it. Anywhere. The plane was methodically winging up and down the corridors of an extra large search grid, the coast guard drift profile had been consulted, and still the yacht remained at large. And as the shadows lengthened on the water, it would only get harder to separate reality from mirage. Time was running out.

So were food supplies. The mood at dinner was strained, and not just because of the sobering update. Peter and I cooked together, mixing frozen albacore with canned soup donated by the departed coast guard crew. We combined this kitchen-sink cioppino with an expired salad, a few potatoes, and some banana cookies that Kristie had baked, and we ate for a good, long time, as though while we were chewing, nothing could possibly be that bad.

Every few minutes, between bites, someone would lament the fact that the storm hadn't been in the forecast. "Lemme tell you," Scot said. "That was a one-two punch. High wind we could've dealt with. Swells we could've dealt with. But both together . . ." He rocked back in his chair. "Anyway, the main thing is we're all here, and we're all okay. And the boat just happens to be—over there. As long as it's floating, it's okay. We just need a little help to get it, that's all."

"Maybe it's underwater," I suggested.

"It's not underwater," Peter said, with conviction.

"Well," I persisted. "What if a container ship just . . ."

Scot finished my thought: "Mows it down."

Peter set down his fork. "We'd hear about that. Even a container ship is going to notice if it plows into a sixty-foot steel-hulled sailboat." Plus, he added, "there would be a bunch of stuff floating."

I couldn't get the image out of my head—the bow tipping skyward as *Just Imagine*'s metal hull was sucked to the seafloor. And then: ling cod weaving through the cabin, starfish glomming onto the naked lady, barnacles atop knotty pine. My books and clothing would slowly rise to the surface in a veil of bubbles, or perhaps they would just disintegrate.

After dinner, Tom called back. He'd had some time to digest the situation. He'd taken stock of what had happened here, and he had one question: "Where was Susan? Why wasn't Susan on the boat?" I got on the phone. "I was on the island," I said, adding testily: "And in bad shape. It wasn't exactly a picnic out there *before* the storm, either."

Tom was unsympathetic. "Yes, but if you were on board, the coast guard would have come out there last night and saved your, excuse my French, pretty little ass."

Well, I wasn't. And furthermore, if I had to choose right now between being lost at sea, in Beaufort Force 9 weather, and the predicament we found ourselves in, there was no contest: I was staying in the kitchen. I tried to imagine my state of mind had I still been on board as the boat had broken loose, but all that came up was a sort of white noise of terror, a disconcerting static blank. On the other hand, I probably wouldn't have survived the day; given the gyrations I'd watched through the scope, it seemed likely that I would've been pasted to the ceiling. I'd been through enough trauma on that scow, thank you very much. Tom's assumption that I should go down with the ship irked me; that wasn't part of the deal.

I thrust the phone at Peter and sulked into the living room, where Scot sat in the tattered La-Z-Boy recliner, strumming a guitar. A mouse explored the area around his foot, whiskers twitching with excitement. I flopped on the couch, tilting my head all the way back until I was staring straight up at the ceiling.

"You know," I said. "Sharks are the *least* wild things around here."

He glanced up, smiled slowly, and kept playing. "They're not too bad, are they? Unless you're a seal."

Peter entered the room and sat beside the marine radio, looking ragged. He was steeling up though, I could see it, gathering strength for what he knew he needed to do: take charge of this debacle, fix yet another broken thing. He flipped on the Weather Voice. With its usual lack of empathy it informed us that for a few hours tomorrow morning, there *might* be a window of opportunity to pull off the landing, to load the shell-shocked crew onto a Farallon Patrol boat, the fresh crew and supplies onto the island, and for me to sneak in among the whale watchers once again. It was the first decent news we'd gotten out of the Voice in quite some time.

Blackbeard called to make plans for another day of searching tomorrow, pushing hard to charge for an additional plane or two. The fee he quoted for this new airpower was astronomical, and I caught the whiff of a hard sell, the grinding insistence of a quota-bound salesman trying to push a round of aluminum siding. The salvage cost was a bargain, he insisted, when you considered the alternatives; for instance, if the boat smashed up on the rocks anywhere near the Monterey Bay National Marine Sanctuary, the cleanup cost could top three hundred thousand dollars. "You'll have divers with tweezers picking fiberglass out of sea anemones." Today's fruitless search had already racked up fifteen thousand dollars in charges on my credit card, and as he spoke, it occurred to me that the sooner we found the yacht, the less money he made. Interrupting the stream-of-consciousness fearmongering, Peter broke the news that the salvage schedule was now in the hands of Tom's insurance company, a piece of information that seemed to turn Blackbeard snarky.

"I think she'll turn up," he said, before signing off. "Of course, it might be in the South Pacific."

• • •

PART OF THE RITUAL WHEN CREWS TURNED OVER WAS A THOROUGH
housecleaning. That included dealing with all the garbage—
torching the burnables and bundling the rest for disposal on the
mainland. Next morning, as the effort to spruce things up got under way, I drew the two bathrooms as my assignment and threw
myself into the task, scrubbing as though it were an Olympic event.
After I finished swabbing the toilets, I went outside and headed toward no particular destination at a fast clip. Wind still raked the island, though not as severely. I walked across the marine terrace,
letting my hair whip me in the face, and felt melancholy. I would
not be coming back to this place—not soon, anyway, and perhaps
not ever. As usual, I hated to leave. Even now, after everything that
had happened, I would've given anything to hit the rewind button
and relive the sharks swimming around me and Kevin tying beautiful precise knots on things and Peter fishing, listening to the Giants and Ron scooping up urchins and telling us stories and Scot
rigging Seal Baby and dipping for jellies while exotic birds appeared in the sky like jewels.

It was time to leave. Much shuttling of people and groceries and
garbage was scheduled in the next hour, so Scot and Peter both
launched—Scot in the whaler and Peter in a Zodiac. *Superfish* planned
to pull into Fisherman's Bay, and I walked to North Landing, where
Peter would pick me up. A pair of sea lions sunning themselves on
the stone steps were put out by my arrival, and they shot me exasperated looks as they slid into the water. A surf scoter, the com-
mando version of a duck, paddled in the shallows. Every ten seconds
or so, waves flooded the gulley. I stood back from the landing,
holding my sleeping bag and a white plastic sack that contained my
few possessions not currently lost at sea. The only clothes I had
were the ones I was wearing—had been wearing, actually, for the
past five days. That ought to keep curious whale watchers at arm's
length, I thought.

The wind was picking up briskly as Peter swept the Zodiac close to the rocks. "Jump, jump, jump!" he said. "There's a set coming in!" I jumped with the usual lack of savoir faire, landing in a kind of modified spread eagle. We didn't speak. No need for goodbyes; we'd be taking the yacht business up on the mainland as soon as we got there. Clambering aboard *Superfish,* I noticed that Scot had tied the whaler to the buoy and was standing, inscrutable in his polarized sunglasses, untangling a rope as he waited for the Farallon Patrol boat to arrive. We waved stiffly to each other across the water.

Mick grabbed my bag and welcomed me aboard. He had a standing-room-only crowd today, due to the whale convention. Also, it was Saturday and Fleet Week had begun, tilting all of the Bay Area toward the ocean. From the looks of several people sitting with their heads bowed low, slumped on the coolers, the rough conditions had already taken their toll. I ducked into the wheelhouse.

"Where's *Just Imagine?*" Mick asked. Obviously, there was a yacht-sized parking spot now open in Fisherman's Bay.

I stared uncomfortably into the middle distance. "Uh, well . . ."

"It didn't get damaged in the storm, did it?" His brow furrowed with concern.

"No, no," I said, waving my hand toward San Francisco, as though the sailboat was there right now, tucked securely in its port. "It went off because of the weather." Technically speaking, this wasn't untrue.

He didn't press me, but I could tell he knew there was more to the story. Though Mick would've been an ideal person to confide in, and may have even been able to help, he was also a member of the Farallon Patrol. We were trying to keep the yacht incident as quiet as possible.

We pushed off from Fisherman's Bay and turned south on *Superfish's* customary circuit of the island. I leaned in the doorway while he drove. Before we'd even rounded Tower Point, his radio buzzed; it was Peter. "*Superfish,* there's a carcass in Mirounga. You might want to check it out. We can't go because we're about to do a landing." I could hear the frustration in his voice.

"Ah, the landlord's collecting his rent," Mick said. He grinned. "Roger." Though they didn't know it yet, today's whale watchers had just scored.

We rounded Saddle Rock about as fast as a sixty-five-foot boat could possibly go, and before we were even past it, I could see that this attack was a big one. The slick spread for thirty yards and was carpeted with gulls; fins slashed away at the surface. Mick cut the engines at a respectful distance, and people pressed themselves against the railing. There were two sharks in attendance that I could see, and possibly more, and when one of them lifted its head, there was a chorus of gasps. In the background, I vaguely heard *Superfish*'s naturalist explaining the scene, but her voice seemed to be coming from far away. We were deep in Rat Pack territory, so I wasn't holding out any last hopes for seeing a Sister, but the action was consuming—this was by far the showiest attack I'd witnessed. One shark seemed especially aggressive, and from my vantage point he appeared to be relatively pint-size. I remembered the guys telling me that the sharks who lost their cool at attacks or snapped at the boat were generally the young ones, while elders like Bitehead and Whiteslash behaved with statesmanlike restraint.

The sharks spent the better part of an hour running around with pieces of the seal. As things quieted down, I heard Mick on the radio enthusiastically describing the attack to another captain.

"There was blood all over the place, and thrashing and splashing, and a big old carcass!"

"That's a beautiful thing," the other captain replied. The radio crackled with static as they reflected appreciatively on the commercial potential of having sixty people go back to San Francisco and report that they'd watched great white sharks tearing apart a seal at close range.

"Love those sharks," Mick said. "Bring on the sharks."

Superfish turned to the next order of business, whales, and as Mick headed to the west, there were suddenly shouts from the back deck. One of the sharks had cruised up to the boat, his curiosity as palpable as that of the neighbor's golden retriever. Video cameras whirred; people yelled with surprise. He was checking us out, and he followed *Superfish* down Shark Alley, hanging at the surface right off the stern, until he decided that we were not food and he left.

The naturalist sidled up beside me. "Susan?" she asked. "Perhaps you could tell us a little bit about these sharks." I'd already been introduced as a Shark Project intern, so there was no escaping it. My head itched under my baseball cap, under the hot sun, under my long-unwashed hair. Sixty faces stared, eager for insider shark information.

"Uh, well, there are a lot of great white sharks here at this time of the year," I said, trying to sound cheery and knowledgeable. "Most of them even have names."

After my highly abridged description of the Shark Project, a guy in his early twenties approached. "Is it boring to be on the island?" he asked, waving dismissively toward it. His nose wrinkled as he spoke, as though being marooned there would be a kind of hell. I replied that, no, it was the opposite of boring.

"Don't you miss the clubs?"

I was rescued from the conversation by a blue whale rising so close to the boat that we pitched up and down in its wake, and its spout misted the people who were standing downwind. Almost simultaneously, another blue whale fed within slingshot distance, raising its magnificent body in a sort of half breach and crashing to the surface with an exuberant splash. They were everywhere, gleaming in the sunlight as the water poured off their flanks.

We were several miles west of the islands now, plowing through seething, roller-coaster swells. I had my hips braced against the wall and ten fingers wrapped on the railing as I watched the whales. Mick's deckhand Morgan, standing next to me, commented that my hands were "trashed," though he voiced it like a compliment. I looked down at them, covered in cuts and scaly rope-burn patches, fingernails chipped and packed with grime—he was right. And the vehicle responsible for trashing my hands was somewhere out here. I stared dumbly at the unquiet Pacific, across a few of its sixty-four million square miles.

The likelihood of finding the yacht dropped off dramatically after forty-eight hours, we'd been told, as the search area swelled. A single-engine airplane could travel only sixty miles due west over the ocean; after that a twin-engine plane was required, the cost of which would quickly exceed the value of the sailboat. I'd been responsible for *Just Imagine,* and I had misplaced it. Everything had come unraveled, undone.

IN NO TIME AT ALL *SUPERFISH* WOULD BE STEAMING BACK INTO SAN Francisco harbor, past the chaos of Fleet Week, past the radio distress calls born of too many gin and tonics, past that grand symbol of civilization, the Golden Gate Bridge, into the thick of human doings. And I was going with it.

I looked back at the Farallones. They sparkled and glinted with an unfamiliar golden cast. I'd seen them washed in a dozen shades of sepia and I'd seen them crusty white and sometimes, from afar, I'd seen them turn as blue as the ocean around them. They'd appeared to me like hazy shadows, and in hard-edged silhouette. But I'd never seen them glow like shards of glass. In the molten light they resembled a forgotten aquatic kingdom, briefly risen from below to bask in the sunshine. Morgan, standing next to me, nodded toward Southeast Farallon. "Looking at those islands, you get the feeling nature could just *take over,*" he said. "Anytime it wanted." There was profound humility in his voice.

Maybe that's what had been missing. Enough humility. The mix just hadn't been right. A human footprint was barely tolerated at the Farallones when it was small; anchoring a sixty-foot sailboat there was like a big, clomping jackboot. Icarus, with his well-intentioned wax wings, learned it the hard way, too.

And as we passed the islands for a final time, I knew that below us things were as they should be. The sharks patrolled and the urchins marched and the rockfish hunkered down for another century or two and the seals looked both ways before crossing. Come winter, Tipfin, Spotty, Gouge, Cuttail, Bitehead, Cal Ripfin, and everyone else who had come around for the season would drop over the edge and head to their secret places, knifing into the unknown. Maybe they would return next September, or maybe, like Stumpy, they would transmute into legend. Like so many creatures in the ocean, they left a trail of mystery behind them. And they left me standing at the surface, looking down into the water.

There's another world, and it's in this one.

EPILOGUE

NOVEMBER 14, 2004

Pale November sun was beginning to light up Monterey Bay when Kevin and I stepped through the back door of the aquarium. Only a handful of people were inside, preparing for the public's arrival later this morning. Walking through darkened rooms filled with glowing tanks and serpentine bodies, we wound our way past the penguins and the otters and the swaying forest of kelp and neon platoons of jellyfish, toward the million-gallon majesty of the Outer Bay tank, where a recent arrival had been causing excitement. The thirty-foot wall of glass rose in front of us, casting the pitch-black anteroom into a kind of azure dreamscape. This vast tank was home to some seventy animals—large fish, for the most part—yellowfin and bluefin tunas, bonito, hammerhead and other smaller sharks, slinky California barracudas, a few black sea turtles as formidable as tanks, and five thousand unlucky sardines, whose numbers were dwindling fast. And this: one baby great white shark.

She was the first thing we saw as we entered the exhibit room, a four-and-a-half-foot-long beauty making dramatic aerials against the glass, flashing her white belly and her black-edged pectoral fins and looking to all the world like an exotic little fighter jet, elegant and fierce at the same time. "There she is," Kevin said. "Displaying in full form." His face was illuminated in the blue underwater light, and he looked at the shark with a slightly awed smile.

This tiniest Sister didn't have a name and wasn't slated to get one. (There was only one great white shark in this neighborhood. Under the circumstances, naming her would be an entirely sentimental gesture, at odds with the aquarium's scientific roots.). She had distinctive facial markings, most notably a bright white clown nose. Earlier, a mask-shaped area of charcoal pigment around her eyes had been rubbed away, but this abrasion had healed nicely and she no longer resembled a piscine bank robber. Most likely, she had gotten scraped during her capture on August 20, when she was accidentally snagged in a halibut gill net near Huntington Beach, hauled aboard a fishing boat, and placed into a live well that wasn't quite long enough to hold her, her face jammed against a corner.

Every part of the plan had worked out perfectly. The scientists rescued her, then made the transfer to their four-million-gallon ocean pen, where she fed, showing no signs of stress. After three weeks of observation she was transported north, to the aquarium. On her first day in captivity she snapped up salmon fillets before a cheering crew of marine biologists, many of them visibly moved by the sight. Since then she had eaten regularly, and with such vigor that she managed to bite the tip off her bamboo feeding pole. SeaWorld's sixteen-day record had been shattered. For now, at least, this white shark was thriving in the tank. Since her arrival in Monterey on September 15, she had gained twenty pounds, grown a few inches, and spurred a 50 percent increase in ticket sales.

Watching a great white interact in an environment filled with other species was fascinating, and we stood for close to an hour, just staring. Her aura preceded her whenever she made an appearance in the window, and beside her the soupfin sharks and Galapagos sharks and hammerheads looked decidedly flimsy. Even the tunas, some of which were absolute battle-axes, appeared submissive in comparison. She swam with her mouth partially open, showing us her pointy baby teeth, which would later broaden into the heftier triangles that adult white sharks use to go about their work. Her back was colored a silvery gray, far paler than the suntanned Farallon sharks, whose lives did not involve spending time under fluorescent lights.

When the aquarium opened its doors at ten o'clock, kids burst into the room, rivering around us, pressing their palms up against the glass. One boy, who rode into the Outer Bay exhibit on his father's shoulders, asked loudly, "Where are the great white sharks?" At that moment the shark emerged from below, buzzing the newly gathered crowd, and provoking a chorus of "wows." "She's small but she's still scary," another child exclaimed to his mother.

Exactly one year and nine days had passed since *Just Imagine* cantered off into the night. After the initial seventy-two hours of concerted searching with spotter planes turned up nothing, it was presumed that the yacht had headed far out to sea, or that it had been stolen. As the weeks wore on without a sign, options expanded to include the possibility that the boat's bilge had become overloaded, that waves had swamped the deck, that *Just Imagine* had, in a word, sunk. Then, on November 9, 2003, when hope had been all but abandoned, Tom Camp had received a call from a navy yeoman, who informed him that "the ship *Just Imagine* has been sighted."

After leaving the island, it turned out, the yacht had drifted for thirty-one days, eventually floating into the U.S. Navy's Pacific Missile Range three hundred miles south of the Farallones and fifty to sixty miles offshore, southwest of the Channel Islands. Astonishingly, it had managed to round Point Conception, a wickedly turbulent stretch of ocean that even boats *with* crews often have trouble navigating. The yacht was making a run for the Mexican border when the navy helicopters descended, hovering low over its bow and barking through a bullhorn that someone had better damn well start responding to their radio hails. More silence. Large, mute, unidentified vessels tooling around in a sensitive military zone are not looked upon kindly, and the gunships were radioing each other, discussing whether to blast the bejeezus out of it when a sharp-eared coast guard operator overheard the plan being finalized and intervened, identifying it as the "derelict boat" from the Farallones.

A salvager from Ventura had braved tempestuous night seas to motor out and corral the yacht, armed only with compass coordinates that were several hours old. He knew, of course, that *Just Imagine* might be miles away from the spot where it was initially sighted, and upon his arrival the situation looked unpromising: his radar swept across a black and empty ocean. After several hours of searching, to no avail, he'd turned to head back toward shore when he received a faint hit on his scope. Something *was* out there, right at the edge of his range. *Just Imagine*. So he'd roped the sailboat like a runaway steer and clambered aboard as it heeled wildly, and then towed it back to the Channel Islands Marina. Damage was not insignificant: the steering system was demolished, various antennas had snapped off, and almost anything that wasn't busted before was busted now. Still, things could have been far, far worse: the bilge was almost full, presaging a long ride to the bottom of the sea. It wasn't pretty inside the cabin, either. Smashed bottles and sodden papers and pieces of garbage had been hurled randomly and exuberantly from fore to aft; coffee grounds lined the floor; mold and mildew flourished, cupboards were jacked open and emptied of their contents, my underwear was strewn across the kitchen. Perhaps most disturbingly, the antique Ouija board had managed to travel all the way from one end of the yacht to the other, somehow maneuvering its ten-pound bulk out of my partially zipped duffel bag, making its way up three steep stairs in the cabin and lodging itself under the dining banquette. This incredible journey unnerved me almost more than anything. (The board has now been safely and permanently disposed of.)

And the verdict for the yacht's delinquency? The anchor had ripped clean off, tearing its beastly thick anchor chain apart like a piece of taffy, and joining the other underwater testaments to nautical hubris that littered the Farallon reefs. All that remained were a few yards of mangled links. Off the stern, a frayed inch-thick rope trailed forlornly: Tubby's tether. The rowboat did not survive the journey, and she would be missed.

Yet while material things like yachts and notebooks and cameras and demonic Ouija boards survived the misadventure basically intact, the personal damage would prove more difficult to repair. During the second week that *Just Imagine* was at large, Tom had placed an ad in a local sailing magazine called *Latitude 49*. REWARD: LOST AT SEA the attention-grabbing headline read, juxtaposed against a photograph of the yacht, and accompanied by a paragraph outlining the situation. Some of the other Farallon Patrol skippers saw it and called PRBO, concerned. At that point the whole story came out, and no one was impressed. Lawyers got involved. As the person in charge of the island, Peter was called onto the carpet, and lost his job. Sadly, he no longer works at the Farallones.

Putting a painful situation into the most positive light, he reckoned that, in any case, it was time to begin a new chapter of his life. "I'm taking a break from predators," he told me, outlining his plans for two new ornithology books. His tenure at the islands, he realized, stretched back to a time before the media caught the irresistible whiff of great white sharks and came hammering at the door, when permits weren't even required—why would they be? You couldn't get onto the island unless someone wanted you there. (The military was right: It would've made a hell of a fortress.) In the seventies and eighties, Farallon biologists were often visited by their wives and children, friends and family members dropped by, local artists were granted internships to write poetry or paint, inspired by the scenery. Individual judgment, rather than regulations, dictated actions. "Because you were just *out there*," Peter explained. "And no one was going to be helping you." Since those early cowboy days, however, out of necessity or design, the mainland rules and bureaucracies had migrated west.

While the Shark Project's future remains in question, there are positive signs. During the 2004 season, previously slated to be the last, white shark research permits were transferred to Barbara

Block's lab. Thus, the tagging goes on, and there is hope that it will continue into the future. Logistics have been difficult though, with both landings closed for repair this fall.

Scot and Peter's partnership has come to an end. It spanned fifteen years; it yielded some of the most intriguing information about great white sharks that has ever been compiled; it was a fortuitous mix of skills and yin and yang balance—but it's over, and both men acknowledge now that the effort had run its course. Scot continues to study sharks wherever he can find them, making trips to Alaska to spend more time with salmon sharks (a species that's also part of Dr. Block's tagging efforts) and thinking about branching out into whale sharks, basking sharks, and tiger sharks: "I'm into them all." But the Farallones are still the epicenter of the white shark world and that means Scot will continue to return there as long as he can, furthering his research, doing whatever it takes to remain in contact with the group of animals that has captivated him for the better part of two decades.

Ron has kept up his diving throughout the 2004 season, though his trips have been less frequent. On the fourteen dives he's made at the island this year, he's seen sharks on all but one. He continues to note a profusion of males, Rat Packers everywhere he looks, and a curious paucity of queen-sized Sisters. Three years have passed since he's seen a truly supersize girl, and he wonders about that. Meanwhile, the urchin market is challenged by cheaper stocks coming from abroad and, in the future, it's likely that Ron will spend time diving at the islands out of choice rather than economics. Make no mistake though, he'll be there. The Farallones remain his refuge and solace, the one place where he feels entirely at peace with himself, where he can think without the din of civilization pounding in his ear. Besides, he hasn't figured out what he wants to do next. He and Carol now have three grandchildren, all under the age of three, and they're a priority. The next thing, whatever it is, will have to balance Ron's love of walking the edge with his love of spending time with his family. In the meantime he's enjoying the chance to slip into the Farallon waters with a video camera, documenting the sharks and other creatures as a kind of living photo album.

Cage diving remains a thriving business in the lee of Saddle Rock, and Groth's company, Great White Adventures, debuted a new boat this year: *Superfish*. Mick and Groth have joined forces, and the thirty-two-foot *Patriot* has been replaced by the sixty-five-foot whale-watching vessel. Now, more people can be accommodated on each trip, and the divers have the benefit of Mick's experience with the island waters. (There's one downside to the larger boat, however: The sharks aren't as likely to approach it.) Groth himself has been spending much of his time in Guadalupe, where the water is a crystal-clear seventy degrees, and clients sign up for three-thousand-dollar weeklong trips in the sunshine.

Everyone continues to surf. Yesterday, in fact, Kevin had ridden waves at Asilomar, near the site of Lewis Boren's attack, and had a fantastic session despite a near closeout, with surf breaking close to the beach. Sidelined for most of the fall after slipping in his boat and bruising a rib while trying to tag a shark, Scot says he intends to make up for lost time when the season winds down. Peter arranges his days according to surf conditions in Bolinas and a few local places that he refuses to divulge, for fear that others will discover them. Ron recently ordered a shortboard to go with his longboard, and has been seen on both at one of the sharkiest places around: Salmon Creek, a fast, steep break where attacks and encounters occur with regularity. On May 28, a Salmon Creek surfer had been bumped from his board and managed to fight off a sixteen-foot shark for several minutes while the animal circled, aggressively thrashing its tail. "I felt like I was in a boiling cauldron," he told a newspaper reporter.

Another surf spot Ron favors is Drake's Estero just north of Bolinas, and Peter likes this wave as well, which is why he was one of the first to hear when, on October 24, a former Farallon intern and friend of his named Pete DeJung was attacked by a white shark while surfing there. DeJung had been sitting on his surfboard when he was jolted forward "like I'd been rear-ended at a stop sign," and then a great white's head had lifted his leg out of the water, its mouth wrapped around his calf, all the way down to his foot. When DeJung whacked the shark, it let go, but not before slapping his face with its tail, opening a deep gash above his eye. Though the fish had done one hundred stitches worth of damage, DeJung remained remarkably cool, paddling to shore on his own. Afterward, he declined to speak to the media regarding the encounter, not wishing to help feed the inevitable shark attack circus. His experiences with the Farallon sharks had given him a different perspective: "I wasn't as frightened," he said. "This wasn't a big one. I've *seen* the big ones."

DeJung's great white encounter was the year's fourth in the Red Triangle. And not everyone had met up with a dinky shark. Near Fort Bragg, an abalone diver named Randy Fry was decapitated by a white shark estimated to measure eighteen feet. It severed Fry's head, neck, and upper shoulders in one sudden and massive swoop as the diver swam near the surface in a cove. The victim, who was fifty years old and the west coast regional director of the Recreational Fishing Alliance, had confided to his friends about a premonition that he would die in the jaws of a great white shark. Two of them were with him at the time of the attack. "When I saw the pool of blood spread across the surface of the water, I knew Randy was gone," his diving partner recounted. "We were in the wrong place at the wrong time."

Great white sharks arrive when you least expect them, and vanish the moment you think you've got them figured out. They don't come into anyone's life in a forgettable way, and once they grab your imagination they don't let go. I was no exception. The professional fallout for Peter, the official censure, the loss of the yacht: None of this was easy to justify in the aftermath. Several of Peter's colleagues speculated that only great white sharks could provoke such irrational behavior; that certainly, no one had ever come a cropper in attempts to study warblers, say, or harbor seals—as though somehow the animal was at fault. But that wasn't the case.

It was purely human behavior that made the wheels come off. Somewhere along the line, right at the beginning I think, I became obsessed with this story. That single-mindedness colored everything I did, and ended up extracting a heavy toll.

And yet, watching the baby white shark in the tank, gliding past the crowds and seeming to revel in her star attraction status, I was awed one more time by how many dimensions there were to these creatures, and how haunting their presence. Exiting the Outer Bay in search of breakfast, we passed a ten-foot-long mural of a great white shark that was thronged with children, all clamoring to have their photos taken in front of it. Across the room, white shark stuffed toys and key chains and books and fridge magnets were being sold from a kiosk. The animal had charisma, all right.

As we threaded our way through the tourists on Cannery Row, the bay was beginning to stir behind us. Car doors slammed; surfboards were lifted down from roof racks. (I had one of my own now, a seven-and-a-half-footer decorated with vibrant fuschia swirls.) All around us, people headed to the ocean.

And eighty-five miles to the northwest, a perfect eight-foot swell was building in Mirounga Bay.

SELECTED BIBLIOGRAPHY

One book in particular was invaluable: *The Farallon Islands, Sentinels of the Golden Gate* (San Francisco, CA: Scottwall Associates, 1995) by Peter White. Along with being the only volume ever compiled about the islands' history, it also happens to be meticulously researched and elegantly written. Any reader wishing to delve into the Farallones' past will find it riveting.

The quote on page 75 comes from Steven Powers's *Tribes of California* (Berkeley, CA: University of California Press, 1976), p. 182.

The following were also helpful:

Ainley, David G., and Robert J. Bockelheide. *Seabirds of the Farallon Islands*. Palo Alto, CA: Stanford University Press, 1990.

Boessenecker, John. *Gold Dust and Gunsmoke: Tales of Gold Rush Outlaws, Gunfighters, Lawmen, and Vigilantes*. New York, NY: John Wiley & Sons, 1999.

Collier, Ralph S. *Shark Attacks of the Twentieth Century: From the Pacific Coast of North America*. Chatsworth, CA: Scientia Publishing, 2003.

Davis, Lisa. "Fallout." *SF Weekly*, 9 May 2001.

De Santis, Marie. *California Currents: An Exploration of the Ocean's Pleasures, Mysteries and Dilemmas*. Novato, CA: Presidio Press, 1985.

Doughty, Robin W. "San Francisco's Nineteenth-Century Egg Basket: The Farallons." *The Geographical Review*, October 1971, 554–72.

Ellis, Richard, and John McCosker. *Great White Shark*. Palo Alto, CA: Stanford University Press, 1991.

Greene, Charles S. "Los Farallones de los Frayles." *Overland Monthly*, September 1892, 226–46.

Hoover, Mildred Brooke. *The Farallon Islands, California*. Palo Alto, CA: Stanford University Press, 1932.

Hoyt, Erich. *Creatures of the Deep: In Search of the Sea's "Monsters" and the World They Live In*. Buffalo, NY: Firefly Books, 2001.

Karl, Herman, J. L. Chin, E. Ueber, P. H. Stauffer, J. W. Hendley II. "Beyond the Golden Gate: Oceanography, Geology, Biology, and Environmental Issues in the Gulf of the Farallones." U.S. Geological Survey circular 1198.

Klimley, A. Peter, and David G. Ainley. *Great White Sharks: The Biology of Carcharodon carcharias*. San Diego, CA: Academic Press, 1996.

McCormick, Harold W., Tom Allen, and William Young. *Shadows in the Sea: The Sharks, Skates and Rays*. New York, NY: Weathervane Books, 1963.

McDavitt, Matthew. Statement for "Sharks: Myth and Mystery" exhibit. Monterey Bay Aquarium, Monterey, California, 2004.

Martin, R. Aidan. *Field Guide to the Great White Shark*. Vancouver, BC: Reef Quest Centre for Shark Reasearch, Special Publication No. 1, 2003.

Meyers, Ransom A., B. Worm. 2003. "Rapid worldwide depletion of predatory fish communities." *Nature* 423:280–83.

Noble, John Wesley. "The Exiles of Howling Island." *The Saturday Evening Post*, 20 June 1953, 24, 87, 89, 90, 93.

Nordhoff, Charles. "The Farallon Islands." *Harper's New Monthly Magazine*, April 1874, 617–25.

Rendon, Jim. "Farallon Feeding Frenzy." *East Bay Express*, 15 January 2003, 12–19.

Robison, Bruce, and Judith Connor. *The Deep Sea*. Monterey, CA: Monterey Bay Aquarium Press, 1999.

Safina, Carl. *Song for the Blue Ocean*. New York, NY: Henry Holt, 1998.

Wilson, Edward O. *Biophilia*. Cambridge, MA: Harvard University Press, 1984.

Wilson, Edward O. *The Diversity of Life*. New York, NY: W.W. Norton & Company, 1999.

SCIENTIFIC PUBLICATIONS ON WHITE SHARKS USING FARALLON DATA

Ainley, D. G., C. S. Strong, H. R. Huber, T. J. Lewis, and S. H. Morrell. 1981. "Predation by sharks on pinnipeds at the Farallon Islands." *Fishery Bulletin* 78:941–45.

Ainley, D. G., R. P. Henderson, H. R. Huber, R. J. Boekelheide, S. G. Allen, and T. L. McElroy. 1985. "Dynamics of white shark/pinniped interactions in the Gulf of the Farallones." *Memoirs of the Southern California Academy of Sciences* 9:109–22.

Anderson, S. D., and K. J. Goldman. 1996. "Photographic evidence of white shark movements in California waters." *California Fish and Game* 82:182–86.

Anderson, S. D., R. P. Henderson, and P. Pyle. 1996. "Observations of white shark reactions to unbaited decoys." Pp. 223–28 in Klimley and Ainley (eds.), *The Ecology and Behavior of the White Shark*. Academic Press, San Diego, 1996.

Anderson, S. D., A. P. Klimley, P. Pyle, and R. P. Henderson. 1996. "Tidal height and white shark predation at the South Farallon Islands, California." Pp. 275–80 in Klimley and Ainley.

Anderson, S. D., and P. Pyle. In press. "A temporal, sex-specific occurrence pattern among white sharks (Carcharodon carcharias) at the South Farallon Islands, California." California Fish and Game.

Boustany, A., S. F. Davis, P. Pyle, S. D. Anderson, B. J. LeBoeuf, and B. A. Block. 2002. "Expanded niche for great white sharks." Nature 415:35–36.

Goldman, K. J., and S. D. Anderson. 1999. "Space utilization and swimming depth of white sharks, Carcharodon carcharias, at the South Farallon Islands, California." Environmental Biology of Fishes 56:351–64.

Goldman, K. J., S. D. Anderson, J. E. McCosker, and A. P. Klimley. 1996. "Temperature, swimming depth, and movements of a white shark at the South Farallon Islands, California." Pp. 111–20 in Klimley and Ainley.

Heneman, B. and M. Glazer. 1996. "More rare than dangerous: A case study of white shark conservation in California." Pp. 481–91 in Klimley and Ainley.

Klimley, A. P. 1985. "The areal distribution and autoecology of the white shark, Carcharodon carcharias, off the west coast of North America." Memoirs of the Southern California Academy of Sciences 9:15–40.

Klimley, A. P. and S. D. Anderson. 1996. "Residency patterns of white sharks at the South Farallon Islands, California." Pp. 365–74 in Klimley and Ainley.

Klimley, A. P., S. D. Anderson, P. Pyle, and R. P. Henderson. 1992. "Spatiotemporal patterns of white shark (Carcharodon carcharias) predation at the South Farallon Islands, California." Copeia 1992:680–90.

Klimley, A. P., P. Pyle, and S. D. Anderson. 1996. "The behavior of white sharks and their pinniped prey during predatory attacks." Pp. 175–92 in Klimley and Ainley.

Klimley, A. P., P. Pyle, and S. D. Anderson. 1996. "Tail slap and breach: Agonistic displays among white sharks?" Pp. 241–56 in Klimley and Ainley.

Lea, R. N. and J. E. McCosker. 1996. "White shark attacks in the Eastern Pacific Ocean: An update and analysis." Pp. 419–34 in Klimley and Ainley.

Long, D. J., K. Hanni, P. Pyle, J. Roletto, R. E. Jones, and R. Bandar. 1996. "Geographical and temporal patterns of white shark predation on four pinniped species along central California, 1970–1992." Pp. 263–74 in Klimley and Ainley.

Pyle, P. 1992. "Sympathy for a predator: White shark studies at Southeast Farallon." Observer 93:1–11.

Pyle, P., S. D. Anderson, and D. G. Ainley. 1996. "Trends in white shark predation at the South Farallon Islands, 1968–1993." Pp. 375–80 in Klimley and Ainley.

Pyle, P., S. D. Anderson, A. P. Klimley, R. P. Henderson, and D. G. Ainley. 1996. "Environmental factors affecting the occurrence and behavior of white sharks at the South Farallon Islands, California." Pp. 281–92 in Klimley and Ainley.

Pyle, P., M. J. Schramm, C. Keiper, and S. D. Anderson. 1999. "Predation on a white shark by a killer whale and a possible case of competitive exclusion." *Marine Mammal Science* 15:563–68.

WEBSITES

For more information on the Farallones and surrounding waters, readers should contact The Farallones Marine Sanctuary Association: www.farallones.org

A fantastic resource for those interested in shark biology, behavior, and conservation: ReefQuest Center for Shark Research: www.elasmo-research.org

Additional websites of potential interest:

TOPP (Tagging of Pacific Pelagics): www.toppcensus.org

Census of Marine Life: www.coml.org

Conservation International: www.conservationinternational.org

Devil's Teeth, a documentary about diving in the Farallones, directed by Roger Teich: www.devilsteeth.com

Environmental Defense: www.environmentaldefense.org

Farallon Island National Wildlife Refuge: http/library.fws.gov/refuges/index

Monterey Bay Aquarium: www.mbayaq.org

Oceana: www.oceana.org

Pew Oceans Commission: www.pewoceans.org

Point Reyes Bird Observatory: www.prbo.org

Surfrider: www.surfrider.com

Wildlife Conservation Society: www.wcs.org

The Great White Shark (1995), the BBC video documentary directed by Paul Atkins that inspired this book, is available on VHS and can be ordered from Amazon.com.

AUTHOR'S NOTE

Words can't express my gratitude to Peter Pyle. His extraordinary talent, warmth, great humor, and devotion to the Farallones made this project a joy, even when it veered into rough waters. I am also deeply indebted to Scot Anderson and Ron Elliott, and to Charlie Merrill, the founder of the Farallon Patrol, whose wisdom and friendship are a gift I'll always cherish, and Paul Atkins, whose vision of these islands still haunts my dreams. Further thanks are owed to the following people, who helped me with island reporting and access: Mick Mengioz, Ed Ueber, Brian Guiles, Tony Badger, Margaret Badger, John Boyes, Mike McHenry, Peter DeJung, Pete Warzybok, Russ Bradley, Jen Greenwood, Meghan Riley, Melinda Nakagawa, Kristie Nelson, Elias Elias, and Josiah Clark. Greg Cailliet, William Gilly, Roger Hanlon, Bruce Mate, David K. Matila, David Festa, and Kathleen Goldstein generously answered research queries. I am especially grateful to biologist R. Aidan Martin, whose love of sharks is surpassed only by his generosity when it comes to sharing his knowledge of them; and to Linda Hunter, the director of the Farallones Marine Sanctuary Association for her vision and support. And I certainly want to thank Paul Amaral of Channel Watch Marine Inc. for finding *Just Imagine*. The retrieval, conducted at night, in stormy seas, was no small feat of nautical expertise and bravery.

Kevin Weng of the Block Lab at Hopkins Marine Station provided invaluable information about white shark conservation, populations, and the inner workings of satellite pop-up tags (and, best of all, taught me to spearfish). Next door, at the Monterey Bay Aquarium, Ken Peterson, John O'Sullivan, and Randy Kochevar were endlessly helpful. Barbara Block deserves everyone's thanks for her brilliant work to prevent the oceans from being reduced to guppy tanks, but she especially has mine.

Over the years, many Farallon scientists whom I've never met have built a legacy: David Ainley, Bill Sydeman, Jim Lewis, Phil Henderson, Bob Boekelheide, Jerry Nussbaum, Burr Heneman, Harriet Huber, Larry Spear, Teya Penniman, Harry Carter, Craig Strong, Stephen Morrell, and Malcolm Coulter are among the names that appear over and over in the logbooks, and in countless papers furthering the study of the islands and their wildlife. Important white shark research was conducted at the Farallones by A. Peter Klimley, Ken Goldman, John McCosker, Scott Davis, and Andre Boustany. Too many interns to name have passed through the Jane Fonda Bedroom, but I wish I could acknowledge them all.

My intention in writing this book was simple: to do justice to a story that captivated me, the story of an unknown place, and the animals and people who were a part of it. Unfortunately, the reporting process turned out to be anything but simple, and some people were angered by my presence at the Farallones. I sincerely regret this. I greatly admire everyone whose job it is to protect and study the islands, and I never set out to jeopardize any part of their work. In the end, I hope I've made clear how extraordinary the stewardship of the Farallones has been in the hands of Joelle Buffa at the U.S. Fish and Wildlife Service, along with Ellie Cohen and Bill Sydeman of the Point Reyes Bird Observatory.

I have the great fortune to work for Isolde Motley, the corporate editor of Time Inc. She was the first person with whom I discussed this story and the first person to green-light it. Her support, guidance, and friendship went beyond what I could have hoped for. At Time Inc. I also owe thanks to Norman Pearlstine, John Huey, and Ann Moore, as well as Steve Koepp and Dan Goodgame for providing the assignment that dispatched me to the islands for the first time, Ned Desmond for toughening me up, Dan Okrent and Dick Stolley for helping me with just about everything, and John Squires, Mark Ford, Martha Nelson, Chris Hunt, Sid Evans, David Petzal, Rick Tetzeli, Rik Kirkland Eric Pooley, Jodi Kahn, Sheila Marmon, Claudette Hutchinson, Milt Williams, and Marcie Jacob. Yet more thanks to Janet Chan, Jim Aley, Mark Adams, Jason Adams, and Mark Golin for razor-sharp humor, sushi lunches, great music, and a steady supply of top shelf liquor. Proper gratitude expressed to my Time Inc. colleagues would fill an entire book in itself.

Terry McDonell, Tim Carvell, Laura Hohnhold, and David Granger read early versions of the manuscript and offered superb insights, as usual. Mark Bryant and John Tayman produced years of elegant, irreverent work that both taught and inspired. Sara Corbett, Mike Paterniti, and Rick Reilly provided insight, encouragement, late-night phone calls, and constant examples of what great writing is supposed to read like.

Martha Corcoran was pivotal to both the book's beginning and its end stages. Gwen Kilvert conducted meticulous research with her typical cool. Katharine Cluverius at ICM and George Hodgman and Sam Douglas at Holt were indispensable readers. La Mura Boelling gave me sage counsel, as always. Mike Casey continued to scare the muskies away.

Writing a book, I discovered, requires asking your friends to go to extraordinary lengths to help you, even as you neglect them. Jenny Doll, Sharon Ludtke, Cathy Cook, Clare Hertel, Deanna Brown, Dean Heistad, Tanya Schubring, Paula Romano, Pam Lazzarotto, Angela Matusik, David Lynch, Kristin Gary, Aroni Reyes, Ann Jackson, Harry Apostolides, Stephen Sumner, and the incomparable Dottie Starr: I love you. Thanks.

And I can't even begin to thank Jennifer Barth, Henry Holt's editor in chief, whose touch is on every page of this volume, and John Sterling, Holt's president, for his deep understanding of this story. I'm saving my biggest thanks for last, though, for my agent, Sloan Harris, who has been there every step of the way, dispensing perfect advice and occasionally talking me down from the ledge. I think I wrote this book in part so that I'd get to talk to him more.

On October 12, 2004, white sharks were listed on Appendix II of CITES (Convention on International Trade in Endangered Species of Wild Flora and Fauna), a global agreement intended to stave off the extirpation of species. This is a step in the right direction. Given white sharks' newly discovered migratory habits, it is clear that local protection alone is not enough: The white sharks that remain are at large in the world's oceans, not conveniently corralled in a few discrete locations. Their mating and pupping grounds remain unknown, they reproduce slowly and produce few offspring, and without strictly enforced, wide-ranging controls on hunting and trade, they really don't stand a chance.

Simple logic dictates that the ocean's resources need to be managed sustainably by international law. To date, this emphatically has not happened. The aquatic environment is being altered radically before we've even begun to understand it, an insane game of brinksmanship with potentially catastrophic results. And even as $10 billion is allocated for interplanetary exploration, ocean conservationists—monitoring 71 percent of the Earth—struggle for funding. Meanwhile, commercial fishing remains a zero-sum game, habitats are being destroyed, species lost forever.

As for the Farallon great whites, they may have adapted to everything that's been thrown at them for the past 11 million years, but here's the question: Will they survive another decade of us?

Susan Casey is the development editor of Time Inc., where she was previously an editor at large, as well as the editor of *Sports Illustrated Women*. She also served as the creative director of *Outside* magazine, which during her tenure won three consecutive, history-making National Magazine Awards for General Excellence. Her writing has appeared in *Sports Illustrated, Esquire*, *Time*, and *Fortune*. A native of Toronto, she lives in New York City.